Kim V. Engelmann

Foreword by John Ortberg

# SOUL-SHAPING SMALL GROUPS

## A Refreshing Approach for Exasperated Leaders

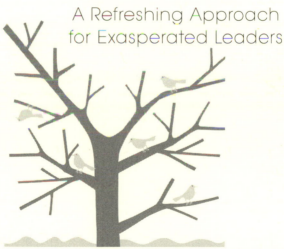

IVP Connect

An imprint of InterVarsity Press
Downers Grove, Illinois

InterVarsity Press
P.O. Box 1400, Downers Grove, IL 60515-1426
World Wide Web: www.ivpress.com
E-mail: email@ivpress.com

InterVarsity Press® is the book-publishing division of InterVarsity Christian Fellowship/USA®, a movement of students and faculty active on campus at hundreds of universities, colleges and schools of nursing in the United States of America, and a member movement of the International Fellowship of Evangelical Students. For information about local and regional activities, write Public Relations Dept., InterVarsity Christian Fellowship/USA, 6400 Schroeder Rd., P.O. Box 7895, Madison, WI 53707-7895, or visit the IVCF website at <www.intervarsity.org>.

All Scripture quotations, unless otherwise indicated, are taken from the New Revised Standard Version of the Bible, copyright 1989 by Division of Christian Education of the National Council of the Churches of Christ in the USA. Used by permission. All rights reserved.

Design: Cindy Kiple
Images: Simon Oxley/iStockphoto

ISBN 978-0-8308-3734-2

Printed in the United States of America ∞

Library of Congress Cataloging-in-Publication Data

Engelmann, Kim.
  Soul-shaping small groups: a refreshing approach for exasperated
leaders / Kim Engelmann; foreword by John Ortberg.
      p. cm.
  Includes biliographical references.
  ISBN 978-0-8308-3734-2 (pbk.: alk. paper)
  1. Church group work. 2. Small groups. I. Title.
  BV652.2.E54 2010
  253'.7—dc22

                                                        2010000189

P   21  20  19  18  17  16  15  14  13  12  11  10  9  8  7  6  5  4  3  2  1

Y   27  26  25  24  23  22  21  20  19  18  17  16  15  14  13  12  11  10

# Contents

# Foreword

$W$hen Jesus was going to launch his ministry, he did not begin by raising an army, raising a budget, starting a university, building a headquarters or writing a manual. He started by forming a small group. He recruited a group of unlikely people to learn together, travel together, live together, eat together, argue together, suffer together, so that they might be knit together and one day change the world. His primary strategy for the extension of his movement was his leadership of a small group.

Life change happens best in small groups. Psychologist Harry Stack Sullivan used to say that it takes people to make people sick, and it takes people to make people well. And while our depravity is such that we all carry a level of responsibility for our own bentness, we can surely never hope to heal apart from the gifts and caring of other human beings.

We live in a day of great hunger for community. Princeton researcher Robert Wuthnow writes that the small group movement is the greatest social revolution in our day. People are God's primary tool when it comes to changing lives. Anybody who has ever preached or taught at a church knows the humbling experience of finishing a message that you believe is absolutely crystal clear, and then talking with someone afterward who not only didn't understand what you were saying, but took away the exact opposite of what you were trying to communicate! Small groups is where people speak, listen, apply, correct, assimilate and have the chance to truly absorb and be affected by learning.

However, here is the dirty little secret of church life: even though churches often praise small groups, form small groups, celebrate small groups and even require small groups—when we get under the hood, when we poke around at people's actual *experience* in small groups, the quality is often amazingly uneven. Making sure small groups are well led and effectively experienced is a Mt. Everest–sized challenge. And Kim Engelmann is prepared to tackle it.

This book is not just a terrific book. It's not just well written and thoughtful and soulish and empathic and well researched and everything else you'd expect a book from Kim to be. It is very badly needed. I can think of few gifts that would have a bigger or better impact on the church than to create more life-giving, life-changing small groups.

In this book you will find not just theory but the kind of "roll-up-your-sleeves-let's-get-it-done" wisdom that real-life small group leaders desperately need. Whether you lead that movement in the church, or lead a single small group, or are a small group member, or are thinking about grouping—this book is the real deal.

So read it and go start a group.

*John Ortberg*

# PART ONE

# Experiencing God's Presence in Small Groups

# 1

## Confessions of a Small Group Deviant

It is Thursday evening—small group night. I pull in the driveway of the host's home and hesitate before getting out of the car. *Do I really want to do this?* I am not the sort of person that likes week-night meetings. I am tired from a long day's work, but I push my car door open and crunch on up the gravel driveway in my usual despondent Eeyore state of mind that I often fall into after 7 p.m.

I convince myself that this is for my own good. I tell myself that I ought to be grateful that I live in a free country where small groups that talk about Jesus and the Bible are allowed. But I am not grateful, not one little bit.

The door is ajar, so I walk in and gather with the others who are standing around a table with snacks and drinks in the living room. I tell myself again that this is good; this is community and I need this.

I pour myself a cup of coffee. It is decaffeinated. Why? It is night. I need to stay awake. An overconfident leader perhaps bought these imposter beans, assuming that the group would be so exciting by doing Bible study that everyone of us in our decaffeinated state would sit there bright and alert on the edge of our seat.

I check my Bible and groan when I realize my homework is not inside. Not that I did it, but having a sheet to look at always adds to my feeling of security—even if it is blank. However, the original piece of paper with the questions on it that we were given at the end of last time has vanished from the place where I wedged it—somewhere between the pages of 1 Corinthians, I am sure of it!

*I should have gotten the Bible with the zipper that I saw on sale last week*, I think. I found myself for a fleeting instant appreciating zippered Bibles, which I had never done before. *Of course! Now I understand—they were to hold extra stuff inside, like small group homework pages that I forget about all week, until its time to go to group. They weren't meant to keep the Bible in, zipped away from the world, stain free.* I'd had a friend once who owned a zippered Bible. Her zipper got stuck. For several days she struggled to open it. Then she just gave up reading the Bible altogether. That is why, until this moment, I had an aversion to zippers around Bibles. This is why I hadn't bought the zippered Bible on sale. To make matters worse it was red-lettered. Everything Jesus said was in little red print. *Why red? Why not gold or green? Gold was heavenly, green was all about life and growth, but red? Red reminded me of hell.*

Someone jabbed me in the shoulder, and I looked around to see Hazel, also drinking imposter coffee. I greeted her, but it was clear to me that Hazel was upset. Her dog Bags might need to be put down. It seems Bags has had a good life up until now, but given the fact that Bags is now seventeen-and-a-half, his back legs just aren't working and he keeps throwing up. Hazel tells me she keeps a mop and a scrub brush handy but her carpets aren't doing well.

Feeling slightly grossed out and guilty that I don't feel more compassionate, I move with the others to the center of the room and sit down on a lime green couch with very stiff pillows. They aren't the kind of pillows that folded nicely under me. Rather the corners stick into my back, making me feel as if Hazel was perpetually jabbing me with her finger.

It's time for an icebreaker. "What is one of the clearest memories you have about your church experience?" the leader asks us, looking expectantly at me. I have no idea why she is looking at me, but the first thing that popped into my mind is nothing I can share aloud.

We read a Scripture passage about the fruit of the Spirit. The questions focus on asking us about ways we think we can grow in order to be more loving and gentle and patient. I am not feeling spiritual enough to answer the questions.

Everyone gets very serious and sort of hunches over his or her Bible and tries to figure all this out. One woman has a highlighter that squeaks, and she keeps underlying things.

At that moment, on that evening, I didn't really care. I knew I was doing the best I could. Anything that I had to do *more of* seemed like a tedious, excruciating exercise in scraping the last vestige of peanut butter out of a pretty well-scraped-out jar.

Just that morning I had scraped the jar in order to create a lunch out of nothing for my ten-year-old. We had two pieces of white Wonder Bread left in the bottom of the bag, but nothing for in-between. Yet with tenacity and great resourcefulness, I had managed to get a tiny line of peanut butter on the end of the knife after an intense moment of valiant scraping. I smeared it on the flimsy bread and heaped on a mound of jelly, slapping the other piece of bread on top in triumph. Lunch was made!

Tonight, my jar was empty—scraped to the max. Not only that, but it seemed we were missing the point. It was the fruit of the *Spirit*, not our own efforts that the passage seemed to be talking about. I was too tired to mention this, however. Besides, I recognized my pessimism and was well aware that one of the fruit of the Spirit happens to be joy.

Generally I am not a particularly joyful person. I have a pessimism that can drive positive, upbeat people nuts. I am one whose tendency is, with cynical indifference, to see the glass half empty—or worse yet—to see no glass at all. As the discussion droned on with very serious people doing this very serious spiritual stuff, I half admired their diligence, while the other half of me sank into a silent slump.

Then it was time to pray. We went around and shared requests, and I heard about Bags all over again. Finally, the leader, a pleasant-faced woman I didn't like because she had served decaffeinated coffee, suggested we all pray for the person on our left. Then she added that we were out of time so please make the prayers short—just a sentence or two.

Panic seized me.

I didn't know what the person on my left had just said. I was thinking about the peanut butter jar. I didn't even know his name except I was sure it was a one syllable name like Bob or Jim or Pete.

"What did you ask prayer for again?" I whispered to the guy with the one syllable name. He was grim-faced and had gnarly hair. I should know his name. He had been to the group three times consecutively, and I had even talked to him once at length, so asking his name would have been a horrible thing.

"For my cousin Ida who is having her jaw wired up next Tuesday because of an overbite." he said.

I was saved! I didn't need to know the one-syllable name, as long as I could pray for Ida and her overbite. When my turn came around, I did a tremendous job praying for Ida, in one perfectly constructed sentence.

# 2

# How Small Groups Can Lead to Spiritual Stagnation

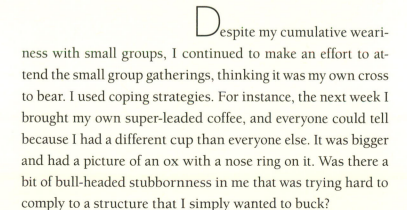

The task of prophetic imagination and ministry
is to bring to public expression those very hopes and
yearnings that have been denied so long and suppressed
so deeply that we no longer know they are there.

WALTER BRUEGGEMANN

Despite my cumulative weariness with small groups, I continued to make an effort to attend the small group gatherings, thinking it was my own cross to bear. I used coping strategies. For instance, the next week I brought my own super-leaded coffee, and everyone could tell because I had a different cup than everyone else. It was bigger and had a picture of an ox with a nose ring on it. Was there a bit of bull-headed stubbornness in me that was trying hard to comply to a structure that I simply wanted to buck?

Whether that was the reason I chose this particular cup, gleaned from a garage sale long ago, I am not sure. What I do know is that I tried. I tried to engage in meaningful ways with the people. I tried to be more humble. I derided myself for not caring that Bags actually did get better.

And then I quit! Yes. You read correctly. The bull with the nose ring and I quit for good.

I just couldn't take it. First off, I felt guilty for not being in the right place spiritually when I went to the group. I kept thinking how shallow and linear all this was, and then kicking myself because I needed more humility and acceptance. Then, I felt dry when I left because I wasn't receiving. Finally, all week long I dreaded Thursday night. I had to do something, so I just didn't go back.

Maybe this was wrong. Perhaps I could have hung in there a little longer; I am not sure. My cynical nature makes it hard for me to eagerly embrace things that don't bring me life or encouragement. Ultimately, if I am entirely honest, I admit I felt as if it was a huge waste of time. And the high-octane coffee just made me more jittery.

When this experience occurred, I was serving Menlo Park Presbyterian Church as an associate pastor and head of the Caring Ministries Department. I oversaw all of the recovery and support groups, and four hundred volunteers who were actively engaged in doing all kinds of caring ministries for those who were hurting. In all of my giving out, I had sought out a place that I was hoping would provide care for my soul. Instead it had become another chore, duty, obligation—something I did not need.

I know others who have found the small group experience to be draining and inconsequential for their spiritual growth. Perhaps this is because a lot of my interaction is with more mature Christians who have been deeply committed to Christ for years. They find themselves looking for something beyond the casual gathering or the question-answer curriculum. They are actually looking for something that goes deeper and nourishes them with the high-octane presence of the Holy Spirit.

There are many church groups out there. I have been in some that I think met a social need or provided content for those becoming acquainted with the Bible and their faith. Others provided help for those who were simply going through a rough time and were looking for supportive community. These are fine, and I am not suggesting that all small groups are meant to operate in the same way.

However, I think the longing of many hearts who have known Jesus for a while is to find a group, or even just a person, who will engage with the divine reality of Jesus' presence with us now.

## HUNGER FOR DEEPER CONNECTION

As Janet Ruffing wrote in a recent article for the *Conversations Journal*,

> We are living in a time of unprecedented spiritual hunger. The very complexity and challenges of our particular moment in history seem to be catalysts for many more people pursuing an explicitly spiritual path and seeking transformation on the basis of personal experience of the Divine.

Willow Creek Community Church is a megachurch in the Midwest that recently came out with a study they call "Reveal." The study used four categories for measurement purposes, which are Exploring Christianity (what we might call a seeker), Growing in Christ (I believe in Jesus and I am working on what it means to get to know him), Close to Christ (I feel close to Christ and depend on him daily for guidance), and finally Christ-centered (God is all I need in my life. He is enough. Everything I do is a reflection of Christ).

I applaud the effort to measure spiritual growth. It is not easy to come up with categories in this area that are simple and definable. After twenty-five years in ministry, I also know there is a great need for pastors and ministry leaders to get a handle on the outcomes of what they spend their time doing.

Willow Creek discovered that as people progressed through these four categories and became more spiritually mature, their satisfaction with the church dropped significantly. Those that were close to Christ and Christ-centered (the two most "mature" categories) described themselves as "stalled" and "dissatisfied" with the church, not getting the spiritual meat they were hoping for. The study showed that *involvement in church activities had absolutely no direct correlation to spiritual growth.*

Well, that really made me want to give up my job! When I thought about the hours of meetings I had been in that focused on program, strategy and incentives for "getting people in the door," I just wanted to push delete and forget I had spent half of my life doing nothing.

Yet the truth (as far as the method went) was staring me

in the face. The great programs designed by well-meaning church leaders (like me!) to help people grow more deeply in love with Jesus and to love others simply did not automatically translate into a transformation of the heart. Something is missing in all of our tactics and procedures. Or Someone! At the same time the study showed that a relational closeness to Jesus (not the church!) was what really changed behavior toward loving God and others.

Most significant for our purposes here is that small groups became far less important to people's spiritual growth as they matured in Christ. Stage two—Growing in Christ—is when small groups seemed to have the most import and significance, as we might expect. In the last two stages, spiritual nourishment and growth happened when people served and spiritually mentored others. These findings were a shock to Willow Creek. Bill Hybels, the senior pastor at Willow, has been a long-time promoter of small groups, believing that small groups are the key throughout our spiritual life and the basis for our spiritual development.

It begs the question: Are small groups the problem, or is it *the way we do small groups* that is the problem?

I would suggest that the latter is the problem, especially when it comes to feeding those who have been Christians for a while.

## A NEW APPROACH TO SMALL GROUPS

Can we create community that nurtures and provides spiritual growth to more mature Christians and those in search of authentic spiritual connection with God? Because Jesus initiated and cultivated small groups, both with the Twelve and at Pentecost, I say yes! Indeed, the Holy Spirit eagerly awaits opportunities to transform hearts and minds, if given a chance.

This book suggests a new format for the small group experience that gives authentic spiritual community a chance. It challenges the compartmentalization of Bible study, prayer, fellowship, even fun (only laugh during ice-breaker time!) and offers creative practical suggestions that can serve to integrate these aspects into more of an experiential framework. It also gives room for the Holy Spirit to work, and trusts that the same Holy Spirit is still longing and yearning to be the primary teacher of us all. After all, John wrote, "You do not need anyone to teach you. . . . His anointing teaches you about all things" (1 John 2:27).

In a postmodern culture where too many voices have caused doctrines and creeds to have a lackluster glaze, we need to find ways to open ourselves up to the reality of experiencing God's presence. God is alive and ready to be known. All we have to do is create both internal and external space for renewal and transformation. Once we have encountered the risen Christ together, then our creeds and doctrines will be understood and validated by our shared experience of him.

God stands at the door and knocks (Revelation 3:20), wanting us to have authentic experiences of renewal and growth with him. When small groups find the door and open it up to God, transformation occurs.

# 3
## Moving into the Presence of God

Unless we are grounded in Mystery—unless we
experience both ourselves and others as co-particpants in
Mystery—we find it almost impossible to live in compassionate
love of one another for any length of time. Unless we have
"new eyes" that can see the others contemplatively, it is easy to
miss the many-splendored thing that is our life together.

CAROLYN GRATTON

I remember the day that I mus-
tered up all my courage and took my three teenagers to a
Taizé service. (Taizé is a style of worship that is built around
contemplation, singing and Scripture reading, with a high
premium placed on the whole community of faith going up
together to the cross.)

Actually, I didn't just take the kids, I dragged them. They didn't want to go, and they expressed that quite clearly, over and over again. Still, I wanted them to experience something that I felt actually might feed them in a way that our very programmed, entertaining, fill-every-second-of-time church worship hour did not.

My kids were not happy. They asked whether they could leave early if they didn't like it. They asked me if I would take them out for ice cream afterward as a reward for making them do "my church thing" on a Friday night. They asked me why the service had such a weird name. My oldest asked me if he could walk there instead of drive, meaning that this would allow him to miss the whole thing.

I was taking a risk. I felt that they might never talk to me again, deny their faith and become advocates for teaching evolution in the schools. Still I was determined and I *made them* go, imagining that years later this would be what they would talk about in therapy.

"She was a religious fanatic," they'd tell their therapist. "She forced church down our throats, and even on Friday night she forced us to do a weird Taizé thing!"

When we arrived at the chapel, the kids flounced out of the car and we went in. We were a few minutes late, and my sullen children settled down on the floor cross-legged with some others who had decided that the pews were not for them. I liked the floor and joined them. The lights were off, the only light coming from some small candles on the floor. Up front, in the center of the platform, a large cross was lying horizontally on the ground.

As we sat there, in complete silence at first, a deep peace and centered awareness of God's intimate presence got my attention. I began to relax. The kids sat waiting, still pouting and sullen.

Then simple music floated up and out in our direction; violin, flute and piano played melodies for words that were sung over and over, again and again. The words were profound in their simplicity "Jesus, remember me, when you come into your kingdom," and "Love is forgiveness. Learn to forgive and God will be with you. Love is forgiveness. Love and do not fear."

The Catholic sister who was leading the singing was frail, blue-veined and looked about ninety years old. She was also off-tune. I started to tense up. Relient K, my kids' favorite Christian band, this was not. I glanced over at my fifteen-year-old son. He had his eyes closed, his palms up in prayer.

*Okay,* I thought. *So far so good. Maybe he doesn't see the ninety-year-old, blue-veined nun.* Then a line formed as everyone got up to wait their turn to bow down at the cross. I had my eyes closed for a while and when I opened them up again, the kids were gone. I looked around. Perhaps they had left in disgust, grabbing a votive candle as they went in order to set the place ablaze. Then I saw them. They were not igniting the rafters but standing in the cross line. I joined them.

My youngest whispered, "This is awesome that we actually get to go up there. And look at all these people who are going up with us." I looked. Virtually every age and stage was represented in that line, from small children to teenagers to young adults and young married couples to families and seniors.

After it was all over, the kids didn't act like they liked it very much at all, until I bought them ice cream with drippy thick fudge sauce and rainbow sprinkles. Then they told me that it was cool (not the ice cream, the service), and they would go back again. My oldest, the fifteen-year-old, had been deeply touched. He told me he wanted to go back again, because at Taizé he *experiences* God's presence in a way that doesn't happen in church.

I pondered this. I wondered what Taizé has that so much of church life misses. And then I thought about the Reveal study and what it had discovered. I wondered whether the small groups that Reveal was talking about actually got into the *experience* of God's presence as a living reality. I remembered how my youngest had liked being with so many other people as he went forward to the cross, how "awesome" my kids thought it was that we actually got to *do* something in worship. I journaled about the peace I had experienced. And I was touched by the space given so the Holy Spirit could actually do a work that was deep and meaningful, if nothing else than to simply remind us of the presence of Jesus with us now.

These services also helped us as a family. Since then we gather together from time to time—especially when things are hectic or rushed—to practice resting in God's presence. Perhaps one of us will read a Scripture, and then we all listen to what God might be saying in the stillness. It is rather exciting. It comes down to the simple practice that can be so easily missed: the living Christ is actually among us. The practice of *treating God like God is actually there* keeps it interesting in terms of letting go and then *actually expecting* something to happen.

## "I THINK I CAN" SPIRITUALITY

When he was very young, my son once asked me why the Little Engine That Could kept on saying "I think I can, I think I can." Why, he wondered, didn't the little engine say "I know I can, I know I can" if God was helping him? I told him I had no idea about the prayer life of a steam engine. He told me that he thought that the Little Engine felt that it was all up to him, and that he wasn't expecting much from God; that's why he wasn't quite sure that he would make it, and why he lacked confidence. As I pondered signing up my four-year-old son up for Theology 101 at a local seminary, I agreed that it seemed to me that the Little Engine That Could was doing it all on his own steam. What's more, most of the time I felt like the Little Engine That Couldn't. That was why I had great expectations about what God could do because I knew that if I relied on my own steam, I was a lost cause. I was too old and rusty.

When we let God take over, experiences of grace invade our lives. As a parent, having raised my children with a biblical understanding, I now needed to teach them to listen and prayerfully create space for God to act in their lives. In their years of programmed Christianity—learning Bible stories and doing good stuff, spending weeks at Christian camps and in small group processing—no one had ever showed them the simple joy of creating space for the Holy Spirit, posturing themselves in quiet receptivity and an open ear.

Countercultural? Perhaps. But maybe it is primarily counter-evangelical church.

Gary Moon interviewed John Michael Talbot for the *Conversations Journal* on the topic of mysticism. In the course of the article, Talbot dispels the myth that mysticism is something that begins in a mist and ends in a schism because it has "I" in the middle. I laughed when I read this, having been in plenty of churches where experience let loose on its own has had disastrous effects. Talbot says:

> To some degree, I think Paul's excitement about the ability to experience the mystery of Christ within has been lost. I'm sure I'm biased, but this loss may be more evident in the evangelical movements in the United States than elsewhere. I certainly believe there definitely should be more spoken about mysticism and the mystery of Christ in us.

Talbot does not consider himself a fan of oblique "touchy-feely" spirituality. Rather, he sees real spiritual experience as making a difference in a person's life for the better (which includes the way we deal with others).

The experience of Christ's presence is never an end in itself. When that happens, all kinds of distortions occur. Essentially, this would be the "I" in the middle—I seek an experience to make me feel good. Rather, Talbot talks about mystery, or mysticism, as something that we cannot fully describe, which is true about all personal religious experiences. It is also true of the nature of love. We can't fully understand or describe love. It must be lived.

The test of a true spiritual experience is how we live out of it, how our heart has been changed by it. And of course the teachings of Christ, faith and morality are important anchors so that the experience has objective truth as its foundation. However, the evangelical church has programmed the more mystical, experiential piece right out of the equation. We assume it is all up to us.

According to the Reveal study, much of what we do in church programming is not directly related to changed hearts and lives. Reveal found that a person's relationship with Jesus—not with the church—is what makes the difference in life and practice. Experiencing Christ's presence is what transforms us.

C. S. Lewis, often thought of as one of the strongest intellectual voices for faith in the modern era, recounts his conversion experience in *Surprised by Joy*. Lewis's spiritual intuition was every bit as powerful as his intellect, according to David Downing in his book *Into the Region of Awe*. Although Lewis saw himself as someone who stayed in the foothills and didn't aspire to the high places where the mystics went, he was greatly inspired by the writings of the mystics, and defined the basic Christian walk not in terms of striving after ethical ideals but of mystical transformation. Lewis defined mysticism as a "direct experience of God, immediate as a taste or color."

However Lewis also asserted that "the Christian is called, not to individualism but to membership in the mystical body." Downing notes that, according to Lewis, "'God communicates His presence' directly to those engaged in praise and adoration, that for many people "'the fair beauty of the Lord" is revealed chiefly while they worship Him together.'"

Here we have one of the greatest intellects championing community as the place where mystical transformation can and does take place.

## TAKING A RISK AND PRAYING TOGETHER

The church I work for has many small groups that pray. We talk a lot *about* prayer. I was the leader of one such small group. And on a certain day I decided to do things differently. I decided to simply let go of my agenda and actually do what I had been talking about all along. I had everyone create space for God. It was a bit risky.

The group members had brought their pencils and tablets ready to take notes on everything I said. (They probably never look at their scribbling again with much interest.) So, instead of giving them content, I asked people to put their pencils down, grow quiet and listen. I explained that listening was simply cocking their ear toward divine love, as well as offering God their receptivity. One of the greatest signs that we love someone is listening to him or her. I asked people to become aware of God's very close and immediate presence.

After we did this, I had those who had specific prayer requests raise their hands, and I had others who wished to pray for them come around and hear the requests. They were surprised. This was the group who officially prayed for others.

"You mean *we* get to be prayed for, ourselves?" someone asked.

"This is more like a prayer meeting than a training," I smiled and nodded.

What I didn't say was that the best training is always experiencing exactly what you are talking about. Until you get something from the inside out, you don't get it.

After we invited the Holy Spirit to come, after we listened and then gave space for God's movement among us, and after we offered auditory prayers, we talked about the whole experience. In the small span of forty-five minutes there were stories of changed people—the official pray-ers of the church already emerging.

"I didn't want to come this morning," one woman said. "I was dealing with a lot. But since I received this kind of prayer, I feel like a huge weight has lifted off my shoulders. I realized that Jesus was saying to me 'Let me carry that load for you.' And when I was willing to give it up, he took it." She was crying. "It's like I want to live again. I feel twenty pounds lighter."

Someone else said, "I realized that God was right here. I didn't have to stretch my spiritual neck muscles of goodness and worthiness to get to God. Jesus had already come to me and was very, very close. So it was easy to be simple, almost childlike, and simply ask. It wasn't complicated. And I have this deep assurance now that God is deeply at work for the request that I had. But it was also great to allow myself to soak in the peace and beauty of God's presence."

No training manual was needed for this. We didn't ponder the complexities of free will and predestination or figure out the three bullet points of successful prayer. All we did was create space for Jesus, and as is characteristic of Jesus, he came and touched hearts. Suddenly, in the space of forty-five minutes we had stories to share.

In our fragmented culture there is a longing for authentic connection with one another and with God. If I could experience in a small group the actual living presence of God in a palpable way, I'd want to go!

What I don't need at the end of a long, hard day is a guilt trip, or a "try harder" list added to my "must do" list—the front of my refrigerator is crowded enough already with to-dos. I also don't need a life application—I need the application of the Holy Spirit for life! A perfunctory prayer at the end of the meeting is a way to end the small group session together—sort of like a smudged period at the end of a sentence—but not a time to encounter the Holy One, who is closer than our breath. Weak, pessimistic and weary at the end of a day, I need Jesus.

This is not to say that I couldn't experience Jesus in the nitty-gritty of listening to Hazel talk about Bags. The truth is that once our eyes are opened, we are able to encounter Jesus in the most mundane, ordinary type of experiences. The transcendent that interfaces with our lives gives a brightness to the ordinary. It is that Source of life that gives our life, day by day, a facelift, a new way of approaching things, a love for Hazel that is not manufactured because I know I *ought* to love Hazel. Rather, touching the hem of Jesus' garment might make me actually care about Bags.

## HOW DO WE CREATE TRANSFORMATIONAL GROUPS?

Given the Reveal data, and my dismal experience with Hazel

and Bags, the whole idea of small groups gave me a stomach cramp for a while. I went into my cynical place and thought about doing away with small groups altogether for the spiritually mature. I knew, though, that lack of community, which this would eventually boil down to, is never the answer for anything.

Community grounds the mystical aspects of faith. The presence of others around me reminds me that Jesus affirmed, as no other religion does, the tangible world. He affirmed flesh-and-blood people in the context of their very real day.

Jesus said the person next to me—the one with the scratchy voice and whose name I can't remember—is a part of his body. This reminds me that I am not seeking an experience of God to take me out of the world. Rather, I am seeking a closer connection to Jesus so that I can be put back into the world in a way that empowers me to live and love sacrificially. The element of service, celebration and joy keeps small groups from growing stale and puts people into contexts where they must be authentic and involved.

I think that rather than not do small groups, the question that needs to be asked is, How do we create quality small groups that lead us into the life-transforming presence of Jesus with us now?

What sorts of paradigm shifts do we need to make in our current structure so that we can learn in a new way what it means to pray together and be primarily connected to one another, not by demographics but by our shared experience of Jesus as risen Lord?

It is fascinating to note that as we read about revivals or movements of the Holy Spirit through history, we find that demographics play no role in how God draws people into community. Experiencing God's presence together *is the super glue* that creates authentic community. The Holy Spirit always leaps over the walls of human propriety and continues to show us something bigger and better than ourselves. Thanks be to God!

I am not suggesting that small groups become experiential factories that try to manipulate the Holy Spirit to do something outside of God's timing. However, small groups need guidance on how to create space for God to move in and among these communities entrusted to our care. The mystics never sought experience for experience's sake. They simply engaged with God with all their heart. They fell in love with their Creator, and once they tasted him, they wanted more. A Roman Catholic priest wrote:

> Nothing is more practical than finding God, i.e. than falling in love in a quite absolute final way. What you are in love with, what seizes your imagination, will affect everything. It will decide what will get you out of bed in the morning, what you do in your evenings, how you spend your weekends, what you read, whom you know, what breaks your heart, what amazes you with joy and gratitude. Fall in love, stay in love—and it will decide everything.

The following chapters will look at some ways to facilitate a "falling in love" experience with our Creator. They will look at some of the group dynamics involved in bringing people into the presence of Jesus, and will give you practical suggestions on how to allow space for the work of the Holy Spirit in your small group.

# 4

# Building a
# Praying Community

When I read the Old Testament, it actually seems to me that when things were going right there was a lot of celebration written into Jewish life that was based around community experience, not the individualistic kind of experience so often associated with encounters with God. Israel was called to "do life" together in a way that regularly and systematically celebrated God's deliverance, transformation and faithfulness. There are calls to feast, to dance, to make music, to be together in community

37

in ways that are actually—dare I say it—fun. In other words, we might actually *look forward* to going, if the experience is life-giving.

I have worked in churches forever and have had a lot of fulfilling moments, but if I were doing a word association with *church*, I am not sure the word *fun* would be in the mix.

Potluck dinners are not fun, they are low cost. Committee meetings are not fun, they are necessary. Fellowship hall sounds like it *could be* fun if it were jazzed up a little bit, with something brighter than brown linoleum on the floor, but it is where the potluck dinners and board meetings happen, so it is not fun. And the word *fellowship* is so antiquated that only churches use it, and the words *fellow* and *ship* smacks of it being a men's boating club. There's got to be a better name for all fellowship halls! Something a little more desirous and jazzed up—like maybe "The Festival Center," as one ground-breaking church has named their gathering spot.

Of course, having fun is not the goal of everything. Jesus didn't say, "I have come that they may have fun and have it more abundantly." But Jesus did say, "I came that they might have life, and have it abundantly" (John 10:10). And when I think about it, the times when I have felt as if I have lived most fully have been the times when I have enjoyed myself with enthusiastic abandon.

## HAVING FUN LIKE THE JEWISH PEOPLE

For the ancient Jews the fun of life was based in celebrating together the faithfulness of God. They knew how to do it right! For instance, when Purim was celebrated, folks gath-

38

ered together as Esther was read, and they stomped their feet, clapped their hands and actually threw out curse words whenever the name of evil Haman was mentioned. Do you know of a church today that holds annual "curse evil people" gatherings, where they hoot, holler, stamp their feet and yell bad words? (This *might* draw in the new people.)

Although this is not completely in synch with New Testament theology, the joy of being together and cheering and booing—validating the good and evil together—is a triumphant celebration of God's faithfulness in and through it all. Other festivals like the Feast of Booths involved families making booths of palms and living in them for a few days, harvesting grapes and enjoying one another as they brought in the harvest. It was like a family camp-out, except that there was work to do and a tangible harvest to celebrate. This created an experience that allowed the people to powerfully act out what they believed. Who could forget it?

This was powerfully illustrated for me when our family participated in a mission trip to Guatemala. It felt a bit like the Feast of Booths because the experience turned into an unexpected festival-like experience.

All day long we lived together in this little shack-like structure that served as church, kitchen, cafeteria, activity center, Vacation Bible School and tool shed. The roof leaked because it wasn't really a roof. The bathroom was up a hill and kept getting clogged. Stray dogs, goats and worn out horses peppered the dusty lanes, along with trash and barbed wire. Not the sort of setting that makes you think of confetti and horns. And yet it was!

We lived together and ate mountains of food prepared by the generous people of a very poor village that virtually had nothing. We spent hours pouring cement for their new church foundation, using cracked buckets and an old cement mixer that was so loud the ringing stayed in our ears long afterward.

We prayed together and the people shared stories with us from their heart. These were stories about how Jesus had rescued them from a life of drunkenness, anger, drugs or despair to a life that was rooted in the hope and confidence of Jesus' presence with them. Every time someone shared, we clapped and cheered. Our team shared as well, and there was immediate resonance. Community was formed overnight, and the tears that we shed when we left, by us and by them, were profound testimonies of the love that had developed between us.

"I had a place of belonging there," someone on our team told me. "I was working to make a difference. I was building a church, both in terms of the building and in terms of connecting with others. Now it is over, and I miss it." Living together, doing work that matters, celebrating God's goodness together—in one of the world's poorest places—was transformational. It was an unforgettable experience of the tangible presence of Jesus. This was community—small groups—being Christ and receiving Christ together.

## PRAYING IN COMMUNITY LIKE
## THE JEWISH PEOPLE

This book probably would not need to be written if we lived

a few thousand years ago in a communal environment. Today we need to learn to be in community, like my group's Guatemala experience. A few thousand years ago, community was part and parcel of the Jewish tradition. It permeated every aspect of life, including prayer, which was one more way of doing life together. In fact, the Jewish tradition today has some very interesting things to say about the value of communal prayer. For instance, the Siddur, or Jewish Prayer book, is essentially the prayer of the community of the people as a whole. In the book *A Guide to Jewish Prayer*, Rabbi Adin Steinsaltz says, "In principle its [the Siddur's] structure, contents and wording are geared to the needs, hopes and sense of gratitude of the community, so that even the individual praying does so as a part of the whole community."

Within Jewish prayer there is a sense of the interconnectedness with ancestors, heritage and history. For the ancient Jew, prayer was not about my needs as an individual and the next person's needs as an individual; rather prayer meant taking into consideration the whole community—essentially the people of Israel as a whole. My identity is found not in me and my concerns, but as a part of a larger context, a communal context that gives me meaning and vision beyond my own myopic concerns. Perhaps this why Paul felt he needed to remind the church that we are surrounded by "a great cloud of witnesses" who have gone before us and are cheering us on (Hebrews 12:1 NIV). When the disciples who walked with Jesus on the Emmaus Road ran back to the other disciples in Jerusalem and found that they had also "seen the

Lord," all joy broke loose (Luke 24). You mean it happened to you too? You mean I can share this extraordinary event with you, and you will understand me? You mean I am not alone with this miracle? This is the joy that we are meant to experience at Easter when we shake each other's hands and declare "He is risen."

Juliet Benner, a guru in individual and group spiritual direction states, "The spiritual journey is a journey we are meant to make with others. The experience of God cries out within us to be shared, and doing so with wise trusted companions is an important part of the way in which we learn to attend to the movement of the Spirit in daily life."

In certain contexts, Jewish group prayer was considered more powerful and more holy than individual prayers. The rabbis declared that when prayers are offered in a congregation or as a community, God will never reject them as he might individual prayers. Some of the more sacred prayers actually can be recited only where a quorum of ten, the *minyan*, is present. The prayers in the standard liturgy, the Siddur or Jewish prayer book, are in the plural form: "Help *us*," "Pardon *us*," "Bless *us*," "*We* give thanks to Thee." Even Jesus begins the Lord's Prayer with "*Our* Father."

An imaginary dialogue between a king and a Jewish sage (Judah Halevi's *Kuzari*—a defense of Judaism) written in the twelfth century has a king asking a Jewish sage why there is so much emphasis on communal prayer. The king thinks it would be better for everyone to say their individual prayers because there is more concentration and purity of thought without distraction from others. The sage counters this by telling the king that someone praying on his own may pray for others to be harmed, but a community will never pray for harm to come to one of its members. Mistakes in prayer that might be made by one person are made up for by others. The community, in essence, offers the checks and balances needed to move individuals into a more corporate awareness of the needs of others and the needs of the world. If love is the nature of God, then it makes sense that prayer must come out of a heart that is passionate about the needs of others and not simply self-enclosed.

Even those who pray individually in Jewish thought still pray in "the name of Israel" and in the environment of community. Rabbi Steinsaltz offers this marvelous image of communal prayer and how it is meant to support and buttress all who participate:

> In a praying congregation, the prayer of each person strengthens and encourages the prayer of every other individual. At moments of emotional weakness or dullness of the heart, one may participate in, and be swept along by, the praying congregation. The congregation acts like a circle of dancers giving constant support to one another, helping the individual to overcome weariness and continue further than each one might do alone. . . . In order to reach the heights, the worshippers create a kind of human ladder, each one standing on the shoulders of the next, thus enabling the individual to climb up high. Anyone who leaves this ladder not only removes a rung, but destroys the entire ladder. On the other hand, one who finds a congregation suited to

his prayers is invigorated and elevated through it and by his participation in it.

A Kabal Kadosh (Holy Congregation) is not simply a collection of individuals, but a new entity in which each worshiper becomes part of a greater unit, drawing strength from others as the person gives back in return.

This also is touched on by Paul through his metaphor of the church being the "body" of Christ—each individual member contributing to the whole in (1 Corinthians 12). Still, sometimes communal prayer for the mainline Protestant is reduced to a unison prayer that is said by rote, printed into a bulletin or flashed up on a screen. The rote-like quality is lifeless for many. One helpful way to approach the printed unison prayer is to ask people to pause, read it once through silently, and then read it together as a group. I have done this for groups, and the way the prayer is read, after just a moment of silent reflection, is transformed. There is usually more of a heartfelt resonance with the words, and the cadence of the prayer is significantly improved.

## DISCERNING GOD'S WILL IN COMMUNITY
A prayerful community recently helped me discern God's will for my life. In this particular group special attention was given to listening to God. In fact, we were given Scriptures to read and then asked to spend a period of time by ourselves to listen, and return to the group with any insights we had. The leaders had been trained in spiritual direction and were as sensitive to the promptings of the Holy Spirit as to the material they chose.

I was contemplating a new call to ministry, wondering if what I had agreed to do was God's will or not. I had received a call from a Presbyterian church to be their senior pastor. I had said yes even though I felt completely inadequate to the task and was scared stiff. I had always been an associate pastor, and people were okay with this. After all, I was a female and always worked under a male. Now I was being asked to be totally in charge! Secretly, I had always wished that someday this would happen, that I would be able to lead, and yet when the opportunity presented itself, I wanted to run away and hide. I couldn't believe this new congregation actually wanted me. I was sick to my stomach with dread.

The first day I walked into the small group a beautiful poem from *Selections* by John O'Donahue was read to all of us—almost before I had a chance to sit down. The poem, "For a New Beginning," advised "Unfurl yourself into the grace of beginning. . . . / Hold nothing back. Learn to find ease in risk; Soon you will be home in a new rhythm."

The words jumped out at me. Every line seemed poignant and true for where I was internally at that moment. I couldn't believe how relevant and clear this was. I keep forgetting all the time that God wants to be intimately involved with every detail of my life. It was as if he were right beside me, encouraging me to be excited about the future, which I never am. I am someone, as I said before, with more of an Eeyore mentality.

After listening in prayer and contemplating the poem, we were given a passage to meditate on. Wouldn't you know it? It was the Emmaus Road story in Luke, which I had been working diligently on for this book. I was sure I would find nothing new. I had combed the text for insights and meaning already. I was a "know it all" when it came to the Emmaus Road, and proud of it!

I went off to pray and contemplate the Scripture, and a new treasure embedded in the text opened up for me. It was a bit of humor, and in the fearful place that I was in—on the cusp of a new beginning—I realized I needed to lighten up with a smile, if not a hearty guffaw! In addition, the bit of humor I saw was directly related to my anxiety. In verse 24 the disciples are explaining to Jesus how the women came back from the empty tomb with a tale about angels that seemed rather bizarre. Then some disciples went to check it all out and "found it just as the women had said; but they did not see him."

"They did not see him" is the last statement Cleopas and his friend make before Jesus takes over the conversation. This is humorous because they are both looking into the face of the risen Christ, telling him that the disciples at the tomb didn't see Jesus, but at the same time they are not seeing him either. The humor touched me and allowed me to realize that I too was not seeing Jesus as alive and active, present in this new beginning. I was doubting and fearful instead. I needed to pray for a new prescription for my spiritual contact lenses that would allow me to recognize Jesus was journeying with me. If I could just *see* with spiritual eyes, I would enter the new opportunity that had been given to me with expectation and joy.

All of this came to me as space was given within the group

for us to listen and discern God's leading through Scripture. When we came back together, I was able to share and be prayed for, and also pray for others. What a difference this small group experience in prayer was from the small group I had been in before! I left not depleted, wanting high-octane coffee, but with my pockets full. I had been infused with new hope and vision.

# 5

# A New Kind of Small Group

[God] comes only through doors that are purposely
opened for him. A person may live as near to God as the
bubble is to the ocean and yet not find him.

RUFUS M. JONES

At this point you are probably looking for some specifics. What are these new groups like? Are they really different? Do they really feed the soul? And what kind of structure is needed to help lead people into an encounter with the living God in a way that makes a difference in their lives?

I have found the Emmaus Road story in Luke's Gospel to be a powerful expression of the transformational small group process. Hidden within it are the steps we need to bring our small groups into the presence of Jesus.

## MEETING JESUS ON THE EMMAUS ROAD

The two disciples hadn't journeyed very far down the road to Emmaus before the stranger joined them. He appeared on their right, keeping pace with them, but they were too engrossed in their conversation to really care or notice all that much. They were having an intense dialogue, but the tone of it was flat with long pauses in between. Both of them, the man and the woman, had a furrowed brow and walked and talked mostly looking down at the ground. Perhaps it was their lack of eye contact that caused the stranger, who kept on looking over at them curiously, to finally ask, "What are you discussing with each other while you walk along?"

The question woke them as if from a dream. They stopped and stared at him, then at each other. Finally their eyes met the ground again and they just stood, still looking sad. "Are you the only stranger in Jerusalem who does not know the things that have taken place there in these days?" the man mumbled.

The stranger had stopped alongside them and was looking at them with interest, head cocked to one side. "What things?" he asked softly, with a shrug.

"The things about Jesus of Nazareth" the woman broke in, "who was a prophet mighty in deed and word. . . . But we had hoped . . ." She couldn't finish because her eyes filled with tears.

"We had hoped," Cleopas finished for her, "that he was the one to redeem Israel." When he said *Israel* his voice cracked and he looked up at the sky to watch a lone bird circling above them. "Our chief priests and leaders handed him over to be condemned to death and crucified him. . . . [I]t is now the third day since these things took place. Moreover, some women of our group astounded us. They were at the tomb early this morning, and when they did not find his body there, they came back and told us that they had indeed seen a vision of angels who said that he was alive. Some of those who were with us went to the tomb and found it just as the women had said; but they did not see him."

Cleopas's words tumbled out in jumbled confusion, leaving the whole matter up in the air with no conclusion whatsoever except a foggy, inexplicable despair etched into the lines of his face. Cleopas did notice, however, that when he said the last part, "they did not see him," the stranger's eyebrows went up in a knowing sort of way that belied a kind of deep wisdom lurking beneath the surface of his friendly nature.

Then the stranger gave a long sigh and looked at them both for a telling moment. "How foolish," he muttered half to himself and half to them, shaking his head, "and how slow of heart to believe." Then, it's as if he said, "Come on, let's walk together and I'll try to explain all this so you can understand."

"But I thought you said you didn't know what happened," the woman probably protested. "How can you explain if you don't know?"

But he did know. As he kept step with them, he began to teach them. He talked like he had studied Scripture all his life. Prophet after prophet, line after line, story after story came spilling out of him as if the whole history of Israel was somehow within him. He explained that the things they were feeling *so badly* about were somehow essential components of an overarching plan.

It seemed to them as they walked along that more was happening to them and in them than they could reasonably understand. They also felt strangely comforted and calmed. It was the sort of feeling we have when we think we are lost and then, quite to our surprise, coming up over a bend, we see our house in the distance. It was with this sort of joyful relief that they listened, as if they were coming home after being gone for way too long. The Scriptures he spoke of were like points of orientation on a map. They held onto each of them like a lifeline.

Seven miles later, the sun was setting, but to them the journey had seemed like seconds. Coming to the outskirts of the small village of Emmaus, the two of them stopped before a small archway that marked the entrance to the inn where they were staying.

The stranger nodded in their direction, but kept walking on, as if he were going farther. This surprised them. They had assumed he would stay at the inn with them. People didn't travel at night on these roads—it was too dangerous. Besides, this was the only inn for miles. They couldn't bear the thought that he would leave now; there was something about him . . .

"Stay with us!" they called out after him. "because it is almost evening and the day is now nearly over."

He turned around to look at them, still seemingly undecided. They urged him again, this time more strongly, insisting that they wouldn't have it any other way. He looked at them steadily for a moment, as if wanting to be sure of their invitation, and then nodded his consent. He had already passed the inn, and as he turned toward them to come back, they noticed that his eyes were very bright. Without knowing quite why, they took a few steps back.

Silently they went in for a simple supper of bread, cheese, dates and figs. As they reclined around a low table in the courtyard the stranger took it upon himself to bless the large loaf of bread, and they watched his hands, bronzed by the sun, tear at the heavy loaf, parceling small pieces out to each of them so that they could dip in the oil or wine. Then they glanced up at his face. Recognition flooded them like an electric charge, and both of them gasped.

For a split second the focus of things had changed, and they could see what they had been unable to see before. They recognized the one who had been familiar to them all along. Jesus Christ, the crucified Messiah, was sitting across the table from them. The broken bread was being held in resurrected hands. He looked back at them with his familiar deep-set eyes and seemed to nod slightly in their direction. Then he vanished.

Cleopas lunged forward, reaching out to grab hold of him, wanting him to stay. But he was truly gone. The woman put her hand on Cleopas's shoulder. "He is not an object in our world any longer," I imagine she whispered, "we are objects in his world. He is here, very close, but not in a body anymore." Then, "Were not our hearts burning within us while he was talking to us on the road?"

Cleopas nodded, mouth open, still staring at the place

where Jesus had been sitting. "We've got to go back" he finally managed. "We've got to tell the others."

Neither of them worried that it was growing dark and therefore dangerous. Neither of them were concerned that it was seven miles away. It was not important. They were turning around. They were going back to Jerusalem. They had to share this news. When the server came back to check on the table, it was empty with only a few scattered pieces of bread left there to testify. The two were already on their way.

When they reached Jerusalem they knew where to go, and they ran, bursting into the upstairs room where the disciples had been hiding, breathless with news. But it was not the somber group they had left behind. Before Cleopas could utter a word, John leaped from his seat and was in front of Cleopas, grabbing him by the shoulders. "The Lord has risen!" he almost shouted at Cleopas. "And he has appeared to Simon." They were all crowding around them both now, Andrew, Thomas, Matthew, Nathaniel—the whole lot of them almost stepping on each other like ebullient puppies, not quite sure what to do, but full of energy for whatever was next.

"I know! I know!" Cleopas declared. "The Lord has appeared to us too. It was the most amazing thing. . . . We recognized him in the breaking of the bread."

## A STORY OF TRANSFORMATION

This is one of my favorite stories in all of Scripture. It is a story of transformation because Cleopas and the unnamed female disciple (we infer that this disciple was female because she is unnamed) have an "aha" experience of seeing Jesus, who had actually been with them all along. Jesus was intimately present with two people who did not recognize him. Two people are "gathered together," and Jesus is in their midst, but they don't figure it out until the very end.

We learn from this that it is in the moment, the *now* of life, that Jesus is present even when we might not *feel* it. In the present there *always* is this remarkable gift of Jesus' presence. It is simply a matter of recognizing the God who is there, taking in what *is*. The disciples finally "took in" the body and blood of Jesus, the bread and wine, and had their eyes opened.

As Jesus held the broken bread in resurrected hands, he was bringing his tangible earthly presence together with his intangible, invisible, resurrected presence. Simple bread was all they could see after he vanished, but the disciples remembered that Jesus had said "this is my body broken for you." There it lay, in pieces, broken for them to see and touch, to take in, to digest and be strengthened. Christ's very presence was now in them, quite literally. This is why at this point they recognize that their hearts had been burning *within* all along (Luke 24:32). They had "taken in" Christ. Implicit in "taking in Christ" is the call to them that they are now his visible presence in the world—God with "skin on."

They were meant to journey with others now, just as Christ had journeyed with them. The person of Christ was also recognized as alive outside of them, and it was validated and confirmed by others in community once they got back to Jerusalem. So both externally and internally we are to represent the body of Christ. In other words, both by a changed heart and by the validation of our small group community, Christ is known to us.

There is then this "turning around" (the meaning of the word *conversion*) when the two of them go back to Jerusalem. The end of the story has all of the disciples testifying together about the truth of the resurrection. Each story shared with joy declares the same reality. Jesus Christ is alive!

When we continue on from this point in Luke, we find that once again Jesus appears to all of them at the same time as they declare together that he has risen. It is when we share our experience of the risen Christ with one another that true community is formed. This kind of joyful exchange ought to be the goal and purpose of all small groups. As we say to each other "You mean you have experienced the risen Christ in your life too?" we find that we are encouraged and affirmed in our faith.

The journey to this joyful exchange is the focus of the next section. How do we get to the place where we have stories to share that testify to the truth that Jesus is indeed alive and meets us in countless different ways on the journey? How do we cultivate small groups that see with the contact lenses of faith? Embedded in this story are important lessons for this kind of small group process. The following points will help guide the leader in creating transformational small groups that lead people into an "aha" recognition of the God who has been there all along. This structure can be modified, and serves only as one possibility. But this structure is intentionally geared toward pulling group participants into an experiential awareness of the God who is with them now and who waits to be recognized.

## A TIME OF INVITATION

"As they came near the village to which they were going, he walked ahead as if he were going on. But they urged him strongly, saying, 'Stay with us, because it is almost evening and the day is now nearly over.' So he went in to stay with them."

Starting with invitation is a faith statement. It declares that it is not about our programs or well-thought-out strategies—the thought for the day or the devotional for the night; rather it is about the power of God and Jesus' presence, the one power on earth that actually changes hearts. Many Scriptures allude to the necessity of invitation, the patience of God and the God who waits for us to call out to him. It is at our initiative and from our desire that we invite first and God shows up. A word to the wise: when we utter the words "stay with us," be forewarned; we ought not to make this invitation lightly. This is the leap of faith, the beginning of the most extreme ride of our lives that will turn us around and change everything. Yet this is where the excitement and joy of the Christian faith begins. So, if you are ready for the ride of your life, at the start of each group meeting, spend time together (10-15 minutes) inviting the presence of Jesus into your gathering.

Invitation is so very important! In the Luke story, when Jesus *appears to be going farther* he doesn't join the disciples for supper until he is asked. Scripture says that they had to "urge him strongly." The same theme comes up in other Scriptures too, such as Jesus standing at the door knocking but not entering until the door is opened and he is invited in (Revelation 3:20). Interestingly, the invitation to come in results in Jesus simply having supper with us. Nothing more. No big earthquake or miracle, simply supper.

God wishes to become our friend—this is the ultimate miracle—and not remain a stranger, to share with us in simple casual moments of relaxation and nurture. It seems that in sharing in these moments "eyes are opened." The invitation is when we say as a small group, "Yes, we are committed to you, Lord. We really do want you to come. We want you here in this small group to lead and guide us. We want to share with you our ordinary lives, our simple moments, our not-so-flashy existences." Henri Nouwen writes:

> Only with an invitation to "come and stay with me" can an interesting encounter develop into a transforming relationship. . . .
>
> Do we say [to Jesus]: "It was wonderful to meet you, thank you for your insights, your advice, and your encouragement. I hope the rest of your journey goes well. Goodbye!" Or do we say: "I have heard you, my heart is changing . . . please come into my home and see where and how I live!" This invitation to come and see is the invitation that makes all the difference.

Given the fact that we are dealing with a rather polite and respectful divine Presence who seeks a close relationship with his creation yet will not intrude, a certain amount of time given to invitation lays the necessary groundwork for a divine encounter. We talk a lot in the evangelical church about "inviting" Jesus into our hearts or "receiving" Jesus. And once we do that at a particular time, on a certain day, we think we're done with the inviting. Actually, this is an ongoing process that lasts our entire life. We continually need to prepare our heart to receive the God who is there.

In one small group that I led, we would start off with a time of invitation. As we began to praise God and invite him into our group, we would say things like "We want you to come and be a part of our gathering here" or "We ask that your presence would make itself known to us in new and transforming ways." When I truly invited God through my prayers, I got a little bit scared. It seems I was getting in touch with the fact that, should Jesus actually show up, I might have to put aside my lesson for the day and simply let the Holy Spirit lead us in a new way. It means surrender, it means trust, and it means getting ready for the unexpected. Still, I came to terms with the fact that God showing up was far better than me showing up and holding tightly to the reigns of my agenda.

I recently acquired an old horse. He is in pretty good condition, and a friend of mine who is a riding champion took it upon herself to teach me how to jump. She told me that when you go over a jump on a horse, the rider momentarily loosens the reigns. Otherwise the horse will be hit in the mouth with the bit. There is a sense of exhilaration in that moment as I fly over the obstacle in front of me and completely rely on the power of the horse to move me up and over, and set me down safely (although perhaps a bit shaken) on the other side.

In the beginning times of invitation, as I let go of the reigns spiritually, I often receive an aha moment. Ideas, thoughts and new possibilities come to me, as well as a more in-depth awareness of the people in the group I am with. Once I looked up at the woman across from me and the words simply flowed out, "I think it is a good thing for you to focus on living out of abundance rather than lack." The woman teared-up because on that particular day she was feeling deprived and alone. These words did not come from me. I didn't know the woman that well at the time because we had just started the group. It was simply that God showed up and worked through all of us in different ways to bring insight, encouragement and truth. The time of invitation is critical and easily leads into aha moments. Nouwen writes,

> We are more inclined to think about Jesus inviting us to his house, his table, his meal. But Jesus wants to be invited. Without an invitation he will go on to other places. It is very important to realize that Jesus never forces himself on us. Unless we invite him, he will always remain a stranger, possibly a very attractive, intelligent stranger with whom we had an interesting conversation, but a stranger nevertheless.

The large Presbyterian church in Korea with almost ten thousand members is built around small groups. A student friend of mine went there to work for a period of time, and she was stunned to find that at the start of each small group there was no small talk, no nibblies, no ice breaker or decaf imposter coffee. People simply came in, sat down and began to pray, even before they said hello to each other. It was their time of inviting Jesus in first. After they were done, they kindly acknowledged one another's presence. The priority was on welcoming God. Afterward they welcomed one another. Given our culture and expectations, I am not saying this is necessary for us to do. But this is an example of the priority of inviting the divine presence into our midst.

## ENCOURAGE HUMBLE, AUTHENTIC SHARING

Another very clear marker point on the journey to Emmaus is Jesus' question to the disciples, which included him in on their conversation. In the same way, he asks us, "What is going on with you? Will you let me in on it?"

> [Jesus] said to them, "What are you discussing with each other while you walk along?" They stood still, looking sad. Then one of them, whose name was Cleopas, answered him, "Are you the only stranger in Jerusalem who does not know the things that have taken place there in these days?" He asked them, "What things?" (Luke 24:17-19)

This is a "let me in on it" desire from Jesus' heart to share in the here and now of our life. In the story, Jesus wants the disciples to *tell him* in their own words, from *their own perspective,* what they are talking about. Of course, from Christ's perspective the problem they are wrestling with has already been solved. In one sense all the problems we are dealing with today have already been solved from God's eternal perspective. Solving the problem as the disciples' saw it was not the issue for Jesus in the Luke story. Otherwise Jesus would have revealed himself right away with "Look guys! It's me!" Rather, Jesus' agenda was to accompany the two disciples on the journey, to listen, to empathize, to explain, to be with them, and to lead them to a point of revelation where they could be converted.

In small groups we usually spend gobs of time sharing what is happening in our lives, but little time sharing it, as a community, with Jesus. There is nothing more deadly in small groups than to have one person hoard too much time with a "request" (unless, of course, it is a real crisis). Instead, I recommend that after one individual *briefly* shares, everyone in the group goes back into prayer to listen and silently lift the person to God. Sometimes I will tell them to imagine the person basking in God's light and receiving God's joy. In my model, listening involves a sixty-second quiet time, after which the group is invited to pray aloud for the individual. Scripture verses, words or phrases can be spoken in this period as well. With four people in a group, the entire process for each person should not last longer than ten minutes (five minutes if you have eight). It is important for the leader to honor this time limit and encourage people to pray for each other for longer periods during the week. (Specific prayer partners can be assigned to individuals for this purpose.) At this point the group will have spent an hour in prayer (invitation, 10-15 mins.; sharing and praying, 40-45 mins.).

Ann Grizzle and David Benner, who lead spiritual direction groups, employ a similar structure. After creating "invitational space" for God (which for them is actually twenty minutes of silence), one person then shares for five minutes or less what is going on in his or her life. At this point no cross talk is allowed, no easy assurances or superficial comments, no advice giving! The rest of the group just listens to the person share, and then everyone goes back into prayer for a couple minutes, listening to the presence of God, who has already been invited into the room. People silently lift the person up in surrender, suspending judgment and the desire to fix the problem. Open listening for another person is a discipline that grows over time, but it is the crux of communal prayer. It is the appropriate response to Jesus asking in the midst of our small group discussion, "What are you talking about as you journey along? Will you include me in the conversation?" Here we have the community of faith at work, validating, confirming and strengthening one another. The Jewish perspective that sees communal prayer as holier than individual prayer makes sense as we engage in this practice.

Authentic sharing and humble surrender to God in small group settings draw us magnetically. God works differently with people, and often there is a pattern of interaction that is unique for each person. Just like God spoke to Daniel in dreams and to David through prophets, so we begin to decipher God's ways with certain individuals, based on the purpose and calling of each. Once, when I was wondering if I should do a certain ministry task that felt enormous and yet seemed like a good thing, I was ambivalent about how to move forward and felt depleted just thinking about it. One of the members of the group said, "If I am remembering, the message God seems to be giving you over and over—it is kind of the theme for you lately—is that you don't need to do things that drain you. If they drain you, you are out of your call, since he has not empowered you to be able to do it out of a sense of joy." This comment came out of a time of listening, and it was said with such humility and genuine care that it resonated deep within my soul. I had lost perspective on my spiritual journey and had forgotten that, yes, this was an ongoing message to me. I am a classic codependent in recovery, and yet I still often find myself feeling obligated to do everything. The community of faith around me helped me to remember this.

With authenticity at the core, groups can become safe places that foster trust between people and ultimately foster trust in God. Humility breeds authenticity. The power of authentic sharing with humility happens when there is trust. This element of small groups is critical, and wherever it is, there will be a magnetic draw.

In one small group that I led, someone asked me why she needed to share. Her point was that God already knew what was going on with her anyway. We talked about this as a group and we agreed that in sharing the specifics of her life with God in prayer she would grow in her relationship with God. She would learn the secrets and insights of God's heart. She didn't share with God to inform God of something he didn't know. Rather, she shared her life specifics with God so that God as "stranger" could be transformed into God as "friend." This is the journey of the Emmaus Road.

It seems to me that Jesus was always calling people to articulate what they needed or wanted. To the blind man Jesus asks, "What do you want me to do for you?" Isn't it fairly obvious? Jesus, knowing what he needed (along with everyone else standing by!), wanted to be asked.

The following story did not happen in a small group. It happened in a worship service I was leading. I think it well illustrates the importance of asking. One Sunday morning, instead of filling up every bit of free space with my words, I asked people to pray, and we did that in silence for a while. The sermon had been on the discipline of asking God for specific things. I had pointed out that sometimes we don't ask for what is on our hearts because we don't believe that we are heard or that God honors those desires. I took some time at the end of the service to give people a chance to do this. We invited God into the things that concerned us, much the way the disciples on the Emmaus Road invited Jesus into the things that were making them sad. I told the congregation that every word they spoke was held by God with great honor, much the way God holds each sparrow that falls, and even if and when requests were wrong, it still delighted God when we trusted him enough to ask. This is much like Jesus wanting the disciples to let him know what they were talking about as they walked along.

At the end of the service a man came up to me. He had tears in his eyes. "I want you to know," he said, "that I have had intense, constant pain in my foot for a long time. It was so bad that I had to park in one of the handicapped spaces when I drove here today. So when you told us to ask God for what was really on our hearts, I asked God to take the pain in my foot away. I hadn't asked because I felt like it was sort of selfish. But when I did ask him, the pain left. Just like that. Right now I am walking for the first time in a long time without pain."

I smiled, but this did not really surprise me. Things like this happen when God is invited into authentic community and open hearts. My response was rather unspiritual, but it made him laugh. "You better pretend to limp back out there," I told him, "or someone will end up giving you a ticket for parking in a handicapped space."

It was far easier to limp than to explain to people that God had actually healed him and done something extraordinary. The unexpected is not usually what we expect to happen in church or in small groups. How dull and uninteresting we have made God to be! It's important for churches to push the reset button, open their eyes, and wait with expectation and hope.

At times, authentic sharing is not easy. The pain in our lives may be too hard to voice. When Jesus first asks the disciples what they were talking about, they "stood still, looking sad." However, when they shared as much as they could, Jesus came alongside and accompanied them on the journey. Jesus joined them not only on the physical journey but also on the psychological/spiritual journey from despair to hope. "We had hoped he was the one" the story begins. The story ends with "he had been made known to them in the breaking of the bread." The breaking of bread signified the very thing they had been hopeless about—the broken body of Christ on the cross. But, ironically, the breaking of the bread was the symbol of hope that opened their eyes to the God, who had been there all along. In leading small groups I have found that when people share authentically with God and with each other, *the very things that have caused the most pain are used by God to bring the most joy and insight in the end.* It is often through the lenses of pain refocused that we see Jesus the best.

## LEARNING TO LISTEN WELL

Listening well is something that is learned over time. In a small group, developing good listening skills is critical, in terms of both listening to God and listening to one another. So the listening piece of the small group process is interlaced throughout every step. I pull it out here as a separate point only because it needs to be highlighted as a priority.

If you look at Luke 24:13-34, you will notice that the longest paragraph of the narrative is the part where *Jesus is listening* to the disciples (vv. 19-24). Nevertheless, for most of the seven-mile journey to Emmaus the disciples are essentially listening to Jesus. As we invite others to share with authenticity, we also must respond by listening carefully to what they say. Listening is one of the greatest gifts we can give to each other in a noisy, preoccupied culture. But this is a challenge. Dietrich Bonhoeffer, the early twentieth-century German theologian, says that there is a distracted kind of listening that we are good at. This is when I am figuring out what to say while the other person is talking. Then I respond in order to be done with that person. True listening is focusing our full attention on what the other person is saying, and being genuinely interested. The only way to be genuinely interested in Hazel and Bags is to listen with ears attuned to Christ's love for them. Small groups are training grounds for this kind of listening. It is harder to be spiritual in groups, where there are real people with idiosyncratic behaviors, greasy hair and "issues," than it is when I am praying alone and "loving the world" in abstraction. In a small group I may not like the person sitting next to me, or I might want to silently criticize what someone has just said. The very fact that the terrain is rough and real is precisely why Jesus deems community necessary. One of the first indications that we are loving real people well is that we listen well.

I remember being in a small group when someone requested prayer for her daughter. Though I was trying to listen, I was also wondering if the chicken in the oven was going to be overcooked when I got home and whether I had anything else for dinner that I could pull out of the freezer. Half listening, I was aware of the woman's anxiety by the way she inflected her words. So when we prayed for her, I asked God to give the woman peace and enable her to trust that she was being held up by Jesus' arms. I suppose it sounded fine, but when we finished praying the woman looked disappointed. "No one prayed for my daughter," she said despondently. I had been a poor listener—distracted and disinterested. I have tried since then to center myself in the love of Jesus for the person and be fully present to whatever situation I am being asked to pray for. Being intentional in this area has helped me track with the person and tune in with more insight and depth.

## BEFRIENDING SCRIPTURE

The last segment of the group time can last anywhere from thirty to forty-five minutes, depending on the group process. I find that sometimes a total of an hour and a half is not quite long enough, whereas two hours is too long. Find your own rhythm with this and allow yourself to get creative in how you use Scripture. For some, the standard Bible study with a question-and-answer format work well. This may be especially helpful for new Christians. However, you may find, as I often do, that this leads the group more into an intellectual discussion of their faith rather than an experiential encounter with God. There is nothing wrong with the intellectual approach, as it may well draw some people closer to God in a different way. However, there are many other methods of using Scripture that are not tried very often in small groups, which you may want to experiment with.

There are exercises in this book that can guide you in new directions. Jesus used Scripture in the Luke story to explain to the two disciples what had happened in his crucifixion. Still, they didn't turn around (convert) until the content came alive in the person of Jesus right before them. Combining Scripture with the opportunity to experience God's presence is often achieved through a more contemplative approach, or through the use of the five senses. In addition, meditating, memorizing and prayerfully saying the words of Scripture can be a way to center on the peace of God's presence. These practices often allow the words of Scripture to move from the head to the heart. There is something about befriending Scripture, getting up close and personal with it, that shapes us from the inside out. It can make our heart "burn within." Doing this in a group is all the more centering.

I recently led a women's retreat and had a potter fashion a beautiful bowl as I gave a talk on surrender. She told us that the beginning of the formation process was very intense, that the potter had to press down on the clay and make sure it was concentrated in the center of the wheel. This had to happen first before further sculpting could be done. It allowed for balance, strength and integrity in the vessel that was to be formed. Befriending Scripture in a more mystical way is one avenue toward experiencing the centering presence of God.

Brian McLaren makes the distinction between knowing a frog through dissection (a more intellectual approach to Scripture) and knowing a frog by experiencing it in its natural habitat, jumping from lily pad to lily pad (a more experiential approach). Both are good ways of knowing, but the latter often touches the heart more profoundly.

Scripture can be seen as either a textbook to be conquered or a love letter to be cherished. The psalmist's line "Oh, how I love your law! / It is my meditation all day long" (Psalm 119:97) was written by someone who was in love-letter mode. A. W. Tozer writes that the Bible

> is not only a book which was once spoken, but a book which is *now speaking.* . . .
>
> If you would follow on to know the Lord, come at once to the open Bible expecting it to speak to you. Do not come with the notion that it is a thing which you may push around at your convenience.

In small groups the half hour or more given to Scripture can be the process of allowing Scripture to read the group and speak to the group, rather than the group reading and analyzing Scripture. If the group follows the steps in order as is suggested in this book, *being read* by Scripture is much simpler to do because this process of opening ourself up to the Word of God is an extension of the prayer time that has gone before. All that has changed is that the Word of God is now a part *of the communion with God.* The communion around the Scriptures makes our hearts burn. If we receive the Scriptures as a love letter, then our contemplation, listening or reading becomes a place of resting in God's presence, who has already been invited in. A group can be read by Scripture only when each person relinquishes control and puts aside any agenda to efficiently get results or conquer the text.

Another way to focus on and pray Scripture is to choose a very small portion of Scripture to meditate on over a period of time. In one of our small groups we spent two weeks meditating, praying and contemplating the familiar words "The LORD is my shepherd, I shall not want." We repeated these words prayerfully and in prayer, and insight from this small verse came bubbling to the surface. What does it mean that the Lord is my shepherd? David wrote this and identified with God. In what ways did David see that what he did was also what God did? How might this have been helpful to him? Is there overlap between my profession and who I know God to be? What does it mean to not be in want? I always want. Why does having the Lord as my shepherd reduce my want? Is this what I really think, believe and live?

Discussion and prayer around these issues was enriching and inspiring. It was intellectual and heartfelt, but it didn't try to conquer the entire terrain of Psalm 23. We were centered around how these few words of Scripture spoke to us about what was going on *with us* in our circumstances. (Refer to the guided prayer exercise on pp. 109-10, which can be adapted to any Scripture.)

There is a profound difference between knowing *about* Jesus and *recognizing* the person of Jesus. This distinction is striking in the Emmaus Road account. The importance of head knowledge is not to be diminished. Jesus taught the two of disciples Scripture on the Emmaus road for seven miles, trying to explain his own death and why it had to happen. We learn from this that we are meant to understand our faith and the workings of God throughout history. We also learn that it is only from the perspective of community that we can get a larger picture of what God is doing in our particular lives.

# 6

# Creating Emmaus
# Road Groups

Prayer, therefore, is God's breathing in us, by which

we become part of the intimacy of God's inner life, and by which

we are born anew. So, the paradox of prayer is that it asks for a

serious effort while it can only be received as a gift. We cannot

plan, organize or manipulate God; but without a careful

discipline, we cannot receive him either.

HENRI J. M. NOUWEN

Early on in ministry I began
to create small groups with the elements from the Emmaus
Road story in mind. I tried to include invitation and the con-
templation/meditation of Scripture, and develop authentic
sharing within the group. I also created celebration moments
or rituals in which we mirrored the joy of transformation by

experiencing joy ourselves in surprising (sometimes even frivolous) ways. Recognizing Jesus on the journey was part and parcel of this structure.

One group was so bonded that seventeen years later they are still meeting with each other. Another group met for over twelve years. In those years one woman felt called into the ministry and was recently ordained. Another participant who was suicidal came out of a deep depression through meditating on Scripture and seeing God at work in the details of life. Someone else who had never really thought much about "religious things" became a Christian educator and did a marvelous job with the kids in the church. In general, with the elements of the Emmaus Road story at work, people became Christians in a deeper way than merely going to church had ever provided. One woman who became a dear friend of mine through this group had been a nominal church-goer for years. As we meditated on Scripture, she fell in love with it. Taking one of the group members out for coffee, she sat down and began to read a Scripture to the woman that she had recently discovered. The other woman just stared at her. "That's nice," she said. My friend stared back at her across the table. "But you don't understand," she said, "this isn't just nice; this is real." Gradually both women grew together in their faith, became fast friends and continually met together to support each other on their journey.

The first woman recently died of cancer and there were seven hundred people at her funeral. She had changed countless lives because she was so aware of the love of Jesus and, without judgment or condemnation, was ready to reach out to anyone who had a need. About ten non-Christians who came to that funeral grabbed her husband after it was over. Instead of the usual "I'm so sorry for your loss," they said instead, "I've never experienced the presence of God so strongly before. Is your church always like this? I'd like to come."

With tears rolling down his cheeks, her husband told me that losing his wife to cancer was awful, terrible, tragic. But years ago, through his wife's prayers he too had experienced Jesus. Previously, he was a borderline alcoholic and complete skeptic. Now, in spite of the tragedy, he had a deep serenity. "All this difficulty has given me a chance to share my faith," he told me. "I've never been very good at that part of Christianity—the sharing my faith part. But now, when people come up to me and ask, 'How can you manage this? How can you go on?' I have a perfect opportunity to tell them where my strength comes from."

All of this illustrates what happens when a small group of people discover the reality of God in their midst. When they realize that what we talk about, sing about, read about in church is *a living reality*, then real things start to happen. There is a ripple effect. One stone thrown into the water creates ripples too numerous to count. One life changed, and more lives are changed. When we move away from formulas, manipulations, three-points-and-your-problems-are-gone simplicities; when we move toward a real God who loves real people; when we put our masks down and humbly trust in a God who tells us that anything is possible, things happen. When God is treated like he is really there, poised and ready to be involved, ready to ask us, "What are you discussing with each other while you walk along?" and we are willing to share and listen, then there will be life, and people will see Jesus.

## EXPERIENCING GOD IN THE MIDST OF THE ORDINARY

Some people ask me whether they need to be a spiritual giant to engage in this kind of group. Will God really come and be a transforming presence in an ordinary group of women who meet on Tuesday afternoons? Will God really meet me in my living room with my group of struggling singles? Will God make a difference for the mechanic, the school teacher, the plumber, the librarian? Ordinary people in ordinary lives? Isn't this kind of a group for the advanced, other-worldly folks who chant and eat organic?

The answer is that making space for God's presence is the only way to help others experience spiritual transformation. So the answer is *yes!* And there is nothing out of the ordinary about listening, friendship with others and with God, sharing real stuff, and surrendering ourselves. We listen, have friends, share and submit in other areas of our lives all the time. And there is nothing more attractive than people who are authentic about their faith and who come together in community without pretense and depend on God, not on themselves, knowing that transformation *is not about what they do but only about what God does*. This small group model is attractive because God is given space to act, to create and to speak to the heart. Most ordinary people leave these kinds of groups with their hearts full.

Jesus affirmed God's value of and love for the tangible world. There is a certain divine delight in the ordinary, which is implicit in the earthiness of the incarnation. In the creation and the incarnation God declares "Yes! Life as I created it is great!" I think there is also a certain desire on the part of God to engage with us *in the ordinary*, because this is the nature of love—to meet others in their world and delight in it with unselfish participation. Thus Jesus' desire to be included in the disciples' ordinary conversation on the Emmaus Road is the epitome of God saying, "Let me into the ordinariness of your life, into all of it—from the conversations to the dusty walk to the questions to a simple supper—all of it." God loves the ordinary and uses ordinary people and ordinary life to make himself visible. This is the message of the Emmaus Road.

Juliet Benner wrote about Caravaggio's *The Supper at Emmaus* painting in *Conversations Journal*. It is famous because of the way the artist used contrasting light and darkness. Out of deep shadows he brings the viewer face to face with the supernatural in the midst of the natural. His art was revolutionary because he did not paint to idealize religious subjects. Instead he presented the real world in all of its commonness—common things and common people—yet he painted with passion and empathy. In the painting, one of the disciples is wearing a shell, indicative that he is just a plain fisherman. The fruit basket on the table is so real and common that there are worm holes in the fruit. In the midst of it all is Jesus. Jesus is recognized in the midst of this common life, where all are welcome.

In the painting, there is an open place at the table that looks just wide enough for someone to pull up a chair and join in. Jesus' hand is outstretched in a welcoming gesture. I must learn to sit and recognize Jesus in the midst of the ordinariness of my journey. As I pull up a chair to join in fellowship around a simple loaf of bread, I join with the two other disciples, who will help me recognize Jesus, as they do. This is the mystical awareness of God's presence in the ordinary—in the humility and authenticity of my own life as I share this with others. I am not seeking to escape from this world—I would not seek out community if this were the case. Rather I am seeking to experience the God who puts me back into the real, raw world in a different way, with renewed capacity to give and receive love. G. K. Chesterton said, "Mysticism keeps men sane. As long as you have mystery you have health; when you destroy mystery you create morbidity. The ordinary man has always been sane because the ordinary man has always been a mystic."

## WHERE DO WE GO FROM HERE?

When the Holy Spirit came and filled the disciples at Pentecost, that was a festival moment! There was no command to be in the temple constantly praising God. There was no mandate to preach or create a church or make something happen that was holy. There was no workbook with a formulaic step-by-step implementation plan. Rather, what was done was a natural outflow of being filled with new wine. The disciples were so happy they acted like they were drunk—giddy, a bit too loud perhaps, too happy, overjoyed. And this irrepressible joy, which came from being intoxicated on the Holy Spirit, is what created the church. I am not suggesting that all Christians should be giddy. I am suggesting a new paradigm. (Amazing, isn't it, churches today are described as boring, strict, too bossy, repressed and out of touch, whereas in Acts the church was described as drunk?)

I believe that there is a strong fermentation of the Holy Spirit in our churches today, and we need new wineskins. The old wineskins of learning *about* God through clever sermons and doctrine will not reach a culture weary of to-dos and on information overload. These old wineskins are bursting open and the beauty of the gospel is being wasted because our systems and programs are not able to stretch and grow with the current needs and attitudes. In the midst of a culture that is hungry for meaning and depth, the new wine of transformation and growth is spilling onto the ground. The three-point sermon doesn't cut it anymore. There is a distrust of authority and a lack of connection with religious organizations. Because human beings are wired for spiritual connection, it is no wonder that many are creating their own "spirituality," using any means available to draw them into an awareness of a higher order of things. It may well be that God is allowing this post-Christian period to wake up the dormant church to the hunger of a spiritually starving generation.

The Christian faith is unique in that it actually celebrates a Person who is at the helm. This relational aspect of divine love couches all of our discontent and existential dysphoria in a divine embrace. If we truly believe in the reality of Jesus' resurrected presence with us now, we ought to be looking for opportunities to make the experience of his presence a reality for others. Empty pews do not speak to a lack of need or desire on the part of our culture but to the emptiness of our convictions. The wineskins are wrong, and as ministry leaders we cannot keep shoving programs, information and didactic Bible studies down the throats of an increasingly dwindling constituency. People are seeking something more authentic. Experiencing the presence of God will give us the vision and passion to reach out to people in new ways with the wineskins of tomorrow.

Our current culture puts a high premium on experience. A person's experience establishes truth—thus the relativism of our culture. We are supposed to respect and tolerate all beliefs that come out of personal experiences. At the same time people feel a desperate need and desire for community. In the midst of the phenomena of social networking—texting, Facebook and the like—many complain that it is difficult to find a "best friend." The new wineskins of the twenty-first century bring the experience of Jesus Christ to the forefront and establish caring communities around this reality. If we only impart information and ignore the Holy Spirit, the change agent of the New Testament, we will put today's new wine into the old skins of yesterday. Although it has its place, doctrine is irrelevant for most people today. Many do not care what others believe, and since everyone's spirituality needs to be respected, there is a "whatever" shrug to the religious beliefs of others.

The evangelical church has been great at imparting information, but not so great in creating the space for people to experience Jesus' love. An important part of this, I believe, is fostering community prayer experiences that are transformational as well as connectional. Prayer as currently practiced is heavily influenced by our culture—it is highly individualized. Unfortunately, even in the small group context, it stays that way. Connectional prayer is not done in these settings.

Jesus said that where two or three are gathered together in his name he would be their midst, which puts a premium on communal prayer. We need a refresher course in what it means to pray as a community, which will bring back a sense of wonder and delight into the prayer experience. This involves drawing on one another's insights and listening to each other, as well as being awed together at the goodness of God.

Authentic community exhibits that our God is available, present and at work in people's lives. He loves surprises and keeps surprising us so we stay on our spiritual tiptoes. We think the story is over, but wait! There is one more chapter, one more bend in the road, one more song to sing, one more move to make. Christian community is meant to be exactly this: a gathering of people who together declare God's surprises, who laugh and rejoice and validate our common experience that we have "seen the Lord." Just when we thought all was lost, he surprises us again with his living presence and turns us around toward authentic joy-filled community.

In the rest of this book you will find exercises for small group transformation. They are designed to help us experience the real and awesome presence of God in the midst of our very ordinary worlds. These suggestions for invitation, sharing and prayer are not formulas for success but are meant to be conduits for the Holy Spirit, who alone can change hearts.

# PART TWO

# Exercises

7

# Invitational Exercises

## UNISON PRAYER

Sometimes it is helpful to start the meeting by reading a unison prayer, which is also repeated to close the invitation segment. To avoid the mindless recitation of empty words, have each person first read through the prayer silently. Then have the group read the prayer in unison. A psalm or Scripture verse can be used, or you can write your own prayer. The following are two suggested prayers:

> Come, Lord Jesus, you are welcome here.
> Come and stay with us, for our days are far spent, and
> we need the refreshment of your presence.
> We do not know what we do, so we are stopping
> our doing.
> And in these moments, we open ourselves up as best
> we can.
> Forgive us, Lord, for all the ways we miss the mark.

And open us to your transforming grace and love that
    covers all of our sin.
We want to let you in on our conversation, our
    thoughts, our dreams.
Come, Lord Jesus.

Lord Jesus Christ, have mercy on us.
We are closed off to your presence so much of the
    time.
We gather in hope that you will let your love burn
    within us.
We invite you to come to us.
Open our eyes, we want to see you.
Open our ears, we want to hear you.
Open our hearts, we want to receive you.
Open our minds, we want to know you.
Open our hands, we want to serve you.
Lord Jesus Christ, have mercy on us.
And meet with us today.

Sometimes the facilitator can lead the group in reading an
appropriate Scripture together, or a chorus can be sung together at the end of this period. Depending on the group, soft
background music may help create a mood of calmness, receptivity and an awareness of God's nearness. Some groups
have closed this time by prayerfully passing the peace. This
practice involves having individuals look into each other's
eyes, shake hands and say "Peace be with you." It is a way to
give a blessing and connect spiritually as a community.

Group members can be reminded that when they look into the eyes of their sister or brother, they are looking into the eyes of Jesus.

## GOD AS SUSTAINER OF LIFE

Grow quiet together as a group and have each person become aware of their heartbeat. (Sometimes it helps if people feel their pulse, either on their wrist or their neck.) The heart is the center of our being, an organ that keeps pumping even when we are not thinking about it. This all-important, life-giving source can remind us of our Creator. Spiritual life gets pumped through us as we allow God to be at the center of our day. God is loving us constantly, even when we are not thinking about him. Praise God for the fact that he has given us life and continues to sustain us even when we are not thinking about him.

Have the group close their eyes and imagine that their heart is a prayer room where Jesus can enter. Direct them to think about Jesus entering their heart in many ways. It may be that they think about this as a light flooding their chest; maybe it would be easier for them to think about Jesus' words "Abide in me" being literally pumped out from the center of their being. Whatever image helps them to "center" on Jesus, to rest in him as the Source of life, have them focus on that. Suggest they ask Jesus to take away any sin that is separating them from him. They could ask him to forgive them and clean up their heart, which is ultimately his home. They also may wish to imagine seeing the others in the group awash in God's love and light, and whisper

"Come, Lord Jesus. Come into our fellowship. We invite you. Stay with us. For the hour is late, and we need your companionship."

## EXPERIENCING GOD'S LIGHT

As people arrive, give everyone a votive candle (or any free-standing candle). Have each person light their own candle and spend some quiet moments watching the candles burn. Let the flame represent God's holiness and the light that exposes all things. Praise God (either silently or aloud) for being the light, for purifying, for bringing illumination and that his light never gets extinguished. Praise him that because of Jesus, humanity does not have to walk in darkness any longer.

Observe that as the candle burns, the top gets deeper at the core. With the candles still lit, pray together (in silence or aloud) for God to burn away anything inauthentic or superficial that may be distancing them from him or from others. Have the group silently confess any sins they may be aware of in this area. Then, invite Jesus to come into the small group gathering and illuminate ways that the group can grow in authenticity and depth as a community. Ask God to burn away anything that is getting in the way of each member experiencing the fullness of his love. Allow the candles to burn throughout the group time, and have people take their candles home as a reminder of God's longing to burn away superficiality and sin and instead make us deep and authentic in our relationships with one another.

## USING SCRIPTURE TO FOCUS
## THE TIME OF INVITATION

Find a Scripture verse that describes who Jesus is. Read it together as a group. Scriptures that emphasize praise or listening (1 Samuel 3:9; John 10:27) are excellent. Another example is, "The LORD is good to those who wait for him, to the soul that seeks him. It is good that one should wait quietly for the salvation of the LORD" (Lamentations 3:25-26). Phrases that state something about the nature of God also work well: "You are the lily of the valley, the bright and morning star," "You are our Comforter," "You are our shepherd," "You are our advocate," "Be still and know that I am God." These kinds of statements help focus our thoughts and direct us to praise and inclining our ear toward God. These statements can be repeated aloud throughout the entire period of invitation.

## USING SYMBOLS FOR INVITATION

Set in front of the group a meaningful symbol as a focal point. If someone's mind starts to wander (everyone's does!), this symbol will help him or her focus. It might be a candle, a cross or even an open Bible. As we posture ourself to be attentive to God, we can look at the symbol as a reminder of God's presence in the center of the group. One especially meaningful symbol for me was a stone representing Christ as the cornerstone. All the names of the group members were written on the stone. We put it in the middle of the table as our focal point. I could look at that and recognize that all of us were joined together by the rock-solid truth of Christ's eternal presence with us now.

## BREATHING IN THE LIFE OF GOD

Have people sit quietly with their palms open in their lap as a gesture of open receptivity to the presence of Jesus. Praise God for a few moments together, thanking him that he is Lord and at the same time is present and available, close and approachable. Lead people to become aware of their breathing and how close God is to them—closer than their breath. Then have the group imagine that as they are breathing in they are inhaling the Holy Spirit. Each person can imagine this in whatever way he or she wishes. Many find that seeing themselves breathing in light and warmth is helpful. As people breathe out, have them exhale any tension or stress they might be holding. Tell the group that very often stress or tension is held in the jaw, shoulders or neck. Have them focus on any other areas of the body where they may be experiencing tension or stress, and consciously relax these areas. Encourage everyone to keep breathing together, inhaling Jesus' presence, exhaling tension or stress. Ask Jesus to forgive any sins that are hindering the group or individuals from experiencing the fullness of his presence. Then invite Jesus to come and bring a sense of his presence to the group as a whole during your meeting time together. Praise God again for his attributes of healing, grace, forgiveness and love.

## RIVERS OF LIFE

As people arrive, have them go into prayer, praising God for his presence with them. Then, have the group see, in their mind's eye, a dam caked with dirt and sticks. On one side of the dam lies crystal-clear water, on the other side a parched desert. Ask the group if there are any parts of them that are parched today. What is walling them off from God's presence? Ask God for forgiveness for anything that might be keeping the members of the group from him. It might be hurt or resentment, doubt or exhaustion. As the group confesses, see the dam breaking down and crystal blue water flowing into the desert in the form of a mighty river flooding the cracked, parched ground and bringing life to withered plants. Praise God that he is the living water, and ask him to flood the group with an awareness of his life-giving power.

## A STONE BEFORE A SCULPTOR

As people arrive, have them come into God's presence by imagining themselves as a stone. Hand people some sharp or misshapen rocks to hold when they come in. As people hold the stones, have them ask God to smooth down any sharp edges and carve something beautiful and meaningful out of the rock. Lead the group in confessing anything they would like God to carve away from their life. Ask God for some quality they would like him to shape in their life. Stay for a moment in the Lord's presence, waiting, given over to God's design for them as Master Sculptor. Have each member ask the Lord to give him or her the ability to attend to his presence in this way, surrendered, open to his plan and design, moment by moment throughout the day. Then they may turn their prayer to the group as a whole. Ask that each person in the group will recognize their giftedness and that as a community they will be able to grow and flourish. Praise God that he is the Master Sculptor, able to shape even stones into masterpieces for his use. You might want to read 1 Peter 2:5, which is a great Scripture on community, joint purpose and call: "Like living stones, let yourselves be built into a spiritual house, to be a holy priesthood."

A variation on this exercise can involve handing group members clay or Play-Doh as they arrive, asking them to knead it in their hands as they pray and invite Jesus into their gathering. Ask God to fashion the group in such a way that all participants would be conduits for the presence of God and represent the body of Christ. Afterward it might be fun to put everyone's piece of clay together to form a joint sculpture of the group, which symbolizes unity and being open and receptive to God's presence. This sculpture, fashioned together, can be a focal point for the group. (It doesn't have to be perfect, just symbolic and representative of everyone's participation together and willingness to be open to what God wants to do in and through them.) Sometimes the sculpture comes out looking ridiculous, but it helps everyone not take themselves too seriously. It reminds the group that God uses us in our weakness, and all of us are a work in progress.

# 8

# Sharing and Praying
# for Others

$\int$mall group sharing and prayer for others can be done without a lot of innovation. As long as people are willing to share and the rest of the group is willing to listen, it isn't all that complicated. However, sometimes we can jump-start praying for others when we have some structure, images and metaphors to help us engage more fully. In addition, I have added some ideas about how to facilitate sharing and listening.

Some people find it very easy to share what is going on in their lives. Others are more reticent. Still others may not be able to fully express themselves with words. Allowing the group to share in different ways can be a helpful way to engage everyone, as well as adding variety, color and life to the process. Here are few suggestions. (Most need to be prepared ahead of time.)

• Have each member draw a time line of their spiritual journey and mark critical junctures along the way where it seems to them that God was at work. What have they learned? Where has God brought them? Where are they now in terms of seeking after God? Where in their life would they like to see God more?

- Have the participants bring a sketch of where they are spiritually. Allow them to show the sketch to the group and share their concerns, joys and requests.

- Before they share their own personal requests, start the time by having people share what their favorite praise song or hymn is and why. This helps everyone in the group to understand what images or phrases about God are most salient for each person, and can help the group know how to pray. A stanza from the song can be used to close the prayer time for that person.

- Have people share by first reading a Scripture that somehow depicts where they are, what they need from God right now or what they are thankful for. (The Scripture should be chosen the week before.)

- Give each participant the prayer of St. Francis, of St. Patrick, the Lord's Prayer or one from a prayer book. Ask them to take it home and highlight the part of the prayer that most closely identifies how they would like the group to pray for them and why.

- Have people share their name and what it means. How does this relate to who they feel they are today? What might God's name be for them, given what their gifts are?

There are many other creative ways a group leader can

facilitate sharing. As the leader gets to know the people and their gifts and abilities, he or she should think about how to *use what participants bring* to build the small group. Every group is different, but every group is chock full of gifts that the Holy Spirit has distributed among them. Many people do not even realize what they have to offer to others. Once these gifts are allowed to unfurl and be used, myriad options will be discovered that will help facilitate authentic community in the group.

# 9

# Listening

$S$omeone once said that the first step in loving someone is learning to listen to him or her. It is important that we learn to listen to each other, because this is the first stepping stone in learning to listen to God. If we can't listen to people who we see, how can we begin to listen to the invisible God? Furthermore, God often speaks through the body of Christ. Some groups listen very well. If a group listens naturally, simply allow the listening to take place. However, if the group is rambunctious or a group member has a hard time not giving advice to others, help is needed.

One tactic I have used to facilitate listening and quiet was used by the Native Americans eons ago: the "talking stick." (School teachers use this very effectively.) A stick (we have also used a cross, a dove, a Bible, an ichthus fish and even a limp stuffed animal with one eye) is passed around from person to person. The person holding the stick (or object) has the floor; it is his or her turn to talk. The rest of the group *must* remain silent as the person shares for three to four minutes. When it is time for the person to stop sharing the, leader takes the stick and places it in the center of the table. This signifies that the group is now to pray—spend sixty seconds listening to God for the person, and then verbal prayers can be offered. This is an effective way to maintain structure, honor the time allotted and also facilitate listening.

The leader must be willing, however, to indicate when the person's sharing time is up, and that by placing the object in the middle of the table, prayers for that person from the group are now in order. In time, the structure becomes second nature, but in the beginning it is sometimes hard to get into the flow.

Structure is important in a group geared toward a more experiential awareness of God's presence. Without it, things can rapidly deteriorate into a touchy-feely kind of mush, and the more talkative members will end up dominating the group.

Another fun exercise is to play three or four informational CDs, tapes or all-talk radio stations at once. Ask members of the group to glean information from only one source. See who is able to hear and retain the most. Use this as an illustration of how we need to learn to tune out the world and tune into God. We need an unflinching resolve to focus our attention until we hear his voice alone. Explain that in time it becomes easier to tune in to one voice in prayer, even with multiple distractions.

Listening well to God can also be facilitated by quiet music, finding a quiet spot outside to meditate or simply listening in the silence. One of the biggest complaints about listening is that a person's mind wanders. This is not unusual—everyone's mind wanders. It is helpful to have a small pad or paper to jot down distractions when they come. This allows us to let go of the distractions and return to listening to God.

# 10

# Interceding for Others

The Spirit helps us in our weakness; for we
do not know how to pray as we ought, but that
very Spirit intercedes with sighs too deep for words.

ROMANS 8:26

Prayer for others naturally flows from invitation. As Paul writes, we do not know what we need. We do not know how to pray. Acknowledging that the Holy Spirit lives in us and knows how to pray for us can greatly relieve performance anxiety and thinking that our prayer for each other is all up to us. As we begin to trust the Holy Spirit more, we will find that the right words come naturally or that it is okay to remain in God's presence and say nothing at all. At these times the Spirit may be interceding with sighs too deep words (Romans 8:26). The Holy Spirit will also lead the group toward doing the right prayer exercises at the right time, and will foster a sense of growth and unity around these practices.

## BRING THE PERSON REQUESTING PRAYER INTO JESUS' PRESENCE IN ORDER TO RECEIVE

Once verbal prayers begin, the leader or a group member may wish to guide the person asking for prayer in the following way:

In Jesus' day people lay on cushions around a low platform table and usually ate propped up on one elbow. Say to the person requesting prayer:

> Imagine yourself "reclining," relaxing in Jesus' presence around a table where a meal is being served. Sometimes in our fast-paced culture it is hard to relax when you commune with God; for many it is more of a tense, fast-food experience. Right now, allow yourself to recline in God's presence internally (breathing deeply, consciously relaxing, willing to stay a while). In this posture, try to stay focused. Sleep later. See Jesus handing you the bread as one friend would hand it to another. "This is my body," he tells you. Then see him handing you the cup: "This is my blood." In a relaxed posture, receive these gifts from the Lord's hand. See yourself literally taking Jesus in. "Remember me," he tells you. "Remember me as loving you always."

After the person has been brought into this place of open receptivity, the prayers for them can be very short, to the point, always reflecting what they have asked from the group initially. This exercise is helpful when someone has been praying for something to happen for a while, with seemingly no change. It can also encourage someone who feels discouraged or depleted.

## SPIRITUAL IDENTITY

This exercise works best after the group members have shared their names (see p. 94).

Many times in Scripture, when people come into relationship with God, their name is changed. This is because a person's name connotes his or her "nature," and God's Spirit transforms our old nature and gradually changes us into the nature of Christ. For example, in the Old Testament, Abram's name was changed to Abraham, and in the New Testament, Saul's name was changed to Paul.

Have the group members close their eyes (or focus on Jesus with their eyes open) and move into an attitude of prayer. As they reflect on the name of the person they are praying for, have them think about how the person's name reflects some of the gifts they see in him or her (based on the earlier sharing time). For those who don't see any connection (and very often there is none), they should meditate on the gifts they see in the person and begin to think about what name might adequately describe his or her identity as a gifted child of God. This may not come right away. We often need to think and pray about it for a while. For instance, maybe a person in the group has a gift of compassion. The spiritual name that might identify the person could be simply "Compassionate One." Or someone may have the gift of hospitality, and his or her name might be "Open to Give." Names connote identity. Perhaps you want to set aside a day when the group shares what gifts they see in each other and what spiritual name these gifts generate.

## GROUP SOLIDARITY: WHERE GOD HAS BROUGHT YOU

This exercise is especially effective when used with the spiritual time line suggestion (see pp. 93-94).

The group leader can suggest that the small group engage in this exercise at the end of the prayers of intercession. (Obviously a shorter time of sharing or Scripture needs to be planned ahead of time.) This exercise sets the tone for further reflection on God's leading and guidance, and allows group members to spend some moments contemplating their life and how God might be using their experiences to encourage and facilitate the group.

Have the group spend some moments in silence, each member thinking about where God has brought and is calling him or her to grow as a part of this small group. Is it growth in terms of trusting God? in awareness of the world's need? in being able to move from bitterness to gratitude, to see all of life as a gift from God, who owns it all? Is it growth in being able to trust others in the group and engage fully in the community of faith? in being able to pray effectively and consistently for others? All should open their hands, palms upward as a symbol of being willing to let go of the stuff of life that keeps them from God's presence and also as a symbol of their willingness to receive from God. Then each should ask the Holy Spirit to help him or her grow in the capacity to receive from this group and to give all that God is asking each to give to this community of believers that he has shaped for a reason and a purpose.

## PRAYING TOGETHER USING THE LITURGY

Liturgy is a tool that is generative for many, giving structure and meaning when words fail. Liturgy also holds a depth of theology that is unparalleled. We have seen that repeating prayers from the Siddur, a collection of Jewish prayers recorded through the centuries, is an important practice. In and of itself, the Siddur represents the larger community of faithful Jews who have gone before, placing the pray-er in community, even when praying alone.

> The constant repetition entailed in prayer constantly reveals new aspects each time, creating in the worshipper feelings, thoughts that he might never have reached on his own, so that he not only utters the words of the Siddur, but they spring from his own mind and heart.

At the same time, despite the value placed on repetition, it was only the prayer of the heart that mattered.

> Prayer should not be recited as if a man were reading a document. (Jerusalem Talmud, *Berakhot* 4:3)

> Always let a man test himself. If he can direct his heart, let him pray. If he cannot, let him not pray. (Babylonian Talmud. *Berakhot* 30B)

With the heart always in mind, and the awareness that

liturgy is never to be recited in a rote way, prayers can be pulled from Scripture (the Lord's Prayer, the Psalms, John 17, Jonah's prayer), from prayer books or from the Book of Common Prayer, and used repeatedly with the group. This helps those who are less familiar with praying aloud, because it gives them a way to participate that is clear and formatted. It provides an anchor that can be said at the same time, in the same way, during the group process. In *Awed to Heaven, Rooted in Earth*, Walter Brueggemann has some wonderful prayers that I use in opening and closing groups. We repeat the same prayers, and after a while their message gets ingrained. One of my favorite Brueggemann prayers is "With You It Is Never 'More or Less.'" He begins with, "We will be your faithful people—more or less" and continues along in the vein. Then he concludes by saying,

> With you it is never "yes and no,"
> > but always "yes"—clear, direct,
> > unambiguous, trustworthy.
> We thank you for your "yes"
> > come flesh among us. Amen

## CENTERING PRAYER

For many, when words fail, simple one-line prayers can be repeated in a way that ushers in the presence of the Holy Spirit. In her classic book *Experiencing the Depths of Jesus Christ*, Madame Guyon offers some suggestions in this regard.

Release such expressions as these to your Lord; "Oh my

God, let me be wholly Yours," "Let me love You purely for Yourself, for You are infinitely lovely," "Oh my God, be my all! Let everything else be as nothing to me." Offer these up and other such words; offer them up from your heart. But I think such expression should be separated from each other by short intervals of silence.

These can be adapted for a small group by praying for one another in this way. For instance, someone might pray, "O Lord, be Karen's all!" as well as praying for him- or herself individually in this way. There are other sentence prayers that can be used in the time of invitation or intercession. Some of them are:

Lord, be merciful to me a sinner.

Come, Lord Jesus. Have mercy on me [or a member of the group].

You are the potter, I am the clay.

Your steadfast love endures forever for [name of group member].

Together the group can focus on one or two of these one-line prayers and say them at various intervals during invitation, intercession or quiet moments alone outside of the group.

# 11

# Befriending Scripture

Sometimes, for the average church attendee, Scripture is something *to learn about*, not to actively *participate in*. These exercises can help people to relax, open themselves up to the power of God's Word, and begin to let Scripture form them from the inside out.

## BEFRIENDING A SMALL PORTION OF SCRIPTURE

Before opening the Scripture, one way to think about the Bible is that it is a love letter from God to us. It reveals great secrets about who our God is and his great longing to be intimate with us. Encourage each group member, in the quiet of his or her heart, to ask Jesus to give the group a longing to read Scripture not as a heavy task but as a joyful response to God's love.

Now, meditate for a moment on some part of Scripture that the group has agreed to study together. For the sake of illustration, let's take the first part of Psalm 23: "The Lord is my shepherd." Each member should say this short phrase several times silently, thinking about each word and the meaning that it may have for him or her. For instance, *my shepherd* makes God's leading and guiding very personal. "The Lord" connotes rulership, mastery and a commanding presence. But when the Lord is "my shepherd," the God of all creation is brought down to a level we can handle. We can realize, then, that this great God wants to make a difference in the specifics of human life. Say it again: "The Lord is my shepherd." Visualize God shepherding the group. What is happening? Where are you being led as a community of people dedicated to serving him? The brevity of the passage makes this a palatable exercise for new Christians who are not as familiar with Scripture.

## IDENTIFYING WITH A BIBLICAL CHARACTER

One of the contributions of the church father Ignatius was his practice of using Scripture as a story in which he was one of the characters encountering Jesus. Using Ignatius's method in our groups, the reader (or group of readers) is asked to *become* the blind man whose eyes Jesus touched with mud. As the group reads a Scripture passage narrative, questions such as the following can be asked:

> Imagine that you are the blind man in Mark 8:22-26. Close your eyes so that you cannot see. Imagine that you have never seen the light of day. You might want to ask yourself, in what ways do I want Jesus to touch me so that I can see more clearly? You are not even sure Jesus will take the time to stop for you, to help you out with your blindness, but he does. What is your reaction

as Jesus smears the mud and spit over your eyes? What does it feel like? What are your thoughts when, as you open your eyes, you still are not able to see clearly? Are there times in your life when prayers seem to be half answered—only part of the answer has been forthcoming? Jesus gives you a second touch. Do you think some circumstances or some people and situations require a second touch? More prayer? Ongoing effort? Why might that be? The second time, after Jesus touches you, what is the first thing or person you see clearly? What is it like to actually see the world and those around you for the first time? Now that your physical sight has been restored, are there also spiritual ways you are able to see more clearly as well? Explain.

After an exercise like this, the group can process what it was like to "become" the blind man and share ideas and insights about Jesus' second touch.

## GUIDED IMAGERY

Another way to befriend scriptural texts is to read the Scripture in such a way that it dramatizes the scene. Sometimes in place of sharing requests, a guided imagery exercise can be a very powerful form of prayer. It is highly communal because each person engages the same narration, and yet each person will be experiencing something different that can be shared at the end of each session.

Earlier in this book I dramatized the Emmaus Road account (see pp. 50-54) and pulled out certain points of insight along the way. If there is a writer in the group, and the group is focusing on a certain narrative, this person might enjoy rewriting the biblical story for a guided imagery exercise, much the way the Mary story is rewritten here. I was able to use this account with a group of Presbyterian women who are not prone to emotion. I guided them step by step through the story of Mary, asking each of them to be Mary and to see themselves encountering Jesus for the first time as resurrected Lord. It was a very moving experience for the group.

Guided imagery is different from asking the participants to put themselves in the text and asking questions about how they would react to Jesus should they encounter him as a biblical character. Guided imagery takes the participant step by step through the entire scene, dramatizing and suggesting connections along the way. This works well for people who are visual and imaginative, but in a group it can work for everyone as they share what they saw, felt or thought about as the story was read. The following dramatization of Luke 20:11-16 is an example of a guided-imagery exercise using the Scripture of Mary, who stood at the empty tomb weeping because she could not find Jesus. Any story from Scripture can be adapted in this way. As people prayerfully contemplate the text, some soft music in the background is often a helpful addition.

> You are Mary. You have come to the tomb this morning, the Sunday after the crucifixion. All Saturday, the sabbath, you have been thinking about this moment. Jesus' death happened so close to the Passover sabbath that you were not allowed, according to Jewish law, to embalm him once the sun went down. You had to wait from

sundown on Friday to sunrise today. Friday evening, as the sun slipped down behind the hills, you promised yourself you would return before anyone else arrived in order to see Jesus one more time and prepare his body in the appropriate way for burial. Offering one more loving gesture to your friend and rabbi pulls at your heart. So here you are. You have brought spices and are standing at the tomb. It is early, the sun has not yet risen. To your dismay, you find his body, the one comfort left to you, is gone. The tomb gapes open, dark and empty. The stone has been rolled to the side. There is no body. Someone, perhaps a Roman soldier, has taken him away. It is the only explanation you can think of. Couldn't they have just left him to lie in peace? Couldn't they have just allowed you this last rite of embalming? They'd taken his life in the cruelest, most barbaric way possible. Wasn't that enough? Did they have to take his body also? Who cared about his body anyway, except those who loved him the most? What gain would they get out of stealing this last vestige of comfort from his friends and followers? You begin to weep. When would all of this end? The heartache, the loss, the dashed hopes and dreams were all just too much to bear.

As you stand crying by the tomb in the gray light of dawn, quite without warning you begin to sense that you are not alone. A figure appears next to you. No one would be out this early in the morning, except perhaps the gardener. Without really looking up you acknowledge his presence with a glance. "Sir," you declare, choking back the tears, "if you have taken him away, please tell me where you have laid him, and I will go and get him." It is a last-ditch plea for the one comfort remaining to you, the dead body of Jesus. You were so set on holding him one last time, of being able to say your final goodbyes to him in this way.

Then the figure at your side, the one you had assumed was the gardener, says your name. Hear Jesus saying *your name*. And as he says it, you recognize him for the first time. In that recognition comes a trembling joy. A too-good-to-be-true awe grabs you and you respond, "Teacher!"

What a lesson! What a revelation! You realize that what you had thought you had wanted—the dead body of Jesus—was not what you really wanted at all. God had something far bigger and better up his sleeve. You realize that what you thought was a hopeless situation—a situation where death and brutality had the last word—was not the case at all. In the midst of all the chaos, the tears, the pain, the loss, life in the resurrected being of Jesus Christ was the final victorious statement for all creation. What you thought was the end of the road, the final goodbye, was only just the beginning. What you really wanted all along was the living Christ at your side.

See the resurrected Jesus with you now, resurrection light in his eyes. Again hear him say your name. Do you have a situation that you want to give to him, a situation where it seems as if there is no hope? What is

Jesus saying to you right now? Spend a moment listening, aware that God's presence is with you right now in the same way that Jesus was with Mary on that first resurrection morning. Is what you are desiring less than what God wants to give you? Is there more hope and life available to you than you thought? Meditate on this for a moment. [Sit in silence for about a minute.] When you are ready, please share with the group any insights you may have had.

Any story in Scripture can be adapted in this way. This kind of imagery work should not be limited to groups of women, although it is sometimes difficult for men to see themselves as Mary or Esther, whereas women seem to more easily identify with David, Moses or Peter. ( I am not sure why this is, except that women are used to identifying with male biblical characters.) If you have men in the group, it is important to keep the makeup of the group and who you are asking them to identify with in mind. I recently led a group of men through the Emmaus Road story, asking them to become Cleopas. We had a very meaningful exchange, and many of the men shared that they experienced God's presence in a renewed way. For some groups, it might help to do a more intellectual study of the same Scripture prior to writing up a dramatization. This allows for the dramatization to maintain historical and theological integrity as you bring the text to life and allow it to "read the group."

Below is one more guided imagery story using Thomas as the main character. Ask the group members to close their eyes and imagine they are Thomas.

You are Thomas, and you have grown up with a twin brother. You are the practical analytical one; your brother is the dreamer. You were not prone to fantasy, and when he wanted to pretend about fights, castles and lands beyond, you waved him away. You are the one who was responsible because you were two minutes older. You took care of him. You are also the one who took responsibility to get food for the ten other disciples who were huddled together, scared and silent, in the Upper Room after the crucifixion of Jesus. When you returned, it was a completely different scene than when you left. All ten were acting in a way you had never seen before. They must have all gone crazy because of the stale air in the room and lack of food. You told them to calm down, but they wouldn't listen. They were too excited and happy. They were acting a bit unruly in their rush and excitement to tell you everything.

In fragments they tell you that Jesus suddenly walked through a wall, appeared to them and declared in no uncertain terms that he was alive. Your cynical side kicks in. You roll your eyes. Impossible! It was a group hallucination.

"Unless I physically put my hands in his wounds and in his side, I will not believe!" you declare. You realize, to your dismay, that you have been following Jesus around with a bunch of lunatics for the past three years. Not okay with you. It was time to get back to reality and stop dreaming!

Much later, you look up and see Jesus standing before

you, showing you his wounds. He had come through the locked door that was still barred and shut tight behind him. You realize that what you had disbelieved so readily was actually the truth. Your eyes grow big and round, you step back and topple the stool you are sitting on. Jesus stands before you, unflinching, and invites you to touch him. "Handle me and see," he tells you. "A spirit does not have flesh and blood like I do." You don't need to touch. It is Jesus, and he is alive. "My Lord and my God!" you stammer, and tears spring to your eyes. It is true. The unbelievable thing has happened.

Ask yourself now where cynicism or doubt has taken root in your life. Perhaps your prayer right now might be the prayer of the father who brought his demoniac son to Jesus to be healed: "Lord, I believe. Help my unbelief." There is something about being human that causes us to believe and disbelieve at the same time when it comes to God's love and mercy. Jesus' wounds remind us themselves of all those who disbelieved, but his resurrection tells us that he is bigger than our biggest doubts. Ask the Lord right now to reveal himself to you in a deep, personal way that assures you of his presence and his awareness of your longing to believe completely and to stake your life on his resurrection power.

## LECTIO DIVINA

Groups can also cultivate the discipline of allowing Scripture to *read them* through some simple exercises in the lectio divina style.

*Read.* The leader reads a chosen Scripture text; the text does not often need to be long. Reading slowly is helpful. Learning to incline the "ear of the heart" and the "ear of the mind" to the passage allows the entire group to be receptive to God's activity in and among them as the words are being read. To allow Scripture to "read the group," I ask two questions: How does this Scripture intersect with who I am and where I am in my life? How does it intersect with the members of my group, and my place in that group? The practice of listening to Scripture with an open and surrendered spirit in a small group extends the listening process that I do for others as well as for myself.

*Respond.* After people read or listen to the text, they are free to ask that it be read again if necessary. Do so slowly and meditatively. Then the group shares with one another by saying a word, phrase or insight that is meaningful, or that they noticed in a special or different way. For instance, take the passage "the Lord is my shepherd." After listening to this contemplatively, one group member shared that it was helpful to see how David allowed God to be what he, David, was—a shepherd. What intimacy David had with God to be able to see him in his own role! What would be the result if we all saw God as doing what we do all day long? The Lord is my lawyer, my doctor, my salesperson, my server, my insurance broker. What qualities of care, advocacy, justice, planning or providing can we come up with? What does this say about how God does things? What does this say about each of us?

Listening to Scripture for encouragement and discernment for other group members takes a good dose of humility, and the person who offers it must acknowledge that what he or she says may or may not be of the Holy Spirit. However, hearing from others can also be life-changing. As we meditated on Psalm 23, one person said that I should write my own psalm: "The Lord is my caring ministries pastor" (my profession). This resonated deep within me, because it had been a difficult week. I had cared for many people, and this word to me was a reminder that as I cared for others, God was also caring for me. If I could remember more often to receive that care and refreshment from God, I knew that I would minister from a position of being filled up inside.

*Closing.* After sharing together, the Scripture can be read again. It is good to close this process with the group reading the text slowly and in unison.

What I have just outlined is my adaptation of the concept of lectio divina. (Don't be put off by this spiritual-sounding Latin term. It's a very simple sort of exercise.) I have also heard of some groups that alternate between allowing Scripture to "read them" and engaging in Bible study the following week. Depending on the people in your group and their knowledge of Scripture, this might be a good option for you. Either way, when we surrender to the Lord and his Word and we don't have to produce results but simply rest in a place of unconditional love, the insights we receive are transformational.

# 12

## Community, Celebration and Service

Not taking ourselves too seriously and keeping ourselves grounded in the world through service and celebration is absolutely critical in maintaining a joy-filled small group. Sometimes these more contemplative gatherings—in which everyone somberly listens, somberly shares and somberly goes home—become so dreadfully serious they undermine the very joy that the Emmaus Road story creates.

### USING CREATIVE COMMUNITY BUILDING

One way to keep joy central is to designate a regular celebration night. Do something completely different. Maybe you should have a "Curse Haman" night like the Jews do when they celebrate Purim! (Probably not.) Have a "dinner together" night or an early breakfast. The purpose is to share stories of how each person has seen the Lord working through the small group. Or go for a walk in nature and have each person pick an object that symbolizes how God is working in the group. Then put the items together and create a new entity—something that signifies the unity of each member of the small group in community with one another. This is something you can use as your focal point for the next time of invitation.

Another fun exercise is to get a large picture of Jesus, a cross or a church and cut it into pieces—as many pieces as you have group members. Then have each person write on the back of his or her piece one thing about the next person that reminds him or her of Jesus. Have people pass the piece to the person they wrote about, and then have everyone put the puzzle together!

Another community-building exercise is to put all of the group's names in a hat and pick someone to pray for that month. To add to the joy factor, everyone has to do something surprisingly pleasant for the person being prayed for. Maybe it's an encouraging note in the mail simply signed "your prayer partner." Maybe it's a gift or cookies specifically for the person at the next meeting. Whatever it is, no one should know who their partner is until the month is over. Then reveal who has been praying for whom and what the surprise has been.

Be creative and come up with new ideas. Note that each of these times of celebration emphasizes the communal element—not simply individuals. This is important to keep in mind as you think about what might be most effective for the people you are working with.

## CHANGED HEARTS THROUGH SERVICE

One of the important elements of the Feast of Booths was significant work done together—essentially harvesting the gifts of God from the land. Nothing bonds a group together with greater spiritual permanence than doing service together, preferably the kind of service that actually provides face-to-face interaction with the people being served. So much of what we do today is anonymous or experienced at a distance. We are specialized, computerized and compartmentalized to the point of being dehumanized. It is fine to sort clothes together for Goodwill, but what is even better is finding a place where we can hand the clothes to the people who need them, talk with them and understand their situation from the inside out. It is great to cook a meal together as a group for the homeless shelter, but it is even better to serve the meal at the shelter and eat with the residents. Sometimes people find the face-to-face interactions awkward. Admittedly, it is easier to write a check. Yet if Christ is found in the "least of these" (see Matthew 25), then the brothers and sisters who have less of the world's goods are part of the body of Christ. It would be good to get to know these folks and learn from them. A face-to-face interaction with one of "the least of these" may be the moment when the small group is able to declare, "We have seen the Lord!"

Linking a contemplative prayer life in community with an outward focus that reaches out with compassion is transformational. You cannot have either practice without the other. Like merging highways, the contemplative life in community and compassionate service to the poor are inseparable.

# Group Discussion Guide

1. What does it mean to know the "love of Christ that surpasses knowledge" (Ephesians 3:19)?

2. Do you think there are many ways to know something? If so, identify some.

   Is one way of knowing higher than another way of knowing? Explain.

3. Use the Emmaus Road account in Luke to answer the following:

   - What do the disciples think they know at the start of the journey?

   - What do they begin to know as they journey with Jesus?

   - What do they know when Jesus breaks the bread at the table with them?

   - What do they know after Jesus disappears?

   - Based on what they know, how does this translate into action?

Look at what you have written for the different things the disciples "knew" during the various stages of their journey. Put each thing you identified in one of the following categories:

- knowing through seeing circumstantial evidence

- knowing through understanding concepts with the mind

- knowing by the power of the Holy Spirit or with the heart

How does God use all three of these categories of knowing to influence your spiritual journey?

4. Do you think that there are different points in our journey when we are called to know God in different ways?

5. What ways of knowing do you gravitate to more readily at this stage in your journey?

6. What ways of knowing are harder for you?

7. Can you think of an "aha" experience that you have had that changed you (or a part of you)? Share the nature of that experience with the group.

# Notes

**Chapter 2: How Small Groups Can Lead to Spiritual Stagnation**

*p. 19*        "We are living in a time": Janet Ruffing, "Prayer," *Conversations Journal* 2, no. 1 (2004): 9.

**Chapter 3: Moving into the Presence of God**

*p. 28*        Talbot dispels the myth that mysticism: John Michael Talbot, "The Way of the Mystics," *Conversations Journal* 6, no 1 (2008): 30.

*p. 29*        Lewis's spiritual intuition was every bit as powerful as his intellect: David Downing, *Into the Region of Awe: Mysticism in C. S. Lewis* (Downers Grove, Ill.: InterVarsity Press, 2005).

*p. 29*        mysticism as a "direct experience of God, immediate as a taste or color": C. S. Lewis, *The Collected Letters of C. S. Lewis*, vol. 3, *Narnia, Cambridge and Joy, 1950-1963*, ed. Walter Hooper (San Francisco: HarperSanFrancisco, 2007), p. 109.

*pp. 29-30*    "the Christian is called": C. S. Lewis, quoted in Downing, *Into the Region of Awe,* p. 165.

*p. 34*        "Nothing is more practical than finding God": Quoted in Rose Mary Dougherty, *Group Spiritual Direction* (Mahwah, N.J.: Paulist Press, 1995), p. 33.

**Chapter 4: Building a Praying Community**

*p. 41*        Rabbi Adin Steinsaltz on Jewish prayer: Adin Steinsaltz, *A Guide to Jewish Prayer* (New York: Schocken, 2002), p. 14.

*p. 42*        "The spiritual journey is a journey we are meant to make with others": Juliet Benner, "O Taste and See," *Conversations Journal* 5, no. 1 (2007): 83.

*pp. 43-44*    "In a praying congregation, the prayer of each person strengthens": Steinsaltz, *Guide to Jewish Prayer*, p. 44.

### Chapter 5: A New Kind of Small Group

*p. 58*    "Only with an invitation to 'come and stay with me'": Henri J. M. Nouwen, *With Burning Hearts* (Maryknoll, N.Y.: Orbis, 1994), p. 57.

*p. 60*    "We are more inclined to think about Jesus inviting us": Ibid., p. 55.

*p. 67*    Distracted listening: Dietrich Bonhoeffer, *Life Together* (New York: Harper & Row, 1954).

*p. 70*    the Bible "is not only a book which was once spoken": A. W. Tozer, *The Pursuit of God* (Camp Hill, Penn.: Christian Publications, 1982), pp. 77-78.

### Chapter 6: Creating Emmaus Road Groups

*p. 77*    Juliet Benner wrote about Caravaggio's *The Supper at Emmaus:* "O Taste and See," *Conversations Journal* 4, no. 1 (2006): 72-76.

*p. 78*    "mysticism keeps men sane": G. K. Chesterton, *Orthodoxy* (New York: Doubleday, 2001), p. 28.

### Chapter 10: Interceding for Others

*p. 105*    "The constant repetition entailed in prayer": Adin Steinsaltz, *A Guide to Jewish Prayer* (New York, Schocken, 2002), p. 14.

*p. 106*    Brueggemann prayer: Walter Brueggemann, "With You It Is Never 'More or Less,'" *Awed to Heaven, Rooted in Earth* (Minneapolis: Fortress, 2003), p. 139.

*pp. 106-7*    "Release such expressions as these to your Lord": Madame Guyon, *Experiencing the Depths of Jesus Christ* (Goleta, Ga.: Christian Books, 1981), p. 141.

# Fast Tract Digestion

# IBS

By Norman Robillard, Ph.D.

**Founder, Digestive Health Institute**

Self Health Publishing
Watertown, Massachusetts

First edition

ISBN 978-0-9766425-5-8

Recipes: Rie Tanaka

Editor: Edward Walters

Figures, Tables and HTML coding: Mahesh Gudapakkam

Book Design KarrieRoss.com

## Disclaimers

The information presented in this book is not intended as medical advice or as a substitute for consultations with your primary care provider. This information should be used in conjunction with the advice of your own doctor. Consult your doctor before changing or discontinuing current medications or initiating any diet.

Any trademarks or product names used herein are the property of their owners, and are for identification only, and no claim is implied by their use.

# Your Gut Health – Fits In Your Pocket

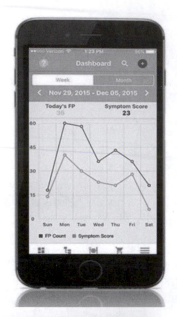

## Fast Tract Diet App
### Everything you need - on the Run!

- FP food list of over 800 items in common household measures
- Meal and symptom tracker
- Custom food and recipe creation tool
- Shopping list tool
- FP calculator
- Fast Tract Diet - what it is, how it works, gut friendly practices, troubleshooting for persistent symptoms, SIBO and more

# ACKNOWLEDGEMENTS

The creation of the Fast Tract Digestion book series was supported by the efforts of several people.

Rie Tanaka was the creative force behind the recipes in each book. Her innate knowledge and creativity in the preparation and presentation of American and Japanese cuisine give the recipes their special appeal.

Dr. Mike Eades was supportive of my research asking key questions that helped me focus on the real problem and develop a method to quantify the symptom risk of foods.

Gary Taubes helped me gain perspective on the limitations of observational studies particularly with regard to the health aspects of fiber.

My editor, Ed Walters, made sure the ideas in the books were organized and simplified to help the reader cut to the chase and gain the maximum benefit from the information.

Mahesh Gudapakkam, my HTML editor, carefully reviewed and improved the HTML coding of each book, and the tables and figures to support their viewing as eBooks across several devices.

Karrie Ross created the cover design for the Fast Tract Digestion book series and designed the book interior for this book.

By Dr. Michael R. Eades, Co-author of the bestseller, *Protein Power*

In writing *Fast Tract Digestion IBS*, Dr. Norm Robillard has turned his own struggles into a mission to help millions of people looking for healthy, science-based solutions to irritable bowel syndrome (IBS). This book puts his passions into an Occam's razor approach arriving at a novel and rational solution to treating this debilitating condition.

The Fast Tract diet evolved from Dr. Robillard's earlier work in which he introduced a new theory about why carbohydrate restriction was effective in treating the related condition, acid reflux. For over 30 years I myself have used carbohydrate restriction to successfully treat gastroesophageal reflux disorder (GERD). However, when patients or even other doctors asked me why it worked, I had to admit I didn't really know.

But that changed some years ago when I first got a call from Dr. Robillard, a microbiologist and GERD sufferer. He was a big fan of *Protein Power* and had, in fact, cured his own acid reflux with a low-carb diet. My curiosity was piqued when he told me he had come up with a mechanism for how such diets worked, which had to do with bacteria in our gut. I got together with him, and he explained his theory. His was the first explanation that truly made sense.

Bypassing 50 years of scientific dogma on trigger foods and alcohol causing relaxation of the low esophageal sphincter, Dr. Robillard proposed that gases produced during bacterial fermentation of malabsorbed carbohydrates create intragastric pressure which drives stomach acid into the esophagus. When these gastric juices come into contact with the delicate membrane lining the esophagus, they cause the discomfort of heartburn, as well as many other symptoms of acid reflux. He posits that small intestinal bacterial overgrowth (SIBO) is the problem driving the process. When carbs are reduced, the gas-producing bacteria in the small bowel have nothing to ferment: therefore they die off, and GERD goes away.

After Dr. Robillard's explanation, I thought it through and speculated that the treatment could maybe be refined a little more. Since the gas-producing bacteria in the small bowel dine primarily on complex carbohydrates and fiber, I wondered if simply reducing the intake of those specific carbs would get rid of GERD. In other words, people could eat certain carbs, yet would not develop heartburn. My reasoning stemmed from my assumption that some easier to digest carbohydrates would absorb through the wall of the GI tract quickly enough to keep from providing food for the bacteria.

I posed a question to Dr. Robillard: "which carbs are more difficult to digest and wouldn't they be the worst offenders?"

He didn't know the answer, but the idea sounded reasonable to him. Unbeknownst to me, he went back to the scientific drawing board, fiddled with the idea for a few years and tested it on himself and others. Based on his work, he derived an entirely new system for treating not only GERD, but any condition caused by SIBO, using a calculation called the Fermentation Potential (FP).

It turns out that IBS is linked to GERD and to SIBO. Dr. Robillard clearly explains the connection between carbohydrate malabsorption, SIBO and IBS. The gases produced by SIBO drive not only the acid reflux and consequent heartburn, but the abdominal pain, bloating, cramps and altered bowel habits associated with IBS. Even constipation can be caused by methane-gas-producing gut bacteria.

People with IBS – and any other SIBO-related condition—can benefit from this book. Dr. Robillard shows the reader why the Fast Track approach is superior to other diets, drugs, antacids and even antibiotics, which are often prescribed in an off-label manner for IBS. The book also contains a comprehensive evaluation of each class of IBS drug and an entire chapter explaining the potential problems with taking antibiotics for anything short of the most severe forms of IBS.

The antibiotic option is one many physicians choose for treatment, but readers of this book will think twice about going on such a regimen until all other options are explored. Most importantly, the Fast Tract approach Dr. Robillard created limits only the most difficult-to-digest carbohydrates. Thus, the means of relief is flexible where both the types and amounts of symptom-causing foods can be adjusted based on personal dietary preferences. Even people with the most challenging symptoms will be pleased with their improvement. I can't recommend this book heartily enough.

Michael R. Eades, MD
Incline Village, Nevada
Co-author of *Protein Power*

Almost fifteen years ago, Elaine Gottschall, in her book, *Breaking the Vicious Cycle*, proposed that "faulty digestion" could lead to the malabsorption of certain sugars, starches and fibers and ultimately result in the overgrowth of bacteria in the small intestine. These overgrowing bacteria can cause injury to the lining of the small intestine thus impairing digestion and causing even more malabsorption. She linked this cycle of overgrowth, injury and malabsorption with several digestive conditions including Crohn's disease, ulcerative colitis, diverticulitis, celiac disease, and chronic diarrhea.

*Fast Tract Digestion IBS*, the second book in the Fast Tract Digestion book series on digestive illness, picks up where *Breaking the Vicious Cycle* left off. Research on the root cause of IBS can be summed up in two conclusions:

(1) *IBS is linked to cycles of carbohydrate malabsorption and bacterial overgrowth in the small intestine. The overgrowing bacteria produce toxins, enzymes and gas that can damage the intestinal surface while causing pain, bloating, diarrhea, constipation, and other familiar symptoms of IBS.*

(2) *Limiting your consumption of five specific types of difficult-to-digest carbohydrates while employing pro-absorption strategies can help you reverse or prevent this bacterial overgrowth providing an effective treatment for IBS.*

Each chapter covers a different aspect of IBS. To help you get you started, my little friend Germaine, a friendly gut microbe, will present a quote relating the the underlying message in each chapter.

The inadequacy of current IBS treatments is explored including an entire chapter on the proposed, if misguided, use of antibiotics for treating IBS.

*Fast Tract Digestion IBS* explains the connection between digestion, malabsorption, bacteria and symptoms of diarrhea-predominant and constipation-predominant IBS as well as acid reflux, which commonly accompanies IBS.

I describe the three basic food groups and how optimal digestion and absorption supports digestive health. Then I explore the various scenarios that can lead to malabsorption and bacterial overgrowth, which can result in the dramatic symptoms of IBS. The biggest problem — difficult to digest carbohydrates driving bacterial overgrowth — is examined in depth.

Finally, *Fast Tract Digestion* provides an innovative dietary treatment plan based on a new concept called the Fermentation Potential which measures the symptom potential of different foods. My Fast Tract Diet offers a complete solution for people suffering from IBS and other conditions resulting from bacterial overgrowth. In most cases, your symptoms will improve in a matter of days.

TABLE OF CONTENTS

Fast Tract Digestion

# IBS

CHAPTER 1:

# What is IBS?

"THE BEST DOCTOR
GIVES THE LEAST
MEDICINES."

—BENJAMIN FRANKLIN

IBS IS SHORT FOR IRRITABLE BOWEL SYNDROME. People who don't suffer from IBS may not fully appreciate how challenging this condition can be. Imagine having dramatic stomach pain, severe cramps, bloating, frequent diarrhea or constipation. Then imagine not being able to predict when your symptoms might start, or even what foods might trigger them. What if you're in a meeting, attending a sporting event, or out on a boat? What if you're not close to a restroom?

If you have IBS, it may be a small comfort to know that you are not alone. IBS affects up to 50 million people in the US alone. Even if you don't have IBS, you likely have close friends or family members who do. What's the cause of this mysterious condition? Are we any closer to finding an effective treatment?

Finding a single cause for IBS has proved to be very difficult. The wide range of symptoms has led to a variety of theories involving gut motility, atypical brain-gut interactions, and immune system reactions. The overgrowth of yeast (*Candida albicans*) was once considered a cause but medical scientists have been unable to establish a clear connection.[1] Others have suggested food allergies or intolerance as a cause, but this, too, has not been supported by research.

Even today, there is no widely accepted diagnostic test for IBS. Instead, doctors evaluate patients for the most common symptoms: abdominal pain, cramping, bloating, gas, diarrhea, or constipation.

IBS has been referred to as a "functional" disorder because doctors often don't find anything physically wrong when they look inside the stomach and intestines (during what's called an endoscopic exam) of people with IBS symptoms. IBS has also been called a diagnosis of exclusion, which simply means that if the doctor can't figure out what's causing your symptoms; he or she may tell you that you have IBS.

Doctors have come up with three basic categories of IBS; Diarrhea-predominant IBS (IBS-D), Constipation-predominant IBS (IBS-C) and Mixed IBS (IBS-M).

In the absence of a specific test, attempts have been made to carefully define IBS based on symptoms and their frequency. Examples include:

Manning criteria[2]

- Abdominal swelling
- Bloating
- Looser stools
- Pain relief with passage of stool
- Sensation of incomplete evacuation and diarrhea with mucus

Rome criteria (Rome III criteria shown)[3,4,5,6]
Abdominal pain or discomfort for at least three days of any three month period in the last 6 months and two of the following:

- Pain relief after having a bowel movement
- Pain linked to bowel movement frequency
- Pain linked to appearance or consistency of stool

These more detailed criteria may be helpful for research and clinical studies, but don't seem to add much value for patients.

Note: Move on to Chapter 2 if not interested in conventional approaches or IBS drugs.

# IBS Treatments

Current IBS treatments include diet modification and dietary supplements; over-the-counter laxatives, anti-diarrhea medications, antacids, and pain relievers; as well as prescription drugs such as antispasmodics and drugs that alter gut motility (how fast digested food moves through the intestines). Due to the lack of adequate treatments, many doctors also write prescriptions for drugs that have not been FDA approved for IBS.

## Dietary treatments for IBS

Dietary treatments for IBS are all over the map. Patients are advised to avoid spicy or fatty foods, carbonated beverages, alcohol, caffeine, dairy, and gas-producing foods such as broccoli and cabbage. Or to avoid insoluble fiber but consume other foods that contain fiber like fruits and complex carbs. These prescriptions (or proscriptions) may provide some temporary relief, but overall they are often contradictory, limiting (in terms of food choices), and based on anecdotal evidence rather than grounded in nutritional science. As a result, most people have to try to figure out what to eat for themselves.

Another popular approach is to avoid foods that cause allergic responses. IBS patients are instructed to eliminate foods from their diet based on extensive antibody testing. Unfortunately, this approach is not very effective. A randomized controlled study with 150 IBS patients, showed only a small (10%) improvement.[7] Given the effort and expense involved, and the poor results, I cannot recommend this approach.

Several more specific but unconventional dietary approaches, while imperfect, have met with more success. They include the elemental, specific carb, GAPs, low-starch, low-carb, Paleo, and FODMAP diets. These approaches are reviewed along with the Fast Tract Diet in Chapter 10.

**Diarrhea medications**

Almost everyone suffers from occasional diarrhea as a result of eating or drinking contaminated food or water, or from any number of intestinal viruses. Typically, the symptoms disappear in a day or so. But for IBS sufferers with IBS-D, diarrhea may occur often and without apparent cause, prompting them to seek medical help or take some form of medication.

The first thing to keep in mind is that diarrhea depletes your body of fluid and salts that must be replaced by oral rehydration therapy (ORT). This is true even if you are trying other treatments. Remember to drink water and consume foods or fluids that contain electrolytes, including glucose, sodium and potassium. Fish stock, herbs, nuts, seeds, avocados and dates contain supplemental potassium. Be careful if you take potassium supplements, as too much potassium can also do you harm.

Common over-the-counter anti-diarrheal products such as Imodium and Kaopectate contain loperamide, a synthetic opioid drug that increases how long food stays in the intestine, allowing more water to be absorbed from the stool. Loperamide can have side effects, including abdominal pain, bloating, nausea, vomiting and constipation.

Pepto-Bismol, which contains bismuth subsalicylate, is another over-the-counter product used to treat diarrhea. The product has been reported to kill some of the bacteria that may cause diarrhea, but I have not confirmed this. Potential side effects include anxiety, confusion, severe constipation and diarrhea.

**Constipation Medications** (Laxatives)

Constipation can be caused by a variety of factors including insufficient fluid intake, excessive use of laxatives, antacids, or pain medicine such as Tylenol 1, 2, 3 and 4, which contain codeine. Health conditions including Parkinson's disease, multiple sclerosis, or colon cancer can also cause constipation.

Chronic constipation can lead to the diagnosis of IBS-C. While no specific cause has been identified for IBS-C, researchers have discovered that IBS-C is often accompanied by the presence of methane-producing bacteria in the gut. This is an important clue, which we'll follow up later on in the book.

The first thing you should try for constipation is increasing your water intake. Also evaluate the medicines you are taking to see if constipation is listed as a potential side effect.

People who find that these basic steps don't help their constipation often reach for a laxative.

Laxatives can include both foods (like prunes) and drugs that loosen stools allowing for easier passage through the intestine. Laxatives include both oral medications and suppositories.

**Fiber Laxatives**

Bulk-forming laxatives, including high-fiber foods and fiber supplements such as psyllium, methylcellulose, and polycarbophil, are often recommended for people suffering from chronic constipation.

The goal is to accelerate the movement of food through your digestive tract. There is considerable doubt as to the effectiveness of this approach. One clinical study looked at the use of bran fiber to reduce constipation. Twenty grams of bran per day did not improve constipation symptoms when compared to a placebo.[8] A systemic review of the effectiveness of different fiber types in treating constipation in IBS patients found only marginal benefits. In some cases, fiber actually worsened IBS symptoms.[9] Another study found that treating 275 IBS patients with psyllium or bran fiber for three months did not improve their quality of life.[10] The group that added bran to their diet experienced a high dropout rate because the participants' IBS symptoms kept getting worse.

Side effects of fiber-based laxatives can include intestinal gas, bloating and diarrhea, as well as electrolyte imbalances and mineral deficiency.

## Osmotic laxatives

If fiber supplements don't work, doctors will often recommend osmotic laxatives which may include over-the-counter products such as polyethylene glycol or PEG (Miralax), magnesium hydroxide-containing products such as Milk of Magnesia, glycerin suppositories (both a lubricating and osmotic laxative), and prescription osmotic medicines including lactulose, a non-digestible sugar. Osmotic laxatives prevent the intestines from removing water from feces resulting in softer stools.

Side effects of osmotic laxatives may include nausea, bloating, cramping, flatulence and diarrhea. Check the packaging of any osmotic laxative you take so that you're aware of any potential product-specific side effects.

## Lubricating laxatives

Lubricating laxatives make it easier for stools to move through the intestines. Examples of lubricating laxatives include mineral oil and glycerin. Lubricating laxatives both slow water uptake from the intestine, and lubricate the stool.

Side effects include reducing the absorption of certain fat-soluble vitamins and minerals as well as bloating, cramps, diarrhea and nausea. (As a result, lubricating laxatives are not recommended for women who are pregnant.) Mineral oil should not be used in young children due to the (rare) possibility of contracting lipoid pneumonia by inhaling droplets of mineral oil.

## Stimulant laxatives

Stimulant laxatives such as bisacodyl are the most intrusive, as they cause the bowel to contract to force the stool out. Stimulant laxatives should not be taken for more than a few days in a row.

Side effects of stimulant laxatives can include discolored urine, abdominal pain, cramping, diarrhea and nausea. More serious side effects include weakness, dizziness, tiredness, severe cramping, rectal bleeding and bloody stools. In the case of serious side effects, stop taking these laxatives and call your doctor.

One final alternative is taking a stool softener, such as docusate, which works by increasing fluid in the stool itself. Side effects include abdominal cramping, bloating and diarrhea.

## Laxative abuse

The overuse of laxatives can lead to serious side effects and health problems, most notably nutritional deficiencies, electrolyte disturbances, and "lazy bowel." Lazy bowel is a condition where normal bowel function, particularly peristalsis, is reduced leading to an increased dependency on even more laxatives. Avoiding or limiting the use of laxatives is the best way to avoid these problems. Consult your primary care provider for guidance on specific laxatives and their side effects.

## IBS-specific drugs

Tegaserod (marketed as Zelnorm) acts like serotonin, a neurotransmitter that stimulates peristalsis (the movement of food through the intestines). Despite relieving some of the diarrhea and constipation symptoms of IBS, tegaserod was taken off the market by the FDA in 2007 due to an increased risk of heart attack and stroke.[11] In July of the same year limited use of tegaserod was allowed for IBS-C in women under 55 years old.

Another serotonin-like drug called alosetron (Lotronex), which blocks nerve receptors, is used to treat severe diarrhea in women. Originally considered a drug that could slow down peristalsis, the drug ended up stopping it almost completely. Not surprisingly, the main side effect is constipation in 25 to 30% of patients that use it. Like tegaserod, alosetron was removed from the market because of the potential for severe constipation and possible damage to the large intestine, but re-introduced in 2002 with strict limits on its use.

Women with severe diarrhea-predominant IBS that has failed to respond to alternative treatments are candidates for alosetron.

Metoclopramide (Reglan), a drug used for heartburn, ulcers and nausea, has also been prescribed for IBS, particularly with constipation-predominant IBS, as it increases peristalsis. The drug works by binding to dopamine D2 and other receptors in the central nervous system, which causes an increase in stomach emptying, which means food will not remain in the stomach as long.

You should use extreme caution in using this drug because it has the potential to cause serious side effects including changes in blood pressure, hormonal imbalances, constipation, depression, headache, and even tardive dyskinesia, a neurological condition involving involuntary movements and facial contortion that can be permanent. I say don't take this drug!

## Antispasmodic Drugs

Antispasmodic medicines such as hyoscyamine and dicyclomine are used to treat pain or the urgent need to empty the bowels after eating. Antispasmodics help relieve cramping by blocking the nerve impulses that control intestinal spasms. Use these drugs with caution as they can have serious side effects, such as dry mouth, confusion, dizziness, headache, forgetfulness, hallucinations, unsteadiness, coma, anxiety, tiredness, insomnia, excitement, mood disorders, blurred vision, eye pain, constipation, diarrhea, muscle weakness, rapid heartbeat, fainting, hives, rash, itching, and difficulty breathing or swallowing.

## Antidepressants for IBS?

Some doctors prescribe antidepressants for people with IBS. There are two main types: tricyclic and selective serotonin reuptake inhibitors (also known as SSRIs).

Tricyclic antidepressants such as imipramine (Tofranil) slow peristalsis by decreasing the rate or number of intestinal muscle contractions and are sometimes prescribed to treat diarrhea-predominant IBS. Though some studies indicate that these drugs may be useful for treating IBS, these drugs are also associated with numerous side effects including constipation, cramps, nausea, vomiting (sometimes severe), weight gain, drowsiness, fatigue, nightmares, headaches, dry mouth, and difficulty urinating.

Selective serotonin reuptake inhibitors (SSRIs) such as Prozac and Zoloft, on the other hand, are sometimes prescribed to treat constipation-predominant IBS, as they reportedly speed up peristalsis. Like tricyclic antidepressants, some studies suggest these drugs may be useful for treating IBS, but potential side effects of serotonin include insomnia, headaches, rash, joint and muscle pain, nausea, diarrhea, bleeding, as well as reduced interest in sexual activity.

These side effects are typically not as severe as those for tryclic medicines, but they are still worth careful attention and caution.

The general rationale for using these drugs to treat IBS is that the condition is sometimes associated with depression. Some medical researchers have proposed that antidepressants might also inhibit misdirected nervous impulses that are affecting the intestines. Some believe that the people with IBS have abnormal or exaggerated pain responses, and these drugs may lesson this "perceived pain."

These ideas make little sense to me. A more reasonable explanation is that mainstream medicine does not have a clear idea of the causes of IBS and is willing to try anything that shows any indication of helping.

IBS, however, is a real disorder with a real biological cause(s). The symptoms are also real, and they can't be treated effectively by random tinkering with the body's control systems. Keep in mind that these antidepressants have not been approved by the FDA for treating IBS. Any such prescription from your doctor would be considered "off label." Doctors will sometimes do this, but you should be aware that the drugs have not been clinically tested in people with IBS.

## Newer IBS drugs

A new type of IBS drug, lubiprostone (Amitiza), was approved by the FDA in 2008 for treating constipation-dependent IBS in adult women. The drug acts by activating chloride channels in the intestine resulting in increased fluid secretion. Clinical studies showed that 18% of the patients treated with lubiprostone showed improvement, compared to 10% of patients treated with a placebo.[12] The most common side effects were nausea, diarrhea, headache, abdominal distention, flatulence, sinusitis, vomiting and dyspnea (difficulty breathing).

Another new IBS drug, called linaclotide (Linzess), was recently approved by the FDA for treating constipation-predominant IBS. This peptide (small protein) drug activates an enzyme called guanylate cyclase-C. Guanylate cyclase-C was targeted for constipation treatment based on observations that this enzyme had the ability to trigger diarrhea following activation by certain bacterial toxins.

Clinical studies involving over 1600 patients showed that linaclotide decreased abdominal pain and increased bowel movements compared to patients treated with placebo.[13, 14] On the surface, the drug appears to have promise, but you should consider the following when deciding whether to try it:

- The number of patients who had a positive response (defined as at least 30% decrease in pain and an increase of one bowel movement per week) to the drug in at least 9 out of 12 weeks during the study was 12% (Study 1) and 13% (Study 2). Five percent (Study 1) and 3% (Study 2) of the patients treated with a placebo showed similar improvements. In other words, the people on the drug showed only an 8% to 10% improvement over the placebo.
- Between 4.5% and 5.7% of the patients dropped out of the study because the drug caused diarrhea.
- The drug has only been approved for use by adults because it has not been tested in children, and because deaths have been observed in newborn and juvenile mice during testing. An FDA warning on the package states that linaclotide cannot be used in

children up to 6 years of age and should be avoided in patients aged 6 through 17 years of age.

While they show promise, lubiprostone and linaclotide need more study. Patients looking for new treatments for IBS should carefully weigh the potential benefits of these medications against the potential risks and side effects.

### Disappointing results

Based on my review of the over-the-counter and prescription drugs used to treat IBS, one thing is clear to me: IBS drugs have missed their mark. They have limited effectiveness, numerous side effects (some potentially dangerous) and fail to address the underlying causes of IBS. The many drug safety issues, in particular, are difficult to ignore.

A statement on the Web MD web site under "medications for IBS" sums it up nicely: "No single medicine has been shown to be effective in relieving IBS over the long term.[15]"

# CHAPTER 2

# The Real Cause of IBS: SIBO

"THREE THINGS CANNOT BE
LONG HIDDEN: THE SUN, THE
MOON, AND THE TRUTH."
—BUDDHA

### Gut bacteria linked to IBS

If IBS is not caused by aberrant brain-gut interactions, non-specific immune system activation, the overgrowth of yeast, or food allergies, then what is the cause? Over the past decade or so, the answer to this question has started to come into focus.

In 1998, Dr. John Hunter's team at Addenbrooke's Hospital, Cambridge, UK, published a study demonstrating a link between the abnormal growth of bacteria in the intestine and IBS by measuring intestinal gas in IBS patients.[16] Their results showed that gut bacteria were more active in people with IBS, and produced significantly more intestinal gas. They concluded that the increase could explain many IBS symptoms such as, cramps, bloating and pain. Another clue was the discovery that antibiotic treatment or gastrointestinal infections often preceded the onset of IBS symptoms.[17, 18] These results suggested that an imbalance of intestinal bacterial populations (gut microbiota) might play a role.

Dr. Mark Pimentel and colleagues at Cedars-Sinai Medical Center in Los Angeles, CA took things a step further publishing a link between IBS and a condition called SIBO (which stands for **S**mall **I**ntestinal **B**acterial **O**vergrowth) after noticing how often patients told their doctors their conditions improved after they were given antibiotics.[19] They found that 78% of patients with IBS had SIBO.[20] Many of these patients treated with antibiotics showed an improvement in their IBS symptoms.

## What is SIBO?

Small intestinal bacterial overgrowth or SIBO is defined as the presence of an abnormally high number of bacteria (more than 100,000 bacteria per milliliter) in the upper part of the small intestine. At this level, the normally harmless bacteria that live in our gut can become harmful. They begin to produce toxins, enzymes, and intestinal gases, including hydrogen, methane, and carbon dioxide that can disrupt digestion, cause intense physical discomfort and even damage the small intestine.

The bacteria associated with SIBO originate from our own intestines; particularly the large intestine. Bacterial types isolated from the small intestine of people with SIBO include: *Streptococcus*, *Staphylococcus*, and *Lactobacillus* — all generally associated with the small intestine; and *E. coli*, *Micrococcus*, *Klebsiella*, *Proteus*, *Bacteriodes*, *Clostridium*, *Veillonella*, *Fusobacterium* and *Peptostreptococcus* — all generally associated with the large intestine.[21] The symptoms of SIBO, like IBS, can include abdominal pain or cramps, diarrhea, constipation, gas, bloating, acid reflux, flatulence, nausea, dehydration and fatigue. More severe symptoms of SIBO (though less often associated with IBS) can include weight loss and "failure to thrive," steatorrhea (the body's failure to digest fats), anemia, bleeding or bruising, night blindness, bone pain and fractures, leaky gut syndrome, and autoimmune reactions, among others.

Note: Symptoms such as vomiting, constant diarrhea, fever or blood in the stool are indicators of even more serious illness and should be evaluated by your doctor as soon as possible.

Symptoms of SIBO will vary from one individual to another and may not be present at all times. Symptoms might go away for one month, only to return the next. However, SIBO is likely to recur until the underlying causes of the bacterial overgrowth are corrected. The only sure way to relieve these symptoms is to bring the balance of bacterial growth between the small and large intestines back under control.

## What Causes SIBO?

There are several factors that can lead to SIBO. They include motility issues (how fast food moves through the digestive tract), antibiotics use, reduced stomach acid, immune deficiency, and carbohydrate malabsorption. Each of these will be closely examined in Chapter 8. Though each of these factors can promote SIBO, carbohydrate malabsorption is the key, as overgrowing bacteria are dependent on malabsorbed carbohydrates for energy.

## The Scientific Evidence that SIBO Causes IBS

The newest research is driving a fundamental change in the way we understand IBS, with critical implications for treatment protocols, and I don't expect you — or the medical community — to just take my word for it. Fortunately, the scientific evidence for this connection has been building over the past decade. My research has uncovered four distinct points of evidence which convinced me that poor carbohydrate absorption (or malabsorption) coupled with SIBO may be the ultimate cause of IBS.

### 1. Carbohydrate malabsorption, SIBO and IBS exhibit the same symptoms.

Many classic IBS symptoms including gas, cramping, bloating, and pain, as well as diarrhea, are also common symptoms of carbohydrate malabsorption and SIBO.[22, 23, 24, 25] Patients who have been diagnosed with functional bowel disease (a conditional similar to IBS) often have trouble absorbing lactose, fructose, or sorbitol, (substances known to fuel bacterial fermentation). These patients display symptoms of abdominal distress that are essentially identical to those caused by IBS.[26]

## 2.  SIBO has been detected in most patients with IBS.

As mentioned above, most adults and children with IBS will exhibit a positive lactulose breath test indicative of the presence of SIBO.[27, 28] In one well-controlled study, 83% of 101 IBS patients tested positive for SIBO.[29] Similar results were achieved in children with IBS where 65% were diagnosed with SIBO.[30] In a study of children with chronic stomach pain (considered pre-IBS) 91% were determined to have SIBO.[31]

Even constipation, the main symptom of IBS-C, has been linked to the overgrowth of methane-producing bacteria in the gut,[32, 33] in other words, a form of SIBO.

## 3.  Limiting the growth of gut bacteria either by diet or antibiotics reduces malabsorption and improves IBS symptoms.

IBS patients diagnosed with SIBO by lactulose breath testing often exhibit malabsorption of lactose, fructose and sorbitol which is improved by antibiotic treatment.[34] Overall symptom improvement in IBS has also been credited to antibiotic treatments that coincide with reduction of SIBO.[35, 36]

In a separate study, IBS patients treated with either the antibiotic metronidazole or a fiber-free diet reduced 24-hr excretion of hydrogen, and IBS symptoms.[37] This study showed you could reduce intestinal gas and IBS symptoms by two means; killing gas-causing gut bacteria with an antibiotic or limiting the growth of gut bacteria by reducing fiber (one source of food for gut bacteria).

Diarrhea-predominant IBS has also been treated successfully with a carbohydrate-restricted diet.[38] Carbohydrates provide the main fuel for the overgrowth of intestinal bacteria, and restricting them would be expected to control overgrowth. Similarly, when fructose-intolerant patients with IBS symptoms limit dietary fructose (which is also presumably feeding SIBO), 85% of them experience reduced symptoms.[39]

Finally, the use of the elemental diet (consisting of pre-digested proteins, fats and carbohydrates) is highly effective in improving IBS symptoms and reducing bacterial overgrowth.[40] Even though the diet contains carbohydrate in the form of glucose, glucose is rapidly absorbed into the blood stream and does not promote the overgrowth of bacteria.

4. *Other digestive health conditions associated with SIBO and carbohydrate malabsorption are linked to IBS.*

**Gastroesophageal reflux disease (GERD).** IBS patients frequently suffer from GERD and GERD patients frequently have IBS symptoms. In my book *Fast Tract Digestion Heartburn*, I provided solid evidence that GERD is also linked to carbohydrate malabsorption and SIBO.[41]

**Celiac disease.** In a study of 200 people with IBS, 40 (20%) showed evidence of celiac disease. This is almost 20 times higher than in the general population. People with celiac disease are often diagnosed with SIBO.[42, 43]

**Restless leg syndrome (RSL).** Approximately 5.5% of people in the general population have RLS.[44] Yet, in a study of 90 patients with IBS, 29% were diagnosed with RLS.[45] In a second study, IBS was diagnosed in 28% of 32 patients with RLS.[46] Sixty-nine percent of the RLS subjects in the second study were diagnosed with SIBO.

**Asthma.** A study of people with asthma showed they had IBS twice as often as non-asthmatics.[47] Asthma is also linked to GERD which is associated with IBS and SIBO.[48] As many as 80% of asthmatics suffer from abnormal gastroesophageal reflux compared to about 20% of non-asthmatics.[49, 50]

**Risk of osteoporosis and bone fracture.** A study of over 300,000 patients diagnosed with IBS showed there was a significant increased risk of osteoporosis and bone fractures in this population.[51] These findings may be related to the malabsorption of vitamins and minerals, including vitamin D and calcium, associated with SIBO. In another study, SIBO patients had lower bone mineral density values and higher bone loss than healthy volunteers.[52]

**Note:** People taking Proton Pump Inhibitor (PPI) drugs, generally for chronic acid reflux, also have a significant increase in bone fractures. This is usually thought to be the result of these drugs lowering stomach acid which inhibits calcium absorption.[53] But given the connection with IBS, there may be a common mechanism at work in both IBS and acid reflux. Both are based on SIBO, which can also have a negative impact on the absorption of minerals.

This is certainly not an exhaustive list of connections supporting a link between SIBO and IBS, but it does demonstrate a clear connection. Digestive and even systemic health conditions linked to SIBO are often linked to IBS, and treatment that improves SIBO or conditions caused by SIBO also improves the symptoms of IBS.

Now for two important next steps: First, I'm going to show you how SIBO causes the symptoms of IBS, and then show how I've used this information to create a comprehensive and effective treatment strategy.

# CHAPTER 3

# How Does SIBO Cause IBS?

"THE CAUSE IS HIDDEN;
THE EFFECT IS VISIBLE
TO ALL".
—OVID.

**Gut Damage?**

SIBO can result in dramatic changes to the small intestine. Remember that most of the bacterial species identified in the diagnosis of SIBO actually originate in the large intestine. Most play an important role in digestion in the large intestine, but are not so "helpful" in the small intestine. These bacteria produce a variety of enzymes and metabolic end-products which include protein-degrading enzymes, an unusual combination of short-chain fatty acids and a variety of endo- and exo-toxins.

These toxins can block water absorption and stimulate fluid secretion by the gut lining, leading to diarrhea. Toxins and other bacterial debris can also cause an inflammatory response, as the intestinal immune system tries to get the overgrowing bacteria back under control. This inflammatory process, in turn, can damage the intestinal surface.

The protein-degrading enzymes produced by these invading bacteria can also damage our own carbohydrate digestive enzymes (because enzymes are made of protein). This can severely decrease our ability to digest carbohydrates. These "extra" undigested carbohydrates become more food for the bacteria, perpetuating the cycle of malabsorption and SIBO depicted in figure 1.

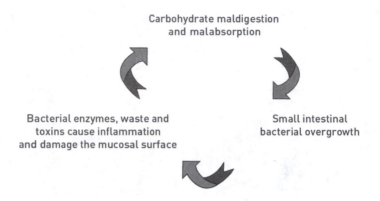

*Figure 1. The vicious cycle of malabsorption, bacterial overgrowth and intestinal damage.*

In the words of Elaine Gottschall, carbohydrate malabsorption and bacterial overgrowth become a "Vicious Cycle". The inflammatory reaction injures the mucosal lining of the small intestine. The injured cells on the mucosal surface are unable to complete the breakdown and absorption of food. This raises the level of malabsorbed carbohydrates, feeding the overgrowth of even more bacteria. This vicious cycle is played out over and over again in the small intestines all over the world.

## Gut Gas?

Most bacteria involved in SIBO produce copious amounts of gas, including carbon dioxide, hydrogen, and in some cases, methane. This gas raises the internal pressure in the small intestine and stomach (the medical term is "intragastric pressure") that I believe is the major cause of several common IBS symptoms, including gas, bloating, abdominal pain and cramps. As discussed in the previous chapter, the production of one of these gases, methane was recently linked to constipation-specific IBS-C.

High levels of bacteria such as *Lactobacillus* and *Bifidobacteria* are considered to be gut healthy because they don't make gas (more details can be found in Chapter 7). If these bacteria are displaced with gas-producing strains in the small intestine, IBS symptoms will follow. Not surprisingly, IBS has been associated with a decrease in *Bifidobacteria* levels.[54] (Refer to the discussion of probiotics in Chapters 8 and 12.)

## The Heartburn Connection

Many people with IBS also suffer with chronic heartburn. Excess gas pressure created by SIBO can push viscous stomach contents into the esophagus. These refluxed stomach contents contain acid, digestive enzymes, bile and even bacteria. The burning sensation, or heartburn, that most people with reflux feel is a direct result of stomach acid "burning" the unprotected esophagus.

In some cases the refluxed stomach acid, digestive enzymes and bacteria reach beyond the esophagus to the lungs and sinuses, creating both new symptoms and more serious health problems — including pneumonia and asthma. This is the reason I believe lung and breathing problems are linked to IBS – through acid reflux. To learn more about SIBO and acid reflux, you may be interested in reading the first book in the series, Fast Tract Digestion Heartburn.

Can bacterial fermentation really create enough (gas) pressure in the digestive system to cause all these symptoms? It certainly can! Years ago, as a research scientist, I routinely grew bacterial cultures of *E. coli*, *Bacteroides fragilis* and other intestinal bacteria in the laboratory.

The growth media we used contained a carbohydrate source (usually glucose) because gut bacteria like to consume carbohydrates for energy. I was amazed at the amount of gas that most strains could produce. As little as thirty grams (the weight of six nickels) of carbohydrate is enough to allow bacteria to produce ten liters of hydrogen gas.[55] Intestinal bacteria can create so much flammable gas that there have been well-documented cases of explosions during intestinal surgery.[56] If bacterial overgrowth can cause that much gas pressure, it can certainly drive IBS and heartburn symptoms.

Dietary malabsorption, bacterial overgrowth, and the resulting gas pressure is a "vicious cycle" that can lead to many of the symptoms experienced by people with IBS. Before we look at how to break this vicious cycle, we're going to take a quick look at how doctors can establish whether or not your IBS is caused by SIBO.

# CHAPTER 4

# Diagnosing SIBO in IBS Patients

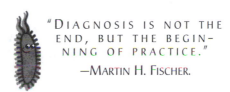

"DIAGNOSIS IS NOT THE
END, BUT THE BEGIN-
NING OF PRACTICE."
—MARTIN H. FISCHER.

If you have IBS and are interested in getting tested for SIBO, you have two choices: bacterial culture or hydrogen breath testing.

## Bacterial Culture Testing

The most definitive test for small intestinal bacterial overgrowth is to actually take a sample of the small intestine contents, culture the sample in a diagnostic microbiology laboratory, and determine the types and concentration of bacteria present. Having more than one hundred thousand bacteria per milliliter in the upper part of one's small intestine indicates overgrowth.

The bacterial culture method is the "gold standard" for this diagnosis, but it is an invasive technique, requiring significant expertise both on the part of the clinician as well as the laboratory analyzing the samples. Getting accurate results can be challenging, due to the difficulty of obtaining a sample from the small intestine, protecting it from contamination, transporting the sample to the lab, and analyzing the sample before the bacterial count changes.

The initial results don't tell you what types of bacteria are present. This requires additional bacteriological typing. The majority of the organisms in the sample will be anaerobic, meaning they cannot grow in the presence of air. Special culturing techniques are needed to detect and identify anaerobic bacteria. And, since a large number of intestinal bacteria simply don't grow in culture, some bacteria would still go undetected. As a result, this method is almost never used in everyday medical practice.

This test does, however, conclusively link SIBO to IBS. The most definitive bacterial culture study to date followed 320 subjects. Forty-two out of 62 people (67.7 percent) confirmed to have SIBO by bacterial culture testing also had IBS.[57] The types of bacteria recovered included *E. coli, Enterococcus* sp, *Klebsiella pneumoniae, Proteus Mirabilis, Acinetobacter baumannii, Citrobacter fruendii, Serratia marscecens, Staphylococcus aureus, Pseudomonas putida, Pasteurella maltocida* and *Enterobacter aerogenes.*

### Hydrogen breath testing

Dr. Pimentel's initial detection of SIBO in IBS patients was based on an indirect measurement of SIBO using a technique called the lactulose breath test, a form of hydrogen breath testing. The test measures the timed release of hydrogen in a subject's breath after consuming a specific quantity of the indigestible sugar lactulose.

The idea is that intestinal bacteria can metabolize the undigested lactulose and produce hydrogen gas, which is absorbed into the blood and exhaled from the lungs. Since human metabolism does not produce hydrogen, any hydrogen detected must come from gut bacteria.

The test is conducted following an overnight fast. After consuming the lactulose sugar solution, breath samples are taken (the patient breaths into a sampling device) every 15 minutes over a three-hour period, and then analyzed for the concentration of hydrogen.

Healthy people are relatively free of bacteria in the upper part of their small intestine. Their test results typically show a single large peak of hydrogen in breath samples taken about 2 hours after the lactulose solution is given, representing fermentation of the lactulose by bacteria in the large intestine.

Test results for people with SIBO will show hydrogen concentrations of 20 or more parts per million in samples collected within 90 minutes or less after the lactulose solution is consumed,[58] representing fermentation of the lactulose by bacteria in the small intestine. This pattern is a strong indication of the presence of SIBO.

One of the challenges in gaining wider acceptance for the use of hydrogen breath testing is the need for standardization of the breath testing technique. Some tests replace lactulose with glucose and as a result can only detect SIBO in the earliest part of the small intestine. Practitioners are also challenged by the differences between analyses at different labs, and the lack of definitive studies comparing the breath test results to microbiological culture methods. More information is needed before we can gauge the sensitivity (how much SIBO must be present to detect it?) and specificity (are some of the results falsely positive?) of the method.

While some researchers achieved conflicting results using hydrogen breath testing,[59] the inconsistency in techniques and the choice of fermentable sugar used in the test could be the cause. Comparing a larger number of lactulose breath test studies (called a meta-analysis) validated the use of this testing for diagnosing SIBO in people with IBS.[60]

### Hydrogen Breath Testing for Individual Carbohydrates

Hydrogen breath testing can also be used to detect the malabsorption of individual sugars other than lactulose.[61] This expanded testing is based on the fact that all digested and absorbed sugars will enter the blood stream and not be available for intestinal fermentation and hydrogen production. Unabsorbed or poorly absorbed sugars, on the other hand, will remain in the intestine and become fermented, releasing hydrogen (demonstrating a hydrogen peak and a positive test for specific sugar malabsorption). This test has even been used to detect the malabsorption of starch.

To conduct this more specific test, the patient drinks a solution containing the suspect carbohydrate, such as lactose or fructose. As in the previous hydrogen test, the administrator will measure the amount of hydrogen present in breath samples over a three-hour period.

Any sugar that is unabsorbed will be consumed by bacteria in the small intestine as well as the large intestine. How soon hydrogen is detected indicates whether the patient has SIBO (an early hydrogen signal indicates bacterial growth in the upper small intestine) or not (a late hydrogen signal indicates fermentation by bacteria in the large intestine) as well as whether or not the specific sugar has been digested and absorbed into the blood stream (and is therefore unavailable for bacterial consumption).

People interested in being tested for SIBO must find a doctor who conducts hydrogen breath testing or the more invasive bacterially culture method. This may not be covered by insurance, as SIBO is not fully accepted as the underlying cause of IBS at this point in time.

Of course, a good and simple alternative to testing by either the bacterial culture method or hydrogen breath testing is to try the Fast Tract Digestion Diet Program and see if your symptoms disappear.

# Treating IBS by Addressing SIBO

There are two major stages in successfully treating IBS symptoms by controlling SIBO. First, the offending bacteria must be killed or inhibited, hopefully without wiping out the healthy bacteria in the process. Second, any existing underlying health problems that promote SIBO must also be identified and addressed. The chapters that follow look at two completely different strategies for achieving this goal.

The first strategy, outlined in Chapter 5, uses antibiotics to control SIBO. This is not an approach I endorse, but it is gaining more headway in medical and regulatory (FDA) circles and could be an approved treatment in the future.

The second strategy (covered through the remainder of the book) focuses on a new diet based on nutritional science, coupled with behavioral interventions designed to deprive bacteria of the "excessive" carbohydrate fuel they need to multiply. Identifying and addressing contributing issues is also an important feature of this strategy.

CHAPTER 5:

# Should I Take Antibiotics for My IBS?

"ANTIBIOTICS, THE GREATEST DOUBLE EDGED SWORD IN MODERN MEDICINE."
—UNKNOWN

How doctors treat IBS could change dramatically in the near future. Two years ago, the pharmaceutical company Salix submitted a supplemental new drug application (sNDA) for the treatment for IBS (non-constipation-dependent) with the antibiotic rifaximin (brand name Xifaxan). In March of 2011, the FDA failed to approve the application on the grounds that more clinical evidence was needed to show that the drug would be effective. The FDA wants to see whether rifaximin will prove effective against the reoccurrence of IBS symptoms in patients who responded to an initial treatment with the drug.[62] Since that time, the FDA has been working with Salix to design additional studies to answer their questions. In the meantime, many doctors are prescribing antibiotics for IBS even before they are approved by the FDA. This practice is called "off-label" prescribing.

One of the newest treatments for IBS patients diagnosed with SIBO is based on the "Cedars-Sinai Protocol," covered in Dr Mark Pimetel's book *A New IBS Solution*. In this protocol, once tests rule out conditions with similar symptoms such as celiac disease or thyroid dysfunction, the patient is given a ten day course of antibiotics. The antibiotic most recommended is rifaximin, which is FDA-approved for traveler's diarrhea caused by certain strains of *E. coli* bacteria. A second antibiotic, neomycin, is sometime recommended as well.

But treating SIBO with antibiotics is not new. Several antibiotics including metronidazole, levofloxacin, ciprofloxacin, doxycycline, amoxicillin-clavulanate, trimethoprim-sulfamethoxazole, cephalexin, and norfloxacin have been tried. A short-term study involving ten SIBO patients indicated that norfloxacin and amoxicillin-clavulanic acid could be effective in the treatment of bacterial overgrowth-related diarrhea.[63] Metronidazole (Flagyl), which is potent against several bacteria associated with SIBO such as *Bacteroides fragilis* and *Clostridium difficile*, has also been used successfully for treating SIBO.[64]

**The case for antibiotics**

There are many medical conditions that require the use of antibiotics. Life-threatening bacterial infections such as pneumonia, wound infections, or septicemia (a serious bacterial infection of the blood) are the most common. Some types of bacteria, such as *Staphylococcus aureus*, are particularly virulent (very effective at causing disease). An antibiotic may be the only way to control these infections. Also, even routine infections can cause serious health problems for people with immune deficiencies. Antibiotics are also used for chronic infections caused by bacteria, such as *H. pylori*, which can lead to stomach ulcers. Treatment of IBS can fall into this category.

There are also other instances where antibiotics are *not* the best choice. The best example is taking antibiotics for a cold or other illness caused by a virus. In these cases, the antibiotics won't help at all, but the body's bacteria will have an opportunity to develop resistance to the antibiotic used.

In most cases, antibiotics are prescribed only when there is clear evidence that the patient suffers from a bacterial illness that is not expected to go away on its own. Doctors often prescribe antibiotics without knowing what specific bacterium is causing the symptoms. Once a specific bacterium has been identified as the source of the problem there is a much better chance it can be controlled. The bacteria can be cultured and tested to find the best antibiotic for the task.

Certainly, there are circumstances where antibiotics are appropriate for SIBO, for example, in situations where SIBO poses a significant and immediate health threat, such as anemia, malnutrition, or other serious medical condition.

On the surface, it would seem logical to treat all IBS caused by SIBO with antibiotics. SIBO, after all, is an overgrowth of bacteria in our small intestine. It sounds logical to "kill the bacteria that are causing the problem."

But are antibiotics the best response to the bacterial overgrowth of SIBO? Unfortunately, when it comes to the human digestive system, solving problems isn't as simple as "killing the bad bacteria." Success really means killing the bad bacteria without killing off the good bacteria the digestive system needs to keep us healthy. And antibiotics represent a shotgun approach that can cause more problems than it solves.

Though I have great respect for Dr. Pimentel and his team's outstanding work on IBS, I have some concerns about using antibiotics as a first-line treatment for SIBO. There are good reasons to reconsider this approach. Let's look at the pros and cons.

**Pros:**

**Lots of people can be helped**. If the Cedar-Sinai Protocol works, it stands to help many people. There are an estimated fifty million people in the US who suffer with chronic IBS. Pimentel's team found that 78% of patients with IBS had SIBO.[65] The statistics are similar for children.[66]

**Antibiotics are often effective and safe**. Dr. Pimentel states in his book that he recommends rifaximin and neomycin because the antibiotics have been shown to be effective for treating SIBO. Both antibiotics are almost completely contained in the gastrointestinal tract, minimizing side effects and drug resistance. Pimentel's team suggests that their treatment protocol is also effective, noting that "patient's IBS symptoms significantly decreased after a single ten-day course of rifaximin" and that "the symptom improvement lasted two months after treatment."

Subsequent to publishing the book, however, Dr. Pimentel has admitted that neomycin, in particular, has limited usefulness because the causative bacteria develop resistance to the drug. He notes that, "Neomycin produces rapid and durable evidence of clinical resistance. In a recent study, 75% of subjects who took conventional antibiotics such as neomycin did not respond to subsequent therapy."[67]

**Preventing the more serious consequences of SIBO**. Antibiotic treatment, if successful, could help prevent some of the more serious complications of SIBO. Like IBS, the symptoms of SIBO include abdominal pain or cramps, diarrhea, constipation, gas, bloating, acid reflux, flatulence, nausea, dehydration, and fatigue. But SIBO can also cause more severe conditions including weight loss, "failure to thrive," steatorrhea (the body's failure to digest fats), anemia, bleeding or bruising, night blindness, bone pain and fractures, leaky gut syndrome, and autoimmune reactions. It is crucial to stop SIBO before it causes these more serious problems.

**Cons:**

While I support the use of antibiotics for treating serious bacterial infections, including the most serious forms of SIBO mentioned above, I have five basic concerns over the use of antibiotics for the routine treatment of IBS.

- Antibiotics lack both short- and long-term efficacy for IBS.
- Antibiotics kill both good and bad bacteria and can lead to *C. diff* infection.
- Overusing antibiotics breeds resistant strains of bacteria.

- Antibiotics are associated with a number of different side effects and can cause allergic reactions.
- There are better ways to control SIBO: specifically, by identifying and addressing the underlying conditions that contribute to SIBO and adopting a diet that limits fermentable carbohydrates and sugar alcohols.

**Antibiotics lack both short- and long-term efficacy for SIBO.** Two double-blind clinical studies funded by Salix Pharmaceuticals showed similar results. Forty-one percent of IBS patients treated with 550 mg of rifaximin three times daily received adequate overall symptom relief, compared to 32% for the placebo.[68] Also, forty percent of those treated with rifaximin reported relief of bloating, compared to 30% of those administered a placebo. While the antibiotic did show a 10% advantage over the placebo, the difference in results should really be more dramatic to justify using the antibiotics.

Antibiotics are not effective for long-term treatment of SIBO, either. A study of eighty patients with SIBO who responded to rifaximin showed a high recurrence rate six months (27.5%) and nine months (43.7%) after therapy.[69] (Refer to figure 2.)

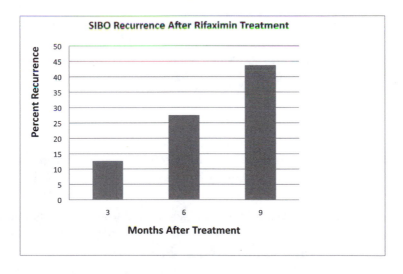

*Figure 2. SIBO recurrence following rifaximin treatment.*

Clearly, this high recurrence rate shows that the rifaximin treatment is not fully addressing the underlying problem. Symptoms often return as soon as the bacteria have a chance to grow back. It may be that the drug does not inhibit all bacterial types, including certain diarrhea-causing organisms, such as *Campylobacter jejuni,* that are naturally resistant to rifaximin. And many of the gut bacteria that cause SIBO and IBS symptoms may quickly develop resistance against the antibiotics (See below).

**Antibiotics kill both good and bad bacteria and can lead to *C. diff* infections.** The Cedars-Sinai Protocol depends on broad-spectrum antibiotics, meaning the drugs are effective for a wide range of bacteria. This is important because SIBO is not caused by a single type of bacteria, but rather, by the overgrowth of many types of bacteria, generally arising from the large intestine. Many of the bacteria involved are likely to be resistant to some of the less potent antibiotics.

But there is a downside to the use of broad-spectrum antibiotics. Broad-spectrum antibiotics are indiscriminate bacteria killers. They will kill both "good" and "bad" bacteria and destroy the natural balance in the intestines — causing diarrhea and other problems.

In fact, broad-spectrum antibiotics have been implicated as a cause of IBS[70] as well as inflammatory bowel disease.[71] In most cases, the natural balance of your intestinal bacteria will return to normal once you stop taking the antibiotic. Unfortunately, this can take a long time, even years. In some cases the original healthy intestinal microbial population never fully recovers.

Once healthy gut bacteria are killed off, pathogenic or "bad" bacteria can take over. The worst of the bunch is *Clostridia difficile*, known as *C diff.* According to a CDC press release,[72] *C diff* infections cost at least one billion dollars each year to treat and lead to approximately 14,000 deaths every year in the US alone. Most deaths are caused by a dangerous condition called pseudo-membranous colitis (a serious and sometimes fatal inflammation of the large intestine). *C diff* infections have increased in incidence (new cases per year), morbidity (illness), and mortality (death) in the last few years.

The major risk factors include use of antibiotics, elderly patients and prolonged hospital or nursing home stays.[73, 74, 75]

*C diff* creates difficult-to-kill antibiotic-resistant spores that can persist in the intestine, on household or doctor's office surfaces, and even on the hands of medical providers. And even more powerful antibiotics may be required to treat it. Elderly patients are most at risk. The best bet is to avoid antibiotics unless they are truly needed so you don't become susceptible to *C diff* in the first place.

**Overusing antibiotics breeds resistant strains of bacteria**. One of the biggest challenges in treating SIBO with antibiotics is drug resistance. Many bacteria are naturally resistant to antibiotics, and all bacteria have the ability to become resistant either through mutation or by transferring genes from other bacteria. I spent a decade of my career studying antibiotic resistance. I can tell you this is a huge problem fueled by the overuse of antibiotics.

Well-known examples of drug-resistant bacteria include methicillin-resistant *Staph aureus* (blood and wound infections and toxic shock syndrome), multidrug-resistant *enterococci* (urinary tract, blood, and other infections) multidrug-resistant *Acinetobacter baumannii* (pneumonia, blood, urinary tract and other infections), drug resistant *C diff* (diarrhea and pseudo-membranous colitis) and most recently, carbapenem-resistant *Enterobacteriaceae* (such as *E coli* and *Klebsiella pneumonia* bacteria) or CRE (blood and wound infections). According to the Centers for Disease Control, CRE have become resistant to even the most powerful antibiotics and can potentially contribute to the death of half of the people they infect.[76]

Drug resistance limits the usefulness of all antibiotics whenever they are used, but the problem is most challenging with SIBO because of the sheer number and diversity of bacteria that reside in the small and large intestines. Resistant bacteria that develop in one person's intestines while on antibiotics can even infect other people through lapses in adequate hygiene.

As resistance to one drug emerges, SIBO and its' symptoms will persist until another effective antibiotic or combination of antibiotics is found. Due to the broad use of antibiotics, new types of antibiotics are not being developed fast enough to keep up with widespread resistance.

**Drug resistance and *C-diff*.** As mentioned above, *C diff* can take over the digestive tract after antibiotic treatments kill the majority of friendly bacteria. *C diff* infection is so often linked to antibiotic use that *C diff* infections are commonly referred to as "antibiotic-associated diarrhea (AAD)." Having a diverse population of healthy bacteria in your digestive system is the best protection against *C diff*.

Many *C diff* strains are already resistant to a number of antibiotics, including rifaximin. Recently, investigators reported the discovery of rifaximin-resistant *C. diff* following rifaximin treatment for recurrent *C. difficile* diarrhea.[77] And the problem is not limited to the US. In another recent study, more than 10% of *C. diff* isolates from three major teaching hospitals in Taiwan were resistant to rifaximin.[78]

Salix, who makes rifaximin, cautions that: "*Clostridium difficile*–associated diarrhea (CDAD) has been reported with use of nearly all antibacterial agents, including Xifaxin, and may range in severity from mild diarrhea to fatal colitis. Treatment with antibacterial agents alters the normal flora of the colon which may lead to overgrowth of *C difficile*.[79]"

The risks posed by *C diff* infections, and the growing resistance of *C diff* to antibiotics in particular, are powerful reasons to seek alternatives to treating SIBO with antibiotics.

**Antibiotics are often associated with side effects and can cause allergic reactions**. As noted on the Salix company web site,[80] patients experienced the following adverse reactions: edema peripheral, or fluid in the tissues of the extremities, causing swelling in 15% of patients, nausea in 14%, dizziness in 13%, fatigue in 12%, ascites, or fluid in peritoneal cavity between abdominal organs, in 11%, muscle spasms in 9%, pruritus in 9%, and abdominal pain in 9%.

The high percentage of patients who experience antibiotic-related side effects makes this a much less desirable approach to treating IBS, especially given its limited effectiveness. Even more serious side effects sometimes occur, though at a lower frequency than those listed above. Web MD lists 15 rare but serious side effects, including a hernia which protrudes into the abdominal wall. And all antibiotics, including rifaximin, can cause serious allergic reactions. These potentially serious side effects are another reason to take antibiotics only when they are absolutely necessary.

**There are better ways to control SIBO**. The biggest problem with antibiotics is that they don't address the root cause. Why has SIBO developed in the first place?

Depending on the answer to this question, correcting SIBO can be fairly simple. For example, a lactose intolerant individual with intermittent diarrhea (caused by SIBO) may recover completely by avoiding lactose or taking the enzyme supplement lactase.

But often the problem is more complex. In these cases, successful treatment of SIBO requires addressing the underlying causes of SIBO, reducing the bacterial overgrowth, as well as treating the symptoms.

Antibiotics should be reserved for the most serious forms of IBS and SIBO; conditions that either fail to respond to diet, or that involve more severe symptoms such as weight loss, failure to thrive, steatorrhea (the body's failure to digest fats), anemia, bleeding or bruising, night blindness, bone pain and fractures, leaky gut syndrome, or autoimmune reactions. Your first response to severe symptoms like these should be a visit to your doctor. The Fast Tract Approach may prove superior to antibiotics even in these cases, but your doctor should be involved in the decision.

# Food Chemistry

"WHAT IS FOOD TO ONE,
IS TO OTHERS BITTER
POISON."

—LUCRETIUS, DE RERUM NATURA.

The Fast Tract Diet that I'm introducing here is based on medical science and biological chemistry. I've researched this approach fully. But unless you're a doctor or nutritionist by trade, you may not understand why the Fast Tract Program is such a breakthrough in treating IBS, or why it's so important that you follow the program carefully to get the results you want.

The purpose of the next two chapters is to provide a basic framework on what food is made of, how each food type is digested, and how our body uses food. Reading these chapters will make it easier to understand the concepts of malabsorption and bacterial overgrowth as we discuss how to treat them.

The basic connection you need to understand is between the digestion and absorption (or, really, the incomplete digestion and malabsorption) of food, how it leads to Small Intestinal Bacterial Overgrowth (SIBO) and, in turn, to the symptoms associated with IBS. In order to understand how they're linked in your body, and why my approach to treating them works, you need to know a little more about the basics of human digestion.

In this chapter I'm going to introduce to the three basic types of food — what they're made of, and how they are digested.

## The Three Basic Types of Food

Given the tremendous variety of foods available, it may seem surprising that all foods fall into only three categories: carbohydrates, proteins, and fats. Fats and carbohydrates satisfy most of our energy needs, but we need protein to grow, repair damaged cells and make new proteins including critical enzymes, antibodies and structural molecules.

Animal-based foods like beef, pork, poultry, fish, dairy products, and eggs are rich in both proteins and fats. Vegetables, fruits and grains are rich sources of carbohydrates. However, many plant-based foods are also good sources of proteins and fats. Animal-based foods contain negligible amounts of carbohydrates.

### *Carbohydrates*

The primary role of the carbohydrates in our diet is to help us meet our need for energy. Plant-based foods such as fruits, vegetables, grains, pasta, flours, potatoes, pastries, candy, rice, sugar and breads contain mostly carbohydrates. Carbohydrates include sugars, starches and fibers and are made up of the elements carbon, hydrogen and oxygen. Glucose, a sugar, is the carbohydrate our cells like to use to get energy. Most of the carbohydrates we eat are eventually broken down to glucose, and burned by our cells for fuel, or stored as glycogen or fat. (A quick note here: carbohydrates are also the preferred food of bacteria. More on this later.)

### Monosaccharides

The basic carbohydrate unit is called a monosaccharide, meaning "single sugar." Single sugars do not really require digestion; they can be absorbed directly from the intestine into your blood. Monosaccharides include sugars like glucose, fructose and galactose. Glucose is the most common and important monosaccharide — it is your body's basic food.

Monosaccharides can link together to form more complex carbo-hydrates that do require digestion. For example, disaccharides (made up of two sugar units) such as lactose and sucrose, or polysaccharides (made up of multiple sugar units) such as raffinose (made up of three sugars), stachyose (made up of four sugars), or starches and fiber (made up of thousands to millions of sugar units).

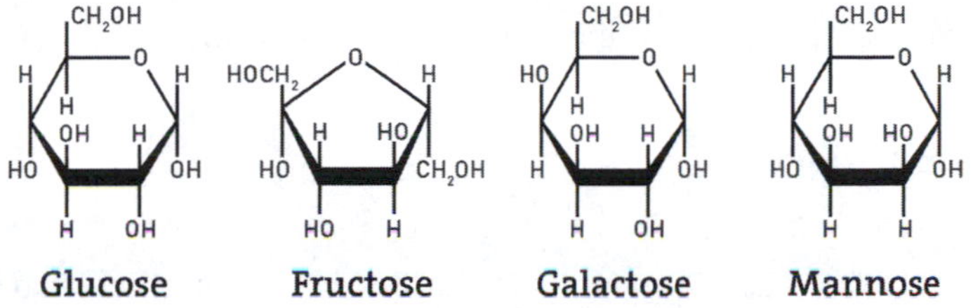

Figure 3. Monosaccharides

## Disaccharides

Disaccharides are composed of two sugars and must be broken down into monosaccharides to be absorbed into the blood stream. Disaccharides include sucrose, made up of glucose and fructose, and commonly known as table sugar; lactose, made up of glucose and galactose, and commonly known as milk sugar; and maltose, produced by the breakdown of starch, and made up of two glucose molecules.

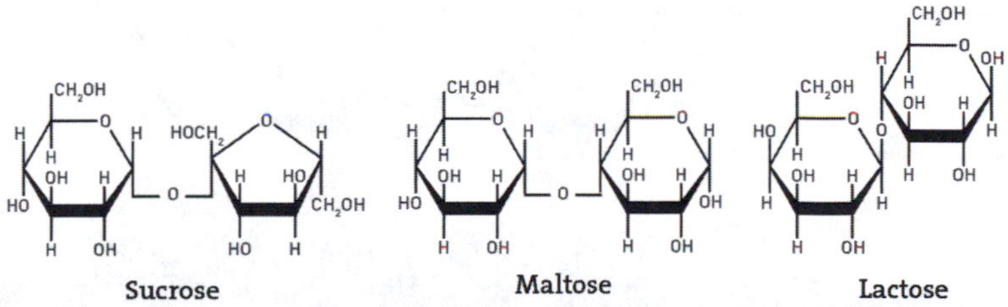

Figure 4. Disaccharides

## Polysaccharides

Polysaccharides are made up of multiple sugar units. Smaller sugar chains called oligosaccharides include stachyose and raffinose. Starches, including amylose and amylopectin, and fibers including cellulose, hemicellulose and pectin are composed of thousands to millions of repeating glucose units. Both of these types of polysaccharides will play extremely important roles in the following chapters.

## Oligosaccharides

Oligosaccharides are short polysaccharides containing between three and ten sugar units. Examples include fructose oligosaccharide (FOS), made from repeating fructose units and found in many plants; stachyose, composed of glucose, fructose, and two galactose sugar units and found in beans and vegetables; and raffinose, composed of glucose, fructose and galactose. Because these oligosaccharides are non- or only marginally digestible, they are defined as dietary fiber.

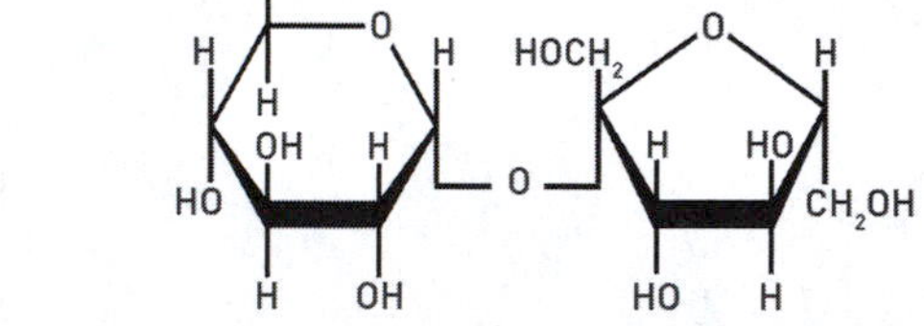

*Figure 5. Oligosaccharide Raffinose*

### Starches

The most common polysaccharide in most people's diet is starch. Starch is the major form of stored carbohydrate in plants, and is present in grain foods like wheat, rice, corn, oats and barley as well as tubers like potatoes.

Most starchy plants contain two types of starch, amylose, an essentially linear polysaccharide, and amylopectin, a more complex and highly branched polysaccharide. Both are composed entirely of glucose sugar units. Most starchy vegetables (including corn, wheat, oats and most barley, as well as many varieties of rice and potatoes) contain 20 to 30% amylose and 70 to 80% amylopectin. Some potatoes, corn and legumes contain higher percentages (up to 65% or more) of amylose. Some plant varieties like waxy rice (also known as short grain, glutinous, sweet or sticky rice) and waxy barley may contain up to 100% amylopectin. This is important for our discussion because one of these starch types, amylose, is very difficult to digest.

## Amylopectin

Amylopectin can contain up to 2 million glucose units. Its structure is more complex than amylose with branches up to 30 glucose units long occurring every 25 to 30 glucose units or so. Due to amylopectin's branching and less dense structure, amylopectin is much easier to break down to glucose than amylose. The main enzyme responsible for the breakdown of amylopectin is amylase, which is found both in our saliva and our small intestine.

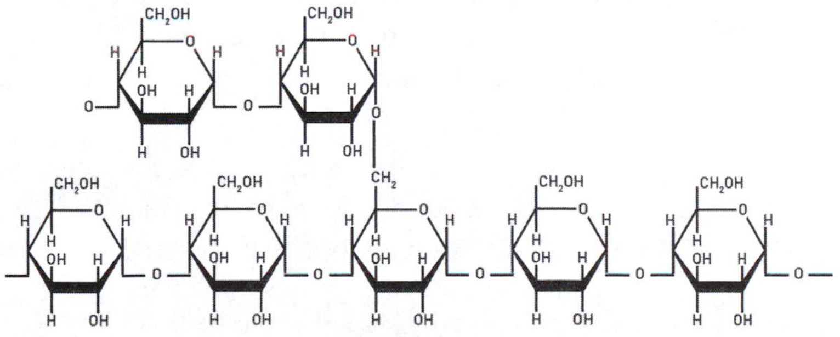

Figure 6. Amylopectin (branching shown)

*Amylose*

Amylose starch molecules are much smaller than amylopectin, containing as few as several hundred to as many as several thousand glucose molecules. Amylose is also broken down by the enzyme amylase, but less efficiently than amylopectin, because the amylose molecule has fewer branch points and can be packed more tightly into starch granules.

The rapid breakdown of amylopectin vs. amylose is one of the key concepts underlying the Fast Tract Diet approach and will be discussed in more detail later in the book.

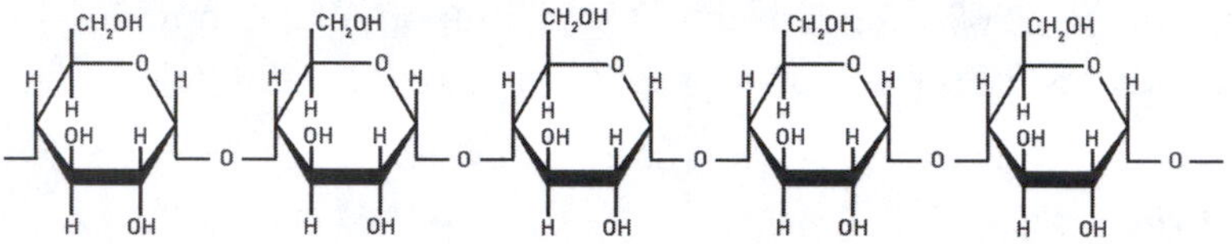

*Figure 7. Amylose (minor branching not shown)*

## Fiber

Fiber is present in plant-based foods and represents structural components such as the cell walls of fruits, vegetables, nuts and legumes, the tough outer layers of grains, as well as any other non- digestible carbohydrates found in plants. Dietary fiber includes cellulose, hemicellulose, lignin (a substance found in plants that binds cellulose fibers together), pectin, gums, polydextrose, raffinose, stachyose, verbascose, and fructans.

Resistant starch is sometimes also considered a class of dietary fiber. But unlike starch, fiber is not digestible by humans. We lack the enzymes to break the chemical bonds between the sugar molecules in fiber. The molecular structure of one type of fiber, cellulose, is shown below.

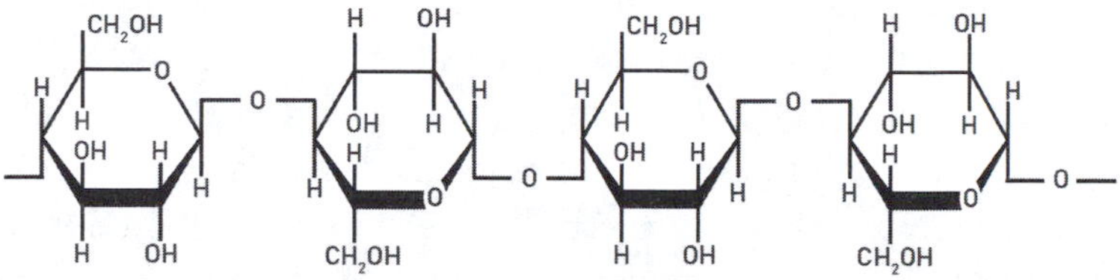

*Figure 8. Cellulose*

## Proteins

Foods such as meats, poultry, fish, eggs and cheese are mostly protein but usually also contain some fats. Protein can also be found in foods such as nuts, beans, grains and seeds. Proteins are generally large molecules that are composed of specific building blocks known as amino acids (see figure 11). As with carbohydrates, proteins contain the elements carbon, hydrogen and oxygen, but proteins also contain nitrogen and sulfur.

Proteins can be used for energy or to make new proteins. Amino acids are required for muscle growth, the repair of damaged cells, and to make enzymes, hormones and structural proteins such as collagen. Approximately half of all amino acids can be made by our body and are known as "non-essential" amino acids. Our bodies cannot produce the other amino acids, and they must be supplied in our diet — or by the microorganisms living in our intestinal tract. These are referred to as "essential" amino acids.

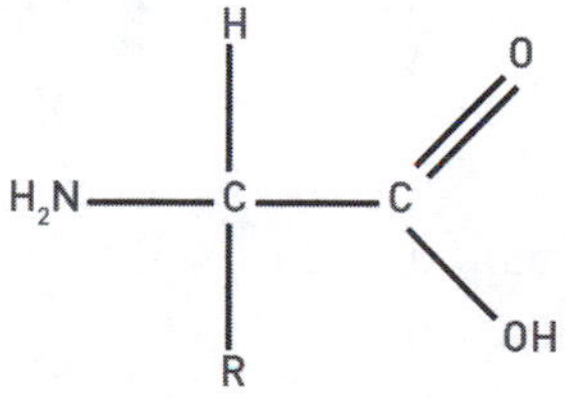

*Figure 9. Amino acid, the building block amino acids have different functional groups (shown as "R") that make each amino acid unique. Glycine's "R" group is a single hydrogen (H) atom, while alanine's R group is a methyl (CH3) group.*

To make new proteins, amino acids are linked together via peptide bonds. The peptide bonds form the backbone of the protein, which can be thought of as a long chain. Twenty different amino acids are used to compose proteins. Proteins range in size from about 40 amino acids (smaller proteins are referred to as peptides) to hundreds of amino acids. The sequence of the amino acids in the protein chain determine its primary structure but proteins can fold back onto themselves in such a way as to have secondary and tertiary structures. The shape of a "re-folded" protein is held in place by a weak force called hydrogen bonding. Proteins are much more complex than carbohydrates or fats because of these secondary and tertiary structures, but their complex shapes make their many catalytic, regulatory, and structural applications possible.

A quick side note about proteins: Proteins that are not digested and fully absorbed can be selectively metabolized by intestinal bacteria but are less likely to contribute to SIBO and intestinal gas.

### Fats

Fats have gotten a bad name in the diet business. In fact, fats comprise a significant part of a normal diet, and you need to eat an adequate amount of healthy fats to maintain your health. Fats provide both an excellent energy source, as well as building materials for cell membranes, hormones and other fatty acid-based molecules.

Good dietary sources of fats include meat, poultry, fish, eggs, cheese, butter, olive oil, nuts, and avocados. Fats are also found in smaller amounts in grains and green leafy vegetables.

Like carbohydrates, fats are comprised of the elements hydrogen, oxygen and carbon. Fatty acids are the "building blocks" of fats. (Just as amino acids are the building blocks of proteins, and sugars are the building blocks of carbohydrates).

Chemically, all fats have the same -COOH (carboxylic acid) group at the end of carbon chains ranging from 4 to 29 carbon atoms in length.

There are four different kinds of fats: mono-unsaturated fats, poly-unsaturated fats, saturated fats and hydrogenated or trans-fats.

These categories are based on the bonding structures within the carbon chains.

Monounsaturated fats (MUFAs, short for monounsaturated fatty acids) are prevalent in peanut, olive, canola, and sunflower oil, as well as meats and butter, while polyunsaturated fats (PUFAs, short for polyunsaturated fatty acids) are prevalent in fish as well as canola, safflower, cottonseed, corn, sunflower and flaxseed oil. Historically, both monounsaturated and polyunsaturated fats have been thought to have significant health benefits, potentially lowering bad cholesterol (LDL) and increasing good cholesterol (HDL). (See additional comments below on essential PUFAs.)

$$CH_3(CH_2)_4CH = CHCH_2CH = CH(CH_2)_7COOH$$

*Figure 10. Polyunsaturated fat linoleic acid*

Saturated fats are found in many foods including butter, cream, coconut oil, palm oil, poultry and meats. They have been associated with an increase in both good (HDL) and bad (LDL) cholesterol. There is a growing consensus that a certain amount of saturated fats may actually be healthy for our bodies, especially our immune systems, and should be consumed along with mono- and polyunsaturated fats.

Trans-fats occur to a small extent in nature but the largest source comes from a process called hydrogenation. This process is used to improve the shelf life of vegetable oils.

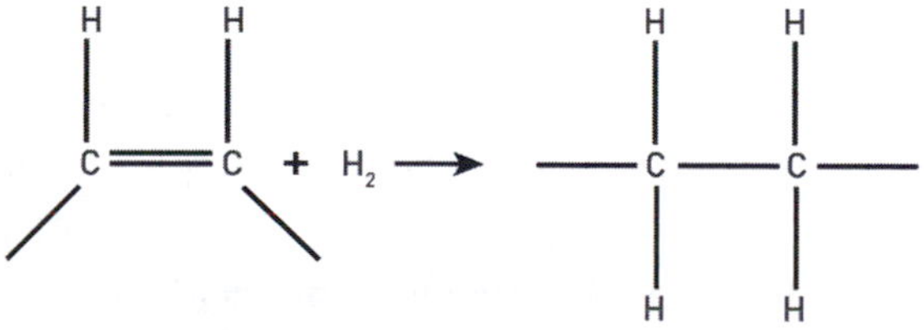

*Figure 11. Hydrogenation Process*

Trans-fats are the unhealthiest fat and have been linked to an increase in bad LDL cholesterol, a decrease in good HDL cholesterol, and a greater risk of cardiovascular disease. [81]

Other than advocating the avoidance of trans-fats, the Fast Tract Diet System does not specifically limit fats as they don't contribute to bacterial overgrowth and resulting inflammation and symptoms.

## Other Essential "Ingredients"

Now let's look at some of the other elements of our diet that are required for good health. Along with proteins and fats, our bodies require water, vitamins, minerals, specific types of essential fatty acids, and amino acids. (Carbohydrates are not technically a nutritional requirement, since fats and protein can meet all of our energy requirements.)

### Water

Water is the most important single metabolic requirement we have. We need water to break down and metabolize every food group; as well as for transporting nutrients and removing waste from around the body. Water is also critical for maintaining body temperature, osmotic balance (controlling salt and other electrolyte concentrations), blood pressure and normal bowel and bladder functions. Lack of water is one of the surest ways to degrade a wide range of normal bodily functions.

### Vitamins

Vitamins are required for a variety of digestive and cellular processes, primarily as co-enzymes (helper molecules for enzymes). Essential vitamins include vitamins A (retinol), Bp (choline), B1 (thiamine), B2 (riboflavin), B3 (niacin), B5 (pantothenic acid), B6 (pyridoxine), B7 (biotin), B9 (folic acid), B10 (p-aminobenzoic acid), B12 (cobalamine), C (ascorbic acid), D (calciferol), E (tocopherol) and K (naphthoquinone). The vitamins present in a balanced diet are usually sufficient for our purposes, taking a daily multivitamin ensures an ample supply of needed vitamins.

## Minerals

Minerals are also required for enzymes to function; giving bones their strength, and cells the ability to regulate fluid levels. Key minerals include; calcium, chloride, magnesium, phosphorus, potassium, sodium and sulfur. Other minerals such as copper, chromium, iodine, iron, manganese molybdenum selenium, zinc and possibly boron, nickel, tin, silicon and vanadium are required in trace amounts. Minerals are generally plentiful in our diet or in the water we drink, but to be on the safe side you can take a daily multivitamin that also contains minerals.

## Omega-3 and Omega-6 Fatty Acids

Essential polyunsaturated fatty acids (PUFAs) include omega-3 and omega-6 fatty acids. Our bodies cannot manufacture these compounds, so you must supply them in your diet. Most diets are rich in omega-6 fatty acids; but omega-3 fatty acids are present in fewer foods. Good sources of omega-3 fatty acids include: alpha-linolenic acid from flaxseed oil, canola or walnut oil; and fish oil-based eicosapentaenoic acid (EPA) and docosahexaenoic acid (DHA) found in fish (fish get EPA and DHA from eating algae). Alpha-linolenic acid can be converted into EPA and DHA in the body though not at 100% efficiency. So it's a good idea to eat fatty fish such as mackerel, trout, sardines, tuna, or salmon a few times per week.[83]

Though PUFAs are essential, too much can be unhealthy. The "unsaturated bonds" in PUFAs make these fats less stable, which means they can become denatured or oxidized (rancid) if exposed to too much heat, or even oxygen in the air. These fats are also more reactive than other fats and can form bonds with sugars and proteins, creating AGEs (Advanced Glycation End-products). AGEs are considered to be unhealthy because they can cause inflammation.

The best rule of thumb with respect to fats and oils is to consume whole foods along with cold pressed oils such as olive and coconut oil. Avoid heavily processed oils, referred to as "industrial oils," that are created using high heat and pressure that can cause oxidation.

### Amino Acids

Essential amino acids include isoleucine, lysine, leucine, methionine, phenylalanine, threonine, tryptophan and valine, but also histidine and arginine in children.

Deficiencies in essential amino acids are very rare. Animal-based protein contains all of the essential amino acids. Even though some plant-based proteins are deficient in amino acids such as lysine, methionine or tryptophan, consuming a variety of plant protein sources can easily give you an adequate supply of all essential amino acids.

## Inessential "Ingredients": Sweeteners

Sweeteners aren't essential like other "foods" in this chapter, but they are used by almost everyone in some form every day.

### Natural Sweeteners

The most common sweetener is sucrose or table sugar. Sucrose is a disaccharide (meaning it's composed of two sugar molecules stuck together) containing equal amounts of glucose and fructose. Sucrose is not used in the recipes in this book because it contains 50% fructose, which is very difficult to absorb (more on this later). The same goes for high fructose corn syrup, which generally contains more fructose than glucose, and honey, which has approximately the same ratio of glucose to fructose as sucrose. Most people can tolerate small amounts of sucrose and honey, but moderation is the key.

Fructose itself is also used as a common sweetener in many foods, snacks and desserts and is almost twice as sweet as sucrose or honey. I would advise strictly limiting fructose as it is very difficult to absorb, particularly in the absence of glucose. This can be challenging given the widespread use of this sweetener.

Gut-friendly natural sweeteners include glucose and maltose. Though less sweet than sucrose and fructose, glucose and maltose are rapidly absorbed into the blood stream and therefore less likely to contribute to SIBO and its related symptoms. These sugars are not available in most grocery stores, but can be purchased in brewer supply stores or online. Maltose is also available in some Asian grocery stores.

Sugar alcohols, also known as polyols, represent a group of non-carbohydrate sweeteners. Sugar alcohols include sorbitol, mannitol, xylitol, lactitol, isomalt, erythritol, and maltitol. In general, sugar alcohols are poorly absorbed and fermentable by gut bacteria, potentially causing diarrhea, gas, bloating, reflux and other IBS symptoms. For this reason most sugar alcohols (except erythritol, refer to chapter 9) should be avoided.

Stevia, marketed as SweetLeaf, Truvia and Stevia Blend, is a natural sweetener that comes from the leaves of the South American plant Stevia rebaudiana. This sweetener has been used for decades in other countries and so far has a good safety record. Like sucralose, stevia is heat stable and can be used in cooking.

### Artificial Sweeteners

There are several artificial sweeteners on the market. Artificial sweeteners generally have few to no carbohydrates and few to zero calories but simply taste sweet. Sucralose (Splenda) is the most popular followed by aspartame (Equal and NutraSweet), and saccharin.

Sucralose (Splenda) was approved for use in the US in 1998. Sucralose is similar in many ways to sucrose, but has been chemically modified so that it is not digestible — by people *or* bacteria. Sucralose is also stable when heated, so can be used for baking or in other hot recipes. People who prefer natural sweeteners should consider using glucose (sold as dextrose) maltose, stevia, monkfruit or erythritol.

Equal and NutraSweet both contain aspartame which was approved by the FDA in 1981. The sweetener can break down when exposed to heat so is not good for baking. Aspartame may also cause mild headaches and other side effects in some people. In general, I would avoid this sweetener in favor of **other low FP sweeteners**. Also, people who have the rare genetic condition known as phenylketonuria must avoid aspartame because it contains the amino acid phenylalanine.

Saccharin (Sweet'N Low) is another artificial sweetener that con-tains just under one gram of dextrose (glucose) as one of its ingredi-ents. Based on testing in rats in the sixties, the sweetener was thought to cause cancer, leading the FDA to require a warning on the product, the cancer fears were determined to be unfounded in humans and the warnings were removed in 2001. Despite its bitter aftertaste, many people prefer it to other sweeteners. Like aspartame, saccharin is not stable when heated and cannot be used for baking.

Now that you have a better idea of just what "raw materials" your digestive system has to deal with, we can take the next step in under-standing digestion: looking into how your body metabolizes all of these different foods.

# CHAPTER 7:

# Healthy Digestion

"HAPPINESS FOR ME IS
LARGELY A MATTER OF
DIGESTION."

—LIN YUTANG.

Next, I'd like to give you a simplified look at how the digestive process is supposed to work. It's much easier to understand how and why IBS develops if you know the basics of how your digestive tract is supposed to act.

Before your body can get the nutrition it needs from the three food groups described in the previous chapter, they must be broken down into their basic "building blocks" through the process of digestion:

*Carbohydrates are broken down to monosaccharides*

*Proteins are broken down to amino acids*

*Fats are broken down to fatty acids*

Once broken down, they can be absorbed into the blood stream and available for use by the cells in our body or stored as glycogen or fat.

First, let's take a step-by-step look at the pathway food takes as it is processed by your digestive system:

# The Digestive Process

### Mouth

Your digestive system starts working even before you take a bite of food. Your senses — primarily smell and taste — trigger the release of saliva and enzymes to prepare your digestive system to process the food.

As soon as you take a bite, your chewing helps break the food up into smaller digestible pieces. At the same time, six salivary glands in your mouth release saliva to help lubricate and liquefy the food. Saliva also contains the enzyme amylase, which begins breaking the chemical bonds between the sugar molecules that hold complex carbohydrates together. When you swallow, rings of muscles around the esophagus push the food towards your stomach through a coordinated wave of contractions, known as peristalsis. At the lower end of the esophagus, a group of muscles collectively referred to as the lower esophageal sphincter (or LES) relax, letting the food pass into your stomach.

### Stomach

By the time the food arrives in your stomach, your body has responded to the smell and taste of the food by releasing histamine. This stimulates the specialized "parietal" cells lining the stomach to produce hydrochloric acid (HCl). The HCl creates an extremely acidic environment that kills bacteria in the food, denatures (unfolds) proteins, and activates the enzyme pepsin, which breaks large proteins into smaller molecules (polypeptides). The stomach protects itself from the acid by producing a coating of mucus. The stomach also produces the enzyme lipase, which helps breakdown fats into triglycerides.

To churn the food together with stomach acid and enzymes, muscles contained in wall of the stomach contract in a coordinated fashion. After a few hours, the partially digested food, called chyme, consists of a mixture of polypeptides (partially broken down protein), polysaccharides (partially digested carbohydrates) and triglycerides (partially broken down fats). The chyme is released from the stomach through the pyloric sphincter, another ring of muscles, to the duodenum, which is the first part of the small intestine.

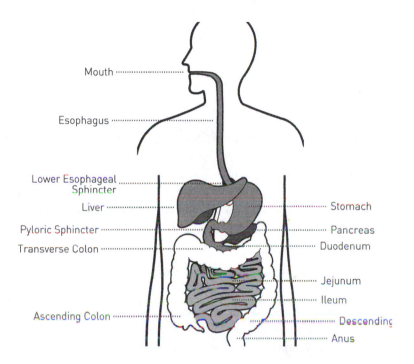

*Figure 12. Human Digestive Tract*

### Small Intestine

The small intestine is approximately 20 feet long and divided into three sections (in this order): the duodenum, jejunum and ileum. The two main purposes of the small intestine are to complete the digestive process started in the stomach, and then absorb the digested nutrients into the blood.

### Duodenum

As chyme enters your duodenum, your pancreas releases bicarbonate to neutralize the stomach acid. It also produces additional enzymes, including amylase for polysaccharide digestion, proteases and elastase for peptide digestion, and lipase for triglyceride digestion. Bile, produced in the liver and stored in the gall bladder, is released to help with the breakdown and absorption of triglycerides. The pancreas also produces ribonuclease and deoxyribonuclease to help digest DNA and RNA.

## Jejunum

Digestion is well underway when chyme leaves the duodenum and enters the highly complex jejunum, where final digestion occurs. The surface of the jejunum is covered with finger-like projections less than a millimeter in length called villi. Epithelial cells that line the villi are covered with even smaller projections called microvilli. These projections maximize the surface area of the small intestine and make absorption of nutrients into the blood stream more efficient.

The villi-covered surface of the small intestine is known as the "brush border." The enzymes produced here complete the final digestion of proteins to amino acids and disaccharides (double sugars) into monosaccharides (single sugars). These broken-down "building blocks" are now small and simple enough to pass through the villi into the bloodstream. Triglycerides (digested fats), coupled with cholesterol and some proteins, enter the bloodstream through villus lacteal capillaries that lead to the lymph system before entering the bloodstream.

## Ileum

Chyme, which at this point contains only undigested food and the by-products of digestion, eventually enters the third part of the small intestine, the ileum, where water, some vitamins and bile salts (used to break down fats) are absorbed. Both water and bile salts are recycled as part of the overall digestive process. At this point the primary digestion and nutrient absorption process is complete. The leftover chyme leaves the small intestine via the ileocecal valve and enters the large intestine.

The number of intestinal bacteria steadily increases towards the last part of the small intestine. Peristalsis, intestinal immunity, and efficient absorption of nutrients help keep these bacterial populations in check. Intestinal bacteria play a key role in the development of IBS, and will be looked at in more detail a little later in this book.

### Large Intestine (or Colon)

Residual material entering the colon has been depleted of many nutrients but still contains resistant starch, fiber and some protein that escaped digestion in the small intestine. As this material moves through the colon, bacteria ferment the remaining starch, protein and much of the fiber. Water and electrolytes (salts) are removed and recycled and the stool is formed and stored until a bowel movement occurs.

By comparison with the small intestine, the human large intestine is a breeding ground for bacteria. On average, it contains over 100 trillion microorganisms representing over 1000 different species. Humans and gut bacteria have evolved together over millions of years. The result is a mutually beneficial relationship: They live on nutrients in our diet that we are unable to digest and would otherwise be wasted. In exchange, bacteria produce some vitamins and other nutrients that nourish our own cells. Bacteria allow us to use food up to 30% more efficiently than we could without them. (This is about the same as boosting the gas mileage in your car from 20 miles per gallon to 26 miles per gallon.)

Healthy intestinal bacteria also compete with and protect us from germs that can cause diseases. Bacteria represent the bulk of intestinal organisms, though some protozoa, fungi and other tiny life-forms reside here as well.

## The Role of Bacteria in Digestion

Most people know that bacteria play some role in the digestive process, but most people are surprised by just how important this role is. Understanding how our gut bacterial populations work is key to understanding the symptoms and proper treatment of IBS.

### Bacteria in the Small Intestine

Bacteria most common to the small intestine include *Lactobacillus, Enterococcus, Staphylococcus*, and *Streptococcus* species, with the most prevalent type being *Lactobacillus*.

The *Lactobacillus* species play a key role in the small intestine. The *Lactobacillus* species, including *Lactobacillus acidophilus* (present in yogurt), ferment small amounts of unabsorbed sugars such as lactose and other disaccharides to produce lactic acid.

Outside the digestive process, lactic acid is a common commercial preservative used to preserve food; just as naturally made lactic acid helps yogurt last a long time in the refrigerator. Inside the small intestine, it maintains an acidic environment that is unfavorable to the many "unhealthy" bacteria.

*Lactobacillus acidophilus* and several related species present in the small intestine are known as homolactic fermenters. These types of bacteria produce predominantly one end produce, lactic acid. Unlike most other bacteria, homolactic fermenters do not produce symptom-causing gaseous end products. This trait is desirable for bacteria living in the small intestine and likely contributes to the success of *Lactobacillus acidophilus* as a probiotic.

Other (heterolactic) bacteria break down starch and sugars to produce a wide variety of end products including lactic, acetic, propionic and butyric acids, but they also produce gases such as carbon dioxide, hydrogen, and sometimes methane. These gases can cause a number of unpleasant symptoms of IBS.

### Bacteria in the Large Intestine

Bacteria common to the large intestine include *Bifidobacteria, Bacteroides, Actinocyces, Fusobacteria, E. coli, Enterocci, Streptococci, Clostridia, Corynebacteri, Enterobacter, Proteus, Klebsiella, Propionibacteria*, as well as *Lactobacilli* and several hundred less common species.

For the most part, we live in mutually beneficial harmony with these highly specialized single-celled creatures for our entire lives. As noted above, they consume food that we fail to digest and, in return, producing high-energy short-chain fatty acids that our cells can use for energy; vitamins, such as biotin, folate and vitamin K; and out-compete disease-causing bacteria like *C. diff*, helping to maintain normal gut function and stimulating our own immunity.

The foods that we either can't digest or digest poorly usually end up in the colon. These include plant fibers such as cellulose and pectin, oligosaccharides stachyose and raffinose as well as the starch amylose and even sugars like fructose and lactose. Some bacteria in the colon can even break down cellulose and hemicellulose fiber. Bacteria that are able to break down these "waste products" clearly have a competitive advantage.

The predominance of *Bifidobacteria* and *Bacteroides* species in the large intestine is no accident. These bacteria have adapted perfectly to the human large intestine with their ability to break down complex and difficult to digest polysaccharides including amylose starch as well as the oligosaccharides stachyose and raffinose (gas-causing fiber types associated with legumes).

As an example of how specialized these bacteria have become, *Bifidibacteria* have the ability to rapidly degrade oligosaccharides using a unique metabolic pathway called the "bifid shunt." Amazingly, *Bifidobacteria* are able to use the oligosaccharides stachyose and raffinose (that we can't digest) more efficiently than they can use simple glucose.

The bacteria living in our colons have adapted to life without oxygen — as there is none in the large intestine. That means that these anaerobic bacteria depend on the process of fermentation (deriving energy from nutrients in the absence of oxygen) to survive.

As part of fermentation, bacteria collectively secrete a large array of enzymes that break down the tough remaining nutrients to produce energy and the raw materials they need for their own existence and reproduction. As part of the process, they also produce lactic acid, acetic acid, propionic acid, ethanol and butyric acid as well as the gases hydrogen, carbon dioxide and sometimes methane.

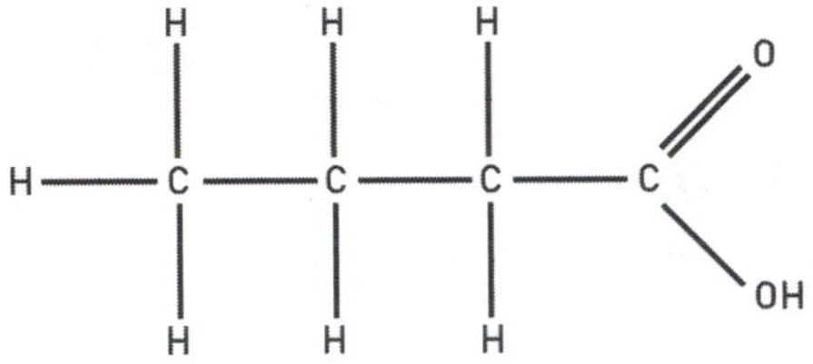

*Figure 13. Butyric Acid*

This fermentation process, as it turns out, is one of the key elements in the development of IBS symptoms. Most people aren't even aware of its existence, yet it plays a critical role in their quality of life!

**A Healthy Balance**

As in most biological or physiological processes, the key to health is maintaining a healthy balance between different aspects of the process.

For example, while the large intestine can deal with huge numbers (trillions) of bacteria, the small intestine can't. Unfortunately, there's a direct physical link between the two — the ileocecal valve! Since the small intestine houses the crucial digestive and absorptive machinery we need to maintain our nutrition, it's essential that the small intestine is protected against potential invasion and overpopulation by bacteria from the large intestine (SIBO). [84]

To maintain digestive health, then, the body must ensure that the bulk of bacterial fermentation occurs in the large intestine and limit fermentation in the small intestine. Besides maintaining a population of friendly, protective bacteria, the small intestine has a number of other defenses that protect it and the digestive process against these harmful bacteria.

These include:

*Stomach acid, bile and mucous secretions.* Stomach acid kills most bacteria swallowed with foods or liquids and maintains acid levels in the stomach and beginning of the small intestine. This acidity reduces the number of bacteria in the upper part of the small intestine and also helps prevent viable bacteria from refluxing into the esophagus, lungs or sinuses, which affects IBS sufferers who also have acid reflux.

Bile helps solubilize fats as part of the digestive process, but it also inhibits the growth of bacteria in the small intestine. The stomach and intestines also secrete a constant supply of mucus that lubricates, coats and protects the intestinal surface.

*Peristalsis.* Peristalsis, also referred to as motility, is a regular muscular contraction around the intestine that keeps food moving through the gut. The movement is mostly unidirectional and the sphincter-shaped ileocecal valve, located between the small and large intestine, helps keep bacteria from moving from the large intestine back into the small intestine. This constant movement of food during digestion also limits the amount and type of bacterial fermentation in the small intestine.

*Efficient digestion and absorption of carbohydrates.* When carbohydrates are broken down and fully absorbed they leave the small intestine and enter the blood stream as glucose. The more efficient this process is, the less "leftover" fuel there is for small intestinal bacterial growth.

Native or "good" bacteria have adapted to survive in the highly competitive environment of our gut by evolving highly specialized abilities to break down nutrients that we can't digest on our own. As a result, bad or pathogenic bacteria, such as *Clostridia difficile* or *C diff,* have a difficult time surviving if nutrients are scarce, because the "good" bacteria can "out-compete" them. "Bad" bacteria, as a general rule, only stand a chance in the digestive system when there are plenty of nutrients to go around. A good analogy is feeding the birds in your back yard. If you put out too much food, or make it too easy to get to, you may end up with more squirrels than birds, or even worse, rats.

*Immune surveillance.* The final layer of protection is active immune surveillance. Specific antimicrobial mucin proteins and alpha defensin peptides (peptides are small proteins) are produced by the intestinal epithelial cells to prevent foreign bacteria from invading.

Pro-inflammatory cytokine molecules help coordinate the activities of white blood cells but are kept in check by other anti-inflammatory cytokines such as IL-10. Antibodies such as IgA and IgM are produced in response to specific identifying proteins on the surface of bacteria. Antibodies identify and protect friendly bacteria and help attack threatening bacteria.

SIBO and IBS get their start when this balance starts to fall apart. One of the goals of Fast Tract Digestion is to show you what you can do to help your body maintain the integrity and balance of your digestive process.

# Treating Underlying Factors

"THE MORE HIDDEN THE
VENOM, THE MORE
DANGEROUS IT IS."

—MARGUERITE DE VALOIS.

Now that we've taken a closer look at the relationship between poor digestion, malabsorption, SIBO, and IBS, we're going to look at how to use this knowledge. Our new understanding of how IBS develops offers some promising avenues for developing more effective treatments.

There is now clear evidence that IBS symptoms are the direct result of small intestinal bacterial overgrowth. Addressing the cause(s) of SIBO therefore represents the most direct treatment for IBS. Let's take a closer look at SIBO and the underlying causes of this condition.

The ratio of "bad" bacteria to "good" bacteria, the overall number of bacteria, and the rate of fermentation in the small intestine depend on many factors. Changes in any of these factors can disrupt the natural balance of the digestive system, creating the conditions for uncontrolled bacterial growth in the small intestine.

## Three Part Strategy

In order to successfully treat IBS, the destructive cycle of malabsorption, bacterial overgrowth, and inflammation must be disrupted. To achieve this goal, I have developed a three-part treatment strategy called the Fast Tract Diet System:

*First, address any underlying condition(s) that promote(s) SIBO on a case-by-case basis (the subject of the rest of this chapter).*

*Second, minimize the malabsorption of difficult-to-digest carbohydrates (see chapter 9).*

*Third, reduce the actual amount of difficult-to-digest carbohydrates with the Fast Tract Diet (see chapters 11 through 13).*

I am convinced that most people suffering from IBS simply consume too many difficult-to-digest carbs. For these individuals the Fast Tract Diet should result in rapid and complete relief of their symptoms. In some cases, there may be other contributing factors or underlying conditions that must also be identified and addressed to allow for a full recovery with the Fast Tract Diet System. This chapter will help you and your health care provider develop a comprehensive treatment plan that addresses any other contributing conditions, should they exist.

Potential causes of SIBO (you likely suffer from one or more of these if you have IBS) can be grouped into five categories:

*Motility issues*

*Antibiotic use*

*Gastric (stomach) acid reduction*

*Immune impairment*

*Carbohydrate malabsorption*

## Motility Issues

Motility is based on the process of peristalsis — the coordination of intestinal muscles to keep food moving through the intestines. Problems with the muscles, the nerves that control the muscles, intestinal scarring or blockages can all slow down motility. Changes in stool consistency, drugs, infections and SIBO itself can also alter motility.

Both constipation and diarrhea are considered forms of irregular motility. Diarrhea-predominant IBS (IBS-D) is linked to the types of bacteria that produce hydrogen but not methane gas, while constipation-predominant IBS (IBS-C) is associated with microbes that produce methane gas.[85, 86]

Problems that can lead to alteration in motility include:

*Structural defects of the intestine*

*Aging*

*Intestinal infections*

*Narrowing of the intestine due to scarring from Crohn's Disease or scleroderma*

*Surgical alteration of the intestine*

*Damage to the vagus nerve*

*Hypothyroidism*

*Drug Use*

Damage to the vagus nerve from years of high blood sugar in type I and type II diabetes can result in prolonged gut transit times because the vagus nerve normally signals the muscles surrounding the intestine to contract. Similarly, intestinal motor dysfunction associated with hypothyroidism has been linked to SIBO.[87] Physical changes caused by surgery, infection, aging and scarring from Crohn's disease can also reduce peristalsis. Various drugs such as antidepressants, diuretics, pain medications or laxatives can also affect intestinal motility.

Regardless of the cause, slower peristalsis means longer gut transit times.[88] Bacteria in the small intestine have more time to break down and metabolize unabsorbed carbohydrates. As bacteria feed, they multiply and produce gas; waste products and cell debris than can damage the intestinal mucosal surface. One study showed that it took food on average 50 minutes longer to go from the mouth through the small intestine in people with SIBO, compared to people without SIBO.[89]

*Treating Motility Problems*

**Constipation predominant IBS – The methane connection**. As mentioned in Chapter 2, recent research has shown that constipation may be caused by the intestinal overgrowth of methane-producing bacteria. This can be confirmed by methane breath testing. Methane-producing microbes associated with IBS-C actually consume hydrogen gas for energy (hydrogen is produced by other SIBO-related bacteria) and produce methane as an end product. The most prevalent methane-producing species in the human gut is *Methanobrevibacter smithii*, a type of microbe known as *archaea,* as opposed to a form of bacteria. Why these *archaea* microbes can cause constipation is not completely understood. However, since constipation is also a form of SIBO, the Fast Tract Diet System should help.

If you suffer from mild constipation, you should follow the Fast Tract Diet, drink plenty of water (at least 6 glasses per day), and eat extra green vegetables. For more severe constipation, stool softeners, laxatives, or enemas may also help. These medicines should only be used occasionally, as overuse causes its own problems. Fiber supplements have also been used for constipation, but I would urge significant caution with these as they sometimes make the problem worse. If severe constipation persists for several days, schedule a doctor's visit. (Refer to chapter 1 for a review of medications that can help constipation.)

**Diarrhea predominant IBS – The hydrogen connection**. Repeated bouts of diarrhea may indicate IBS. Hydrogen-producing bacteria have been linked to IBS-D.

Diarrhea caused by food poisoning, contaminated drinking water or intestinal infection will usually end naturally, but severe cases, especially involving high fevers, may require a doctor's attention. Make sure to stay fully hydrated. (Refer to Chapter 1 for diarrhea treatments and the section on rehydration for gastroenteritis under the Damage to the Intestinal Epithelium section below.) Your doctor may also prescribe an antibiotic. (Be sure to read chapter 5 on antibiotics for IBS.) The diarrhea should end as your gut heals and your normal healthy population of gut bacteria is reestablished. I would not recommend using anti-diarrheal drugs such as loperamide, alosetron or diphenoxylate to treat diarrhea as these medications can have serious side effects.

Complex motility issues associated with diabetes (vagus nerve damage), hypothyroidism (hormonal and neuromuscular problems), scarring of the intestinal mucosal surface (Crohn's disease or scleroderma), surgery, and trauma should be discussed with your medical provider as these motility issues are outside the scope of this book.

**Some drugs influence motility (causing either diarrhea or constipation).** Besides laxatives, drugs such as antidepressants, diuretics and pain medications can influence motility. Changing medicines or reducing the dosage is an option you can explore with your doctor's help. Prescription pro-motility drugs do exist, but I would use them with caution, and discuss them with your doctor, because they have their own side effects, some serious.

### Antibiotic Use

Chapter 5 discusses the use of antibiotics for treating SIBO, but antibiotics can also cause IBS. Symptoms such as abdominal pain, cramps, gas, bloating, diarrhea, reflux, etc. are indicative of SIBO, but if your symptoms come after you've taken a course of antibiotics, they could be indicative of something called post antibiotic IBS.

### *Treating Complications From Antibiotic Treatment*

If possible, avoid antibiotics unless they are absolutely needed. This is the best way to avoid their complications and side effects.

Reestablishing the healthy balance of bacterial populations after taking antibiotics can take weeks, months, or in some cases, years. The Fast Tract approach can help you recover more quickly by limiting the amount of fermentable nutrients in your diet (which favors good bacteria over bad, less well adapted bacteria).

You may also try adding a high-quality probiotic supplement to your diet. High-quality probiotics typically contain live (freeze-dried) lactic acid bacteria such as *Lactobacillus acidophilis, Lactobacillus plantarum, Lactobacillus bulgaricus, Bifidobacterium breve, Bifidobacterium longum, Bifidobacterium infantis,* and *Streptococcus thermophilus.* Most brands contain at least two billion cfu (colony forming units) per dose. In choosing a probiotic supplement make sure the following criteria are met:

*The label should state the potency (how many bacteria per dose) and the expiration date. Probiotics manufactured in Canada are required to have an expiration date (supported by shelf life testing) but there is no identical requirement in the US.*

*The probiotics should be shipped and stored under the recommended storage conditions.*

*The probiotics should be protected with an enteric coating or capsule to ensure the bacteria survive exposure to stomach acid.*

One note of caution: Some brands of probiotics are associated with bloating. Bloating can be caused by including bacterial strains that (unlike *Lactobacillus acidophilis,* a "homolactic fermenter" which produces no gas) are capable of producing gas from carbohydrates under certain circumstances. These strains include: *Lactobacillus brevis, Lactobacillus casei, Streptococcus thermophilus* and probiotic yeast strains. Gas from probiotics should be less of a problem on the Fast Track Diet which limits difficult-to-digest but fermentable carbs.

Instead of probiotics, some people consume a daily serving of yogurt that contains live gut-healthy bacteria including both *Lactobacillus acidophilis* and *Bifidobacteria.* One drawback of yogurt is that a large number of the bacteria will be killed by stomach acid.

Both probiotic supplements and yogurt contain only two to five different types of bacteria where the healthy gut contains hundreds of different species. So supplementing with two to five types may not provide a complete solution. If you decide to add daily yogurt to your diet, be sure to consult the tables in appendix B to select a type with limited fermentation potential.

The most important advice I can give you to recover from antibi-otic-induced IBS is to keep your microbes on a nutrient-limited diet using the Fast Tract Diet Program.

## Gastric (Stomach) Acid Reduction

Low stomach acid, called hypochlorhydria, is a common problem that puts people at a greater risk for developing SIBO, while increasing the difficulty of treating it. Without adequate stomach acid, bacteria eaten with food or liquids are no longer killed in the stomach. The stomach and upper intestine also become less acidic and more hospitable to the kind of bacterial growth that causes SIBO and IBS.

If you are taking PPI drugs to treat GERD (half of people with IBS also suffer from GERD) or another condition, you don't need to be tested. You know that you have low stomach acid. That's what PPI drugs do.

If this is the case, I suggest you discuss the Fast Tract Diet System with your doctor, and consider weaning yourself off PPIs that you're taking over a period of two to three weeks. Stopping PPI treatment without gradually decreasing your dosage can cause a potentially painful rebound effect. You may also want to read book one in this series, *Fast Tract Digestion Heartburn*.

Normally, the stomach plays a dual role: It both protects the intestines against outside threats from bacteria, viruses and parasites and protects the esophagus, lungs and sinuses from bacteria present in the digestive tract. Without stomach acid, this dual protection no longer exists. You'll not only be more susceptible to SIBO and related conditions, but also to pneumonia, asthma and sinus infections.

In this light, the well-documented connection between SIBO and asthma makes perfect sense as does the connection between PPI drugs and pneumonia. Low acidity promotes SIBO, SIBO promotes IBS symptoms often with gastroesophageal reflux, and reflux allows intestinal bacteria to enter the esophagus and lungs.

Several conditions can reduce or eliminate stomach acid. They include:

### Most Common

*Chronic use of acid-reducing medicines (antacids, H2 or PPI drugs). One study showed that as many as 50% of people taking PPI drugs suffered from bacterial overgrowth.*[90]

*Aging. As people get older, they often produce lower amounts of stomach acid, which is another reason (besides motility issues) why older people frequently suffer from SIBO-related illness.*

*H. Pylori infection. The bacterium that causes ulcers can reduce the amount of acid in the stomach. There is a test for H. pylori, and the infection is treatable with antibiotics. This is one example of the proper use of antibiotics.*

### Less Common

*Gastric bypass surgery.*

*Autoimmune disorders.*

*Stomach cancer. Stomach cancer can affect acid-producing parietal cells sharply reducing stomach acid production.*

*Radiation therapy. This is another way to damage acid-producing parietal cells.*

### Treating Reduced Stomach Acidity

Aging and the pervasive use of acid-reducing drugs are the most important factors. Older people may produce less stomach acid due to an autoimmune condition, chronic *H. pylori* infection or even cancer. Anyone, but particularly people over 50 with SIBO-related conditions, can be tested using the Heidelberg Stomach Acid Test.

If testing shows you have low stomach acid (in the absence of a definitive cause that may require specific treatment), you might want to take betaine hydrochloride supplements (also known as betaine HCL) at the beginning of every meal. This will increase the overall level of stomach acid while you eat. Make sure not to take the supplements on an empty stomach. Avoid antacids while trying this approach as they exert the opposite effect.

## Immune Impairment

The success of the human immune system depends on complex inter-actions between white blood cells, antibodies, cytokine-modulating factors and bile salts produced in the liver. Protective barriers such as your skin and your intestinal mucosal surface are considered to be part of your immune system. Our immune system protects us from viruses, bacteria, protozoa, and other pathogens but also helps enforce order amongst our intestinal microflora.

A healthy immune system is critical to maintaining a balance of the type and number of bacteria present in the small intestine. Our immune system is able to tell the good bacteria from the bad (although the exact mechanism(s) are not clear). Though highly redundant, the system can be disturbed or damaged by a variety of factors. Cancer therapy, autoimmune conditions, the drugs to treat them, allergy and other medicines, HIV infection, illness and aging all can affect immunity. Immune impairment can result in or contribute to SIBO.

### Treating Immune Impairment

If possible, treating conditions that damage or disrupt your immune system will improve your ability to control SIBO. If you suspect you suffer from immune deficiencies, diagnostic testing is available that can help you determine what if any, immune impairments exist, and offer a path for treatment.

Many drugs can impair the immune system. The most common are drugs that treat autoimmune diseases and to some extent allergies, because autoimmune diseases and allergies are caused by an overactive or mis-directed immune system. Before making any changes to your medication, be sure to consult with your health care provider. It may be possible to change the type or dosage of any medication that's caus-ing the problem.

## Carbohydrate Malabsorption

In a general sense, malabsorption is the failure to absorb specific nutrients from the small intestine into the blood stream during digestion. Malabsorption can affect all three food groups — proteins, fats and carbohydrates — as well as vitamins and minerals. This can lead to a variety of illnesses, conditions, and nutritional deficiencies. [91]

Malabsorption has been referred to as the hallmark of SIBO. Not only does SIBO cause malabsorption, but malabsorption of carbohydrates is required for SIBO. Without malabsorbed carbohydrates, bacteria do not have the fuel required for overgrowth. In the next few chapters you'll see how this key concept provides the basis for the Fast Track Diet System.

Carbohydrates make up a significant portion of most people's diet. Many of these carbohydrates are difficult to digest, so carbohydrate malabsorption is common.

Carbohydrates range in size and complexity from small single-unit monosaccharides and double-unit disaccharides to very large polysaccharides linking together thousands of sugar units. Size is not always the determining factor in how easy carbohydrates are to break down and absorb. The types of molecular bonds holding the sugar units together also determine how digestible they are.

Many people have difficulty digesting and absorbing carbohydrate foods due to short-term illnesses, surgery or underlying chronic conditions. Also, many carbohydrates are inherently difficult to digest and absorb even for people with fully functional digestive systems.

Carbohydrate malabsorption can be caused by the following:

*Damage to the intestinal epithelium (from drugs, infections, SIBO or inflammation).*

*Difficult-to-digest carbohydrates and sugar alcohols. These carbohydrates often escape digestion and absorption but are fermentable by intestinal bacteria.*

*Overconsumption of carbohydrates, in general.*

*Digestive enzyme deficiency (caused by pancreas problems, cystic fibrosis, or genetics).*

## Damage to the Intestinal Epithelium

The interior surface of the intestine is lined with specialized epithelial cells that can be damaged by drugs (such as neomycin), SIBO, or intestinal infections or inflammatory reactions. The key areas of concern are the "brush border" areas in the duodenum and jejunum portion of the small intestine. Damage to these areas destroys digestive enzymes and nutrient transport systems necessary for the final steps of digestion.

Several types of bacteria identified with SIBO, such as *Bacteroides fragilis, Clostridium perfringens,* and *Streptococcus fecalis,* possess protein-degrading enzymes that can destroy brush border enzymes including lactase, sucrase, and maltase, which are necessary for the final breakdown and absorption of carbohydrates.[92]

The ability of bacteria to damage critical digestive enzymes on the surface of the small intestine helps explain how SIBO causes carbohydrate malabsorption. Malabsorption of fats and fat-soluble vitamins may also be affected because many of the bacterial strains associated with SIBO can metabolize bile salts (needed for fat digestion).

Autoimmune diseases such as celiac disease and Crohn's disease can also damage cells lining the small intestine. One study examined lactose malabsorption in Crohn's disease, an autoimmune disease characterized by intestinal inflammation. Crohn's disease patients showed a higher rate of lactose malabsorption.[93]

**Post-infectious IBS.** Post infectious IBS refers to IBS that develops following an episode of gastroenteritis, an intestinal infection caused by one of many disease causing bacteria such as *C diff, Campylobacter, Salmonella, Shigella, Yersinia* or *E. coli,* or parasites like *Giardia.*

Unlike SIBO (described above), which is caused by a general overgrowth of the bacteria normally present in our intestines, gastroenteritis is typically caused by a single strain of disease-causing bacteria, parasite or virus that is not normally present in the digestive tract.

Gastroenteritis is usually caused by exposure to disease-causing microorganisms, whether through food poisoning, drinking or swimming in contaminated water or other means of exposure, often through a fecal-oral route.

Gastroenteritis also often occurs after antibiotic treatments which can upset the balance of the healthy intestinal microbe population, allowing "bad" bacteria to overgrow. *C diff* is just one example of these "bad" bacteria.

Most people experience several bouts of acute gastrointestinal illness throughout their lifetimes.

The symptoms tend to be sudden and dramatic, including stomach pain, vomiting, fever, weakness and watery or even bloody diarrhea. Most of the time these symptoms will resolve without treatment, as the infection runs its course, but sometimes antibiotics or other drug treatments are required. The primary treatment is giving oral rehydration salts, such as Pedialyte, to replace the water and electrolytes lost due to the diarrhea.

According to the World Health Organization (WHO), each of the electrolytes in oral rehydration salts has a specific purpose:

- Glucose facilitates the absorption of sodium (and hence water) in the small intestine
- Sodium and potassium are needed to replace these essential ions which are lost during diarrhea (and vomiting)
- Citrate corrects the acidosis that occurs as a result of diarrhea and dehydration.

The best response is to start rehydration therapy as soon as the diarrhea occurs. The Mayo Clinic Web site[94] provides the following improvised home formula for emergency use. They advise measuring carefully or having a second person check the measurements.

Home Oral Rehydration Salts: 1/2 teaspoon table salt, 6 level teaspoons of sugar and 1 liter (about 1 quart) of safe drinking water.

Gastroenteritis kills millions of people each year, and is a leading cause of death in infants and young children. But gastroenteritis can also damage the intestinal epithelium, making it more difficult for the digestive system to absorb carbohydrates, and increasing the likelihood of SIBO and IBS for months or even years to follow.

**Post-infectious case study.** A clear demonstration of post-infectious IBS was documented in the Walkerton Health Study. The researchers followed 2069 adults, with no prior history of IBS, who lived in the town of Walkerton, Ontario, Canada during a tragic contamination of the town's water supply in 2000.[95] One of the town's main wells was contaminated with farm water runoff containing the infectious bacterial strains *Escherichia coli* strain 0157:H7 and *Campylobacter jejuni*. Many of the town's 5000 residents became sick with symptoms of acute bacterial infection such as bloody diarrhea, abdominal cramps and weight loss.

Two years after the event, 36% of people who had gotten sick showed signs of IBS, while only 10% of those who had not become ill showed symptoms. Most people did eventually recover from the post-infectious IBS.

The authors of the study proposed that the post-infectious IBS may occur because the body is unable to reduce the inflammation that occurs during the initial infection. Inflammation has been associated with IBS, and IBS symptoms have been reported in people who went on to develop inflammatory bowel disease (IBD).[96]

I have a slightly different interpretation. During the original infection, the disease-causing bacterium (*E. coli* or *Campylobacter* in this case) is able to grow rapidly, displacing the healthy bacteria normally present, causing inflammation and damage to the cells (villi and microvilli) that line mucosal surface of the small intestine. These cells, when healthy, play a key role in the digestion and absorption of proteins, fats and carbohydrates.

Infected individuals would continue to experience IBS symptoms for the as long as the cell damage persisted. This shows how a single case of gastroenteritis can cause dysbiosis (unbalanced gut microbes) the result of which can lead to chronic SIBO.

### Treatment For Intestinal Surface Damage

There is no quick fix for damage to the surface of the small intestine. But the body has remarkable healing abilities. The important thing is to stop the cause of the damage, which can involve bacterial overgrowth, intestinal infection or food poisoning, or an autoimmune reaction from gluten (in the case of celiac disease). The small intestine can heal in one month or many months depending on the seriousness of the damage and the effectiveness of the treatment.

### Volume-Based Carbohydrate Malabsorption

Early in the history of the human race every scrap of food was important. Calories were the key to our survival. Based on mutual survival needs humans evolved in partnership with microorganisms. By harboring a diverse population of microorganisms in our gut, we gained the ability to digest a wider variety of carbohydrates. These bacteria possessed unique enzymes that could help break down complex carbohydrates that our bodies could not digest. We were able to do this by adapting to use bacterial end products to help meet our own energy needs.

Fast forward to modern Western cultures. Today, we find ourselves surrounded by dietary excess. We can eat pretty much whatever we want whenever we want. The problem is that our survival instincts are like little voices telling us to eat as much as possible whenever we get a chance. In the Paleolithic part of our brains, it may be the last meal we have for days. We all know "less is better," but our cravings and our instincts tempt us to overindulge. Deciding what foods to eat in what quantity and what foods to avoid can be challenging.

Too often, people indiscriminately overeat to the point where they suffer from a variety of serious health problems. In terms of digestive health threats, difficult to digest carbohydrates are the biggest problem, but volume-based malabsorption can also cause SIBO. Even though our body possesses very efficient digestive machinery, it can be overcome by sheer volume. I believe this is why obesity is linked to GERD,[97] which is linked to IBS as well as to symptoms such as bloating and diarrhea — hallmarks of malabsorption and IBS.[98]

Obesity often involves the consumption of large amounts of snack foods loaded with difficult-to-digest carbohydrates. Malabsorption is almost certain to occur, leading to conditions linked to SIBO, such as GERD and IBS.

### Treating Difficult to Digest Carbohydrates

Finding ways to reduce the impact of difficult-to-digest carbohydrates is the main focus of this book, and the central design principle of the Fast Tract Diet System. Almost every chapter in this book discusses ways you can improve the efficiency of your digestion!

### Digestive Enzyme Deficiency

Finally, the disappearance of digestive enzymes as a result of pancreatic diseases, cystic fibrosis, lactose intolerance, or damage to the enzymes of the small intestine can also cause malabsorption and SIBO.

We know that digestive enzymes play a central role in the breakdown of fats, carbohydrates and proteins. Digestive enzymes are secreted with saliva in the mouth, produced and secreted by cells that line the stomach, and produced by the pancreas for secretion into the intestines. The cells that line the intestinal brush border produce still more digestive enzymes. While the loss of any digestive enzyme can contribute to nutrient malabsorption and digestive problems, the loss of carbohydrate- degrading enzymes (especially amylase, lactase and brush border enzymes) limit starch and sugar digestion and absorption providing the most powerful fuel for the development of SIBO.

### Treating Digestive Enzyme Deficiency

The good news is that replacement enzymes can be taken as supplements to address two types of enzyme deficiencies — amylase and lactase deficiencies.

Enzyme replacement therapy may be appropriate for conditions such as lactose intolerance, cystic fibrosis, pancreatic cancer, and chronic pancreatitis. SIBO is common in these cases, because of the failure of the digestive enzymes and the malabsorption that follows.

Unless these enzymes are replaced with supplements, SIBO will be more difficult to treat and will require further dietary restriction. Without sufficient amylase enzyme, even amylopectin starch, allowed on the Fast Tract diet, can potentially cause symptoms.

If you believe you suffer from lactose intolerance or a condition resulting in amylase enzyme deficiency, talk to your health care provider. You may need to add a high-quality enteric-coated lactase or amylase enzyme supplement to your diet. Generally, you'll take one tablet or capsule before each meal. Be sure to check the expiration date, and store the supplements as directed on the label.

## Future Trends in Treating SIBO

We're just beginning to fully recognize the complexity of intestinal microflora and its importance in human health. No less than thirty diseases involve an out-of-balance gut *microbiota*. (*Microbiota* refers to the gut microbe population as a whole).

My research supports the view that limiting malabsorption and addressing the underlying conditions that promote SIBO can successfully treat SIBO-related conditions, but medical scientists are also trying a more radical approach.

Can a "normal" or at least more balanced population of gut microbes be restored by "transplanting" the contents of a healthy person's digestive tract?

This relatively new treatment is called fecal bacteriotherapy. The patient's entire microflora is replaced with the microflora of a healthy person. Amazing as this sounds (and maybe a little unsettling to some), it may turn out to be the best way to treat intestinal infections and possibly other SIBO related conditions.

The treatment is common in veterinary medicine and is now being performed successfully in humans. The sick person is treated with antibiotics and bowel lavage to remove their own gut microbes followed by the introduction of a fecal suspension (containing gut bacteria) from a healthy donor who has been prescreened for a variety of illnesses and pathogens.

Fecal bacteriotherapy has been used to treat hundreds of patients suffering from *C diff* (some critically ill) with a success rate of greater than 90 percent.[99] Encouraging results have also been obtained in the treatment of patients with inflammatory bowel disease, IBS, and chronic constipation.[100]

More work needs to be done to understand the exactly how this treatment works, but two things are clear: The patient responses are long lasting and the transplanted microorganisms are able to survive and persist in the recipients. In one case, transplanted microbes were recovered 24 weeks after the procedure.[101] Who knows? One day fecal transplantation could be a routine treatment for IBS.

My goal in this chapter was to review several underlying factors or conditions that can contribute to SIBO and IBS. In the chapters that follow, we'll look at what this implies for treating IBS, and offer the details of the Fast Tract Diet System — specifically designed to make it easier for you to reduce or eliminate your symptoms.

First, let's take a look at how your choice of foods affects your risk for SIBO and IBS. A typical diet consists of an extremely broad range of foods, some of which are easy to digest, and some of which are extremely difficult to digest. You can reduce your IBS symptoms by identifying and limiting your consumption of foods that will overwhelm your digestive system with undigested (and therefore fermentable) carbohydrates.

# CHAPTER 9

# Foods that Lead to SIBO

 "FORBIDDEN FRUIT
ALWAYS TASTES THE
BEST."

—SWEDISH PROVERB.

Now that you have a better idea of how underlying digestive issues can increase the likelihood of SIBO and IBS, I'd like to take a closer look at the critical dietary aspect of this problem — the foods that are more difficult to digest, and how they contribute to the problem.

A number of studies have shown that some carbohydrates are digested and absorbed better than others. The carbohydrates most subject to poor or incomplete absorption include:

*Lactose*

*Fructose*

*Resistant starch*

*Fiber*

*Sugar alcohols (which are similar to carbohydrates)*

While digestive health problems associated with lactose, fructose and even sugar alcohols have been widely documented, resistant starch and dietary fiber is widely considered to be healthy for the colon.

This is especially true for fiber, which is widely marketed in many forms as a key ingredient for digestive health. I was surprised to find little support for these claims in my research and now believe them to be exaggerated, dogmatic, and heavily promoted by companies that sell fiber-based products.

But the key issue for our purposes is that resistant starch and many types of fiber resemble lactose, fructose and sugar alcohols in their ability to persist in the intestine, providing a source of fermentable carbohydrates that can promote bacterial overgrowth.

For many people, the problem is simply over-consumption of these difficult-to-digest carbohydrates. But some individuals also have problems with digesting even small quantities of foods containing specific kinds of carbohydrates due to a variety of contributing factors. With that in mind, I'd like to give you a closer look at these prime "candidates" for malabsorption as well as the best available strategies for reducing their impact on your health.

## Lactose

As discussed in chapter 6, lactose is a disaccharide (or double sugar) made of galactose and glucose that is present in milk, ice cream, cheese, and other dairy products made from milk.

Lactose intolerance and lactose malabsorption are essentially the same thing. Lactose intolerance is the inability to digest and absorb lactose. It's usually caused by a naturally occurring shortage or absence of the enzyme lactase, produced by the cells that line the small intestine. Lactase breaks down lactose into glucose and galactose that can then be absorbed into the bloodstream.

Most infants possess ample amounts of lactase, which helps them to digest and absorb the lactose in breast milk. For most people, lactase levels decrease with age after weaning. While most Northern Europeans are lactose-tolerant, the majority of people in many other parts of the world, such as Africa and Asia, are lactose-intolerant. Up to 50 million people in the US exhibit some level of lactose intolerance, and it affects approximately 75% to 80% of African and Asian

Americans, and 90% of Native Americans (according to the National Institute of Diabetes and Digestive and Kidney Diseases (NIDDK)).

If your body does not produce enough lactase enzyme, you cannot digest lactose sugar or absorb it into your blood stream. The unabsorbed sugar is then fermented by bacteria in the small or large intestine. Lactose is an easy target for the bacteria in the small intestine and fully capable of fueling SIBO. The symptoms of lactose intolerance are identical to IBS symptoms and include nausea, cramps, bloating, diarrhea, gas and reflux following meals or snacks containing lactose.

If you experience IBS symptoms (cramps, diarrhea, etc.) after consuming milk or milk products, you may be lactose-intolerant and suffering from SIBO. If you see a doctor about these symptoms, he or she will most likely encourage you to avoid foods that contain lactose. If your symptoms improve after you remove lactose from your diet, you are almost certainly lactose-intolerant. Specific tests are available, but they are usually not necessary.

However, you may be affected by more than one cause (or contributing factor) of SIBO. In this case it can be useful to have more specific testing done. Conditions that damage intestinal villi such as celiac or Crohn's disease can also lead to lactose malabsorption since the cells that produce the lactase enzyme have been damaged. Lactose intolerance caused by damaged villi can usually be reversed if treatment of the underlying causes, such as celiac or Crohn's disease is effective.

Your health care provider can confirm lactose intolerance with a lactose tolerance test. After you drink a solution containing lactose, your blood glucose level is measured over a few hours to see how much lactose was converted to glucose and absorbed into your blood. If only a small amount of glucose enters the blood compared to the amount of lactose consumed, you will be diagnosed as lactose-intolerant. Hydrogen breath testing is another way to test for lactose malabsorption (refer to section on how to diagnose malabsorption and SIBO in chapter 4).

### Treating Lactose Intolerance

Lactose intolerance can be treated in several ways. One approach is to avoid milk and other lactose-containing foods, replacing them with lactose-free or reduced lactose products. A second approach is to take lactase enzyme supplements, which are available in both pill and liquid form, whenever you consume lactose-containing foods. This strategy can be very effective but requires diligence on your part.

Fortunately, most lactose-intolerant people still make some lactase and small amounts of lactose typically do not cause symptoms. Reducing the total amount of lactose you consume to less than 10 grams per day may be enough. If you fall into this category, you may be able to minimize your symptoms by avoiding milk that contains lactose (which has the highest level of lactose in common foods) while consuming moderate levels of other dairy products. You'll probably be best off with fermented dairy products such as cheese and yogurt where bacteria have already consumed most of the lactose during the fermentation process.

Yogurt, for example, contains lactase enzyme released by the bacteria while fermenting lactose. Studies have shown that the lactase in yogurt can make up for missing human lactase, making lactose digestion safe for most lactose-intolerant people when consumed with a yogurt "supplement." [102]

The Fast Track Diet System should solve the problem for most people. Dietary lactose increases fermentative potential, and lactose-containing foods are automatically limited with the Fast Track Diet System.

### Fructose

Fructose is a monosaccharide (or single sugar) that requires no breakdown or digestion before it enters the bloodstream. Fructose intolerance and fructose malabsorption both refer to the body's inability to absorb fructose from the intestine into the blood stream.

Fructose malabsorption is common, affecting 39 to 50% of the population.[103] This condition is not related to hereditary fructose intolerance where the enzymes needed to breakdown fructose are simply missing. Hereditary fructose intolerance is a rare and serious condition beyond the scope of this book.

The symptoms of fructose malabsorption can include nausea, cramps, bloating, gas, reflux and diarrhea, which reflect the link between malabsorption, IBS and SIBO.

As with lactose malabsorption, fructose malabsorption can be detected using a hydrogen breath test. In this case, fructose is given orally in place of lactose during the test.

Unlike glucose, which is absorbed directly into the blood stream as soon as it reaches the small intestine, fructose requires a much slower process, known as "facilitated diffusion," before it can be absorbed. Fructose connects with a protein called Glut 5 to pass through cells called enterocytes that line the intestine. You can compare glucose and fructose absorption to a daily commute to work via either a high-speed train (glucose) or riding a skateboard (fructose). Fructose has to "ride the skateboard" to go to work in the bloodstream.

Making the relatively slow and inefficient process even worse, people who have difficulty absorbing fructose may also be deficient in Glut 5, meaning that they, in effect, are trying to ride a broken skate board.[104]

Secondary causes of fructose malabsorption include damage to the intestinal surface caused by Crohn's disease, celiac disease, or SIBO itself.

### Treating Fructose Intolerance

The most common treatment for fructose malabsorption is avoiding fructose and the related fructans. Fructans are categorized as fructo-oligosaccharides (chains of fructose containing less than ten fructose units), and inulins (chains of fructose containing more than 10 fructose units) and are actually more closely related to dietary fiber.

Unlike lactose intolerance, there is no supplement or enzyme that can help reduce fructose malabsorption. And avoiding fructose is a challenge because this sugar is present in so many foods and sweeteners. Fructose is the sweetener of choice in the food industry because it's much sweeter than glucose and other sugars. Even dietetic foods use fructose because less fructose is required to achieve the same sweetness.

Fructose makes up 50% of the sugar in sucrose and honey and just over half of the sugar in high fructose corn syrup. Glucose represents the balance of the sugar in these sweeteners. Other sweeteners containing fructose include maple syrup, molasses, and corn-based sweeteners. Fructose is also found in a wide variety of foods including candy, fruit, especially dried fruits such as raisins, figs, fruit juices, soda, and vegetables.

Studies have shown that 85% of patients with IBS could reduce their symptoms by avoiding dietary fructose.[105] I am not surprised by this as the glycemic index (the glycemic index is explained in Chapter 11) for fructose is only 20 meaning 80 percent of fructose (if consumed alone) is malabsobed in healthy people. This value is may be even higher in people with IBS.

Though the exact mechanism isn't clear, fructose absorption seems to improve dramatically in the presence of glucose. One study of 10 healthy volunteers showed evidence of fructose malabsorption with as little as 15 grams of fructose. When the same 10 subjects were given 100 grams of sucrose (a disaccharide made up of one unit of glucose and one unit of fructose), or 50 grams of fructose with 50 grams of glucose, there was no evidence of malabsorption.[106]

These results suggest that glucose stimulates or assists in the absorption of fructose. That's why sucrose, which is composed of equal amounts of fructose and glucose, is less likely to result in malabsorption than pure fructose. Similarly, high fructose corn syrup (HFCS), containing close to equal proportions of glucose and fructose, is less likely to cause malabsorption than pure fructose.

There is also evidence that fructose not only plays a role in digestive problems, but also in diabetes, heart disease, high cholesterol, high blood pressure and blocked arteries – all more good reasons to limit fructose. One approach to treating fructose intolerance is to make an exhaustive list of all the foods that are high in fructose — and avoid those foods. The alternative is to use the Fast Tract Diet System, which makes it easy to limit all difficult-to-digest carbohydrates, including fructose.

**Resistant Starch**

Starch is a large complex carbohydrate used by plants such as oats, corn, potatoes, wheat, and rice to store energy. Foods that contain starch make up a large part of many people's diet.

For many years it was believed that starch was completely digested and absorbed in the small intestine. But studies published in the 1980s, based on hydrogen breath testing, showed that oats, wheat, potatoes, corn, and beans contained 10 to 20% malabsorbed, fermentable material.[107] In another study of the digestion of starch, samples were taken from the terminal ilium (the end of the small intestine) of healthy individuals after two different meals containing starch. This study showed that eight to 10% of the starch escaped absorption.[108] Even the digestion of bread, long known as the "staff of life," has been shown to end in malabsorption by hydrogen breath testing and symptom scoring.[109] Starch that isn't absorbed, known by scientists as "resistant starch," is estimated to represent at least 10% of the total starch in a typically Western diet. If 10% of starch is malabsorbed in healthy people, how much is malabsorbed by people with digestive problems? The amount is certainly much higher.

Resistant starch is found in seeds, nuts, whole grains, cereals, bread, pasta, most rice varieties, most potato varieties, corn, certain fruits such as unripe bananas, and legumes such as beans and lentils. Undercooked, or cooked, then cooled foods contain more resistant starch than fully cooked or hot foods. In many ways, resistant starch is similar to and behaves like fermentable fiber in the digestive tract.

Resistant starch (RS) has been assigned to four groups based on the properties that allow it to resist digestion:[110]

> *RS1 – Physically resists digestion because of a protective matrix or coating surrounding the granules found in whole grains, legumes and seeds.*

RS2 – *Is intrinsically resistant to digestion before cooking. RS2 includes unripe bananas, uncooked potatoes, along with many other foods.*

RS3 – *Retrograded starch is formed when starchy foods are cooked and then cooled.*

RS4 – *Refers to starch that is chemically modified to resist digestion and absorption. RS4 starches are often developed for use in processed foods.*

Several factors contribute to the formation of resistant starch, and, the relative amount of resistant starch in foods influences the level of malabsorption. The most important, yet often overlooked, factor is the ratio of the two molecular types of starch, amylose and amylopectin. Each type of starch possesses a unique structure and different properties that affect how easily they can be digested and absorbed.

Amylopectin starch, which is easy to digest and absorb, is a much larger molecule, containing 10,000 to 100,000 glucose units. At the molecular level amylopectin is highly branched. (See figure 14.) The large size and branching forms starch granules that are less dense and gelatinize (absorb water) easily when heated in water. Gelatinized starch is easier to digest. The branched, less dense structure also allows the digestive enzyme amylase to work more efficiently, breaking amylopectin down quickly into glucose, which is absorbed rapidly.

Amylose starch, which is more difficult to digest and absorb, is both smaller, containing only 100 to 10,000 glucose units, and less heavily branched compared to amylopectin. (Again, see figure 14.) This linear shape allows amylose to pack more tightly into the less accessible regions of starch granules where it's more difficult to digest.[111] A high ratio of amylose in starch granules also makes it more difficult to gelatinize (it gelatinizes at a higher temperature), making digestion by amylase enzyme even more difficult.

Resistant starch (types RS1 through RS3) can contain both amylopectin and amylose. But comparing amylose content with the glycemic index (how quickly foods are converted to blood sugar) reveals that amylose clearly represents the predominant component of resistant starch. In RS3, linear or straight portions of amylose can re-associate, forming insoluble crystallites that are difficult to digest. [112]

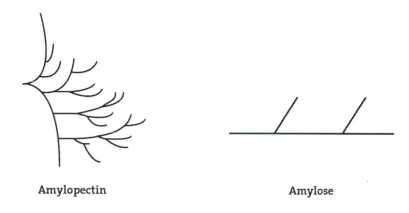

**Amylopectin**                                    **Amylose**

*Figure 14. Branching nature of amylopectin (highly branched) and amylose (fewer branches) starch.*

In general, foods that contain more amylopectin (higher glycemic index), such as jasmine rice, short grain sticky rice (also known as glutinous or sushi rice) as well as some varieties of potatoes, such as Russet Burbank, are much easier to digest and absorb than foods containing more amylose (lower glycemic index), such as basmati rice, most long grain rice (except for jasmine), pasta, most wheat, corn, oat and barley products, most potatoes and bananas (more on this below).

We know that a typical diet contains lots of resistant starch and we know that starch malabsorption is common. How does the presence of resistant starch affect the development of SIBO, and in turn IBS symptoms?

Resistant starch escapes digestion and absorption yet is fermentable by the bacteria common to the large intestine, including *Bifidobacterium, Clostridium, Bacteroides, Fusobacterium* and *Butyrivibrio*. These bacteria contain efficient starch-degrading enzymes and most can break down both amylopectin and amylose starch. [113]

The majority of bacteria found in the small intestine, on the other hand, are best at consuming single and double sugars such as glucose, fructose, lactose, mannose and sucrose. In one study, for example, none of the eight species of *Lactobacillus* and several other types of bacteria common to the small intestine were able to break down amylose or amylopectin. [114]

Moderate levels of resistant starch are not a problem for most healthy people, but consumption of large amounts of resistant starch, particularly in people with underlying digestive illnesses, increases the risk that malabsorbed starch will fuel the overgrowth of bacteria in the small intestine, or SIBO.

One study linked IBS symptoms to bread consumption. Of 34 IBS patients placed on a gluten-free diet, 19 were given two slices of bread and a muffin each day, while 15 were given no bread or muffin. Sixty-eight% of the bread and muffin group continued to have symptoms compared to 40% of the group that avoided bread.[115] While the study was evaluating gluten, bread and muffins contain a significant amount of resistant starch, which could just as likely be the driver of symptom persistence. The fact that gluten-free diets contain variable levels of difficult-to-digest carbohydrates including resistant starch may help explain why 40% of the gluten-free group continued to have symptoms.

We know that low-carbohydrate and "elemental" diets (see the following chapter for a more thorough discussion), which limit resistant starch, can reduce SIBO-related intestinal gas production and IBS symptoms. [116]

As I mentioned earlier, there is also a strong link between cystic fibrosis and gastroesophageal reflux disease (GERD), a condition tightly linked with IBS. About 80% of cystic fibrosis patients suffer from GERD compared to about 20% in the general population. No one has been able to figure out exactly why.

Cystic fibrosis patients, however, have a well-known deficiency of digestive enzymes, including a lack of pancreatic alpha amylase, an enzyme required for starch digestion. (The amylase present in saliva gets destroyed in the stomach.) The pancreatic amylase cannot get out of the pancreas, where it's produced, because the pancreatic ducts are often plugged up with thick mucus, a hallmark of CF.

Not surprisingly, this amylase deficiency results in starch malabsorption and SIBO. A study of CF patients with pancreatic deficiencies showed that SIBO was diagnosed (based on hydrogen breath testing) almost three times more frequently when compared to patients without cystic fibrosis. [117]

Believe it or not, there are actually products on the market that promote starch malabsorption. Weight loss products that block the absorption of starch are intentionally designed to inhibit amylase, the enzyme that normally breaks down starch. The idea behind these products is that blocking starch from being absorbed into the blood stream will prevent weight gain.

While the goal makes sense, the approach is short-sighted because it does not consider the possible consequences of malabsorption: diarrhea, cramps, bloating, abdominal distention, and excessive gas. Not so surprisingly, the side effects caused by these starch blockers include the symptoms of SIBO and IBS. The nearly inescapable conclusion is that starch malabsorption can cause SIBO, and ultimately contribute to IBS symptoms.

### Amylose vs. Amylopectin Starch

There's one more critical aspect of this connection: As mentioned above, I believe amylose (rather than amylopectin) starch to be the real culprit — because of its greater ability to resist digestion.

The key role of amylose malabsorption can be demonstrated by comparing the ability of different kinds of rice, containing different ratios of amylose and amylopectin, to raise blood sugar levels. Rice containing a higher ratio of amylose to amylopectin raises blood sugar less than rice containing amylopectin but no amylose.[118] A greater rise in blood sugar level indicates better digestion and absorption; a lesser rise in blood sugar level indicates malabsorption.

This difference is reflected in the glycemic index (again, more on this later), which determines the ability of carbohydrate-containing foods to raise blood sugar levels. Foods high in amylopectin, such as Asian short grain or glutinous rice, have a high glycemic index (98 percent) because they are digested and absorbed almost as efficiently as glucose — which has a glycemic index of 100 percent. Foods high in amylose, such as basmati rice, have a much lower glycemic index (58 percent), indicative of starch malabsorption.

According to researcher Peter Born, abdominal complaints (indicative of carbohydrate malabsorption and SIBO) affect 30% or more of Western populations, but only 10% of Asian populations.[119] Fewer symptoms in Asian populations could be due in part to Asian preferences for short grain rice over long grain rice and other starch containing foods. Short grain rice contains no amylose (only amylopectin) while most long grain rice varieties, such as basmati rice, and other starchy foods consumed by Western and other non-Asian cultures contain 20 to 30% amylose.

If you follow this evidence to its logical conclusion, it's clear that amylose starch is difficult to digest and absorb, but easy for bacteria associated with SIBO to metabolize. This can lead to severe gastrointestinal symptoms including symptoms of IBS. Any program with the goal of reducing the symptoms of SIBO and IBS will need to find some way to reduce the impact of amylose starch on digestion.

Unfortunately, there doesn't seem to be a specific medical test for amylose starch malabsorption. Technically, an amylose intolerance test could be given the same way a lactose or fructose intolerance test is given — by using high amylose starch in place of lactose or fructose — either by monitoring the rise in blood glucose (measuring the efficiency of digestion and absorption) or by using a hydrogen breath test (measuring how much bacterial fermentation is occurring in the small intestine). The lack of such a test is probably due to the general lack of recognition of the role of amylose starch in carbohydrate malabsorption and IBS symptoms.

### Treating Amylose Malabsorption

Because amylose starch is present in so many starchy vegetables, desserts, sauces, and baked goods, it would be difficult to avoid it completely. The best approach is to reduce how much amylose starch you consume by following the carefully designed Fast Tract Diet System. The Fast Tract Diet System works by limiting all difficult to digest carbohydrates, including resistant (mostly amylose) starch.

**Fiber**

Fiber is the indigestible part of plant-based foods, consisting of structural components such as the cell walls of fruits, vegetables, nuts and legumes, the tough outer layers of grains, as well as any other non-digestible carbohydrates, as well as lignin — a substance found in plants that binds the cellulose fibers together. The quick list of dietary fibers includes:

> *Fructans (including inulin and other polymers of fructose)*
>
> *Pectin*
>
> *Beta glucan (polydextrose)*
>
> *Gums*
>
> *Stachyose*
>
> *Raffinose*
>
> *Verbascose*
>
> *Hemicellulose*
>
> *Cellulose.*
>
> *Lignin*

Resistant starch (which we've just looked at in detail) is sometimes categorized as a type of dietary fiber because it exhibits similar properties, particularly in terms of indigestibility and fermentability. Similarly, some sugar alcohols (mannitol, sorbitol, xylitol, etc.), but not erythritol, are not classified as fiber, yet like fiber, resist digestion and are fermentable by gut bacteria.

### Soluble and Insoluble Fiber

Most plants contain both soluble and insoluble fiber. Soluble fiber includes pectin, polydextrose, some hemicelluloses, raffinose, stachyose, verbascose and fructans. Soluble fiber increases the viscosity of semi-solid materials moving through the intestines, increasing the time it takes to travel the entire route.

Insoluble fiber includes cellulose (beta-glucan), lignin and some hemicelluloses. Insoluble fiber is believed to increase bulk, soften stools and decrease gut transit time, potentially helping relieve constipation.

Because both soluble and insoluble fiber increases stool bulk, fiber can make you feel fuller. This has been proposed as an explanation of why fiber might help with weight loss.

### Fiber Intake and Health

The Academy of Nutrition and Dietetics (AND) recommends consuming between 20 and 35 grams of fiber per day. Most people consume 14 grams per day or less.

It's proven to be extremely difficult to confirm the many reported health benefits of fiber in the diet. Companies that market foods that contain fiber certainly publicize these reported benefits, but supporting evidence is hard to find.

For example, in a clinical study looking at the use of bran to reduce constipation, 20 grams of bran per day did not improve constipation symptoms compared to the placebo. [120]

Fiber is also, by reputation, an important tool in lowering cholesterol. In the eighties, for instance, a small study reported that 60 grams of oat bran or oat meal per day lowered cholesterol levels by roughly 3% after 12 weeks — when combined with a low fat diet.[121] However, another study found that fiber had no cholesterol-lowering effect in men with high cholesterol who did not follow a low-fat diet.[122] A third study, at Brigham and Women's Hospital in Boston, Massachusetts, found that oat bran and low-fiber wheat had the same moderate effect on cholesterol levels, suggesting that fiber itself is not responsible.

What about fiber and heart health? Two studies, one based in Finland and one in Japan suggest that people who eat lots of fiber (30-35 grams per day) may reduce their risk of coronary heart disease. [124]

I asked Gary Taubes, the author of *Good Calories Bad Calories*, about these studies. Gary cautioned me about reading too much into them. Observational studies follow large groups of people (22,000 subjects in the Finnish case, and 58,000 in the Japanese study) over time to see how their health develops. Then they compare, for example, the subgroup who ate the most fiber with the subgroup that ate the least, measure the occurrence of disease in each, and then draw conclusions about cause and effect connections.

He pointed out that the problem with this kind of study is that fiber consumption may not be the only factor shared by members of the subgroups. For example, the subgroup that ate more fiber may also be more health-conscious in general, and a more careful look at them might reveal that they also drink less, or smoke less, or exercise more. If true, this means that you cannot make a cause-and-effect connection between fiber consumption and heart health based on these studies (At least not without a lot more information about the individuals).

For more information on the effect of biases on observational studies, you might be interested in a cover story Gary wrote for *The New York Times Magazine* in September 2007 entitled, "Do We Really Know What Makes Us Healthy?" Gary's point is that many hypotheses generated by observational studies later turn out not to be true, and setting broad dietary guidelines without randomized, placebo-controlled clinical studies can lead to unintended and sometimes unhealthy consequences.

Another example: The idea that high dietary fiber may lower the risk of colon cancer came from studies in the 1970s that made a connection between low colon cancer rates in developing countries and diets higher in fiber.[125] A more recent study of 88,757 women found no association between dietary fiber consumption and the risk for colon cancer.[126] Similar results were obtained from the Fukuoka Colorectal Cancer Study,[127] and another large study of men. [128]

I have to admit that these results surprised me. Like most people, I grew up believing in the health benefits of fiber. If fiber did no harm it might not matter. But unfortunately, that's not the case for many people with digestive problems. For these people, excessive dietary fiber can create significant health challenges, because it can lead to excessive intestinal fermentation, SIBO, and IBS.

For one thing, it's nearly impossible for most people to consume enough fiber on a daily basis to realize any potential health benefits.

And commercial fiber supplements often contain large amounts of added sugar, which can increase the potential for fermentation in the small intestine. For instance, the recommended dose of the fiber supplement Metamucil, which contains fiber from psyllium husk, is one tablespoon three times per day. This daily dose equals 9 grams of dietary (insoluble) fiber, 7 grams of soluble fiber, and 21 (!) grams of sugar.

Note: Metamucil is now available as a sugar-free product, though as you will see below, I don't advise fiber supplementation.

By definition, the fiber in our diet is not digested or absorbed. The fiber we consume resists absorption and must pass through both the small and large intestine. Along the way, fiber is subjected to fermentation as a wide variety of bacteria try to break it down for energy.

Most fiber fermentation occurs in the large intestine and is generally considered normal and healthy. But consuming too much fiber can also cause excess fermentation in the small intestine. This can lead to serious gastrointestinal problems. Excessive fermentation in the small intestine increases the presence of bacterial endo- and exo- toxins as well as hydrogen, carbon dioxide, and methane gas. Symptoms can include pain, bloating, distention, gas, reflux, cramps, and diarrhea (and is some cases, constipation, especially in the absence of sufficient water).

### Fermentability of Fiber Types

The "fermentability" of fiber depends on the chemical makeup of the fiber, as well as the amount and types of bacteria present in the small and large intestines. Bacteria normally present in the small intestine can ferment smaller disaccharide sugars along with some easier-to-digest types of fiber. Bacteria normally present in the large intestine use a range of enzymes to ferment even the most resistant fiber types.

Fructans are long chains of fructose that include fructooligosaccharide and inulin. They are found in wheat, artichokes, garlic, onions, unripe bananas, asparagus and green beans. Fructans are highly fermentable by some bacteria, notably *Bifidobacteria*, which is considered to be a healthy inhabitant of the large intestine but is also associated with SIBO. It has been suggested that fructans can promote intestinal health, but there is also solid evidence linking fructans to SIBO. One study, for instance, found that fructans cause abdominal symptoms that can be reversed by limiting their consumption. [129]

Pectin, on the other hand, tends to be fermented slowly. In one study it took up to six hours to detect metabolic end products that indicated that gut bacteria in the large intestine had consumed the pectin.

Beta-glucan, present in oat flour, has been found to be highly fermentable resulting in gases as an end product.[130] Acacia gums used as food additives are also rapidly fermented by intestinal bacteria. [131]

Raffinose (trisaccharide), stachyose (tetrasaccharide) and verbascose (pentasaccharide) are found in legumes, especially beans. These fibers are well known for their role in causing flatulence, indicating that they are fermented in the large intestine. They are broken down by bacteria that possess the enzyme alpha-galactosidase (also present in the digestive supplement Beano).

In a study of fiber fermentability, cellulose was compared to water-insoluble hemicellulose and lignin.[132] The results show that 80% of the cellulose was fermented, with up to 15% of the fermentation taking place in the small intestine. Over 95% of the water-insoluble hemicellulose was fermented with up to 72% of the fermentation taking place in the small intestine. Lignin was not fermented at all.

*Table 1. Relative Fermentability of Fiber Types.*

| Fiber Type | Fermentability |
|---|---|
| Beta glucans | High |
| Fructans | High |
| Gums | High |
| Stachyose | Medium |
| Raffinose | Medium |
| Verbascos | Medium |
| Hemicellulose | Variable |
| Pectin | Low (safer form of fiber) |
| Cellulose | Low (safer form of fiber) |
| Lignin | Low (safer form of fiber) |

## Fiber and IBS

For decades, fiber was widely recommended as a treatment for Irritable Bowel Syndrome (IBS). But a study of wheat bran for IBS symptoms was inconclusive. [133] Along the same lines, treating 275 IBS patients with psyllium or bran fiber for three months did not improve their quality of life. The bran group actually suffered a high dropout rate because the participant's IBS symptoms kept getting worse. [134]

On the other hand, IBS patients who eliminated fiber from their diet showed a significant improvement in symptoms as well reduced production of hydrogen.[135] Avoiding fiber was actually more effective at reducing hydrogen gas than the potent antibiotic metronidazole.

## Treating Fiber Malabsorption

There's no real point in testing for fiber malabsorption since fiber, by definition, is not digested or absorbed. But if excessive fiber causes excessive fermentation, a lactulose breath test should be able to detect SIBO.

Moreover, trying to limit the different types of fiber in the diet can be difficult. There are so many different kinds of fiber that it is difficult to link symptoms with any specific type.

My advice would be to follow the Fast Tract Diet, which limits fiber. Enjoy plenty of green, leafy, and stalked vegetables as well as nuts and seeds that contain the less fermentable types of fiber. But consume beans, lentils and other legumes in limited quantities.

## Sugar Alcohols

Sugar alcohols, sometimes referred to as polyols; include sorbitol, mannitol, xylitol, lactitol, isomalt, erythritol, and maltitol. Sugar alcohols taste sweet, but are poorly digested and absorbed. One benefit is that they don't raise blood sugar as much or have as many calories as sugar. For this reason, sugar alcohols have been used for weight and diabetic control and for preventing dental cavities. Sugar alcohols are generally accepted as sugar-free alternatives for people on low-carb diets.

While several sugar alcohols including xylitol, mannitol and sorbitol, are listed as GRAS (Generally Regarded As Safe) food additives by the FDA, not all sugar alcohols are included. The FDA requires that mannitol and sorbitol have warning labels indicating that over 20 grams per day for mannitol and 50 g per day for sorbitol can give a laxative effect. But these warnings don't appear to go far enough. For instance, early studies on sorbitol using hydrogen breath testing indicate that bacterial fermentation was observed with as little as 5 grams and that at 10 grams, subjects experienced gas and bloating. The symptoms became more severe, including cramps and diarrhea, when 20 grams were ingested.[136] In another study, 84% of people ingesting 25 grams of sorbitol had a positive breath test for malabsorption and 57% exhibiting malabsorption reported symptoms.[137] Clearly people experience GI symptoms well below the 50 grams per day deemed by the FDA as acceptable. Even smaller amounts would be expected to invoke symptoms in people with digestive issues.

Clearly, most sugar alcohol sweeteners cause bloating, cramps and diarrhea as well as excessive fermentation, hallmarks of IBS. Any effective diet for IBS must limit these sweeteners with the exception of erythritol (see below).

Avoiding sugar alcohols can be hard to do as they are often added to cough syrup, mouthwash, toothpaste, baked goods, syrups, candy, gum, chocolate and other "sugarless" or diet products. To determine if products you buy contain sugar alcohols, check the labels. Luckily, the FDA requires food labels to list the amount (if not the specific types) of sugar alcohols. The Fast Tract Diet System includes sugar alcohols when calculating fermentation potential and does not use or include sugar alcohols in the Fast Tract Diet recipes.

Important Exception: One sugar alcohol, erythritol, has some unique properties which makes it a good choice as a natural (it's produced by yeast) alternative sweetener. Unlike the other sugar alcohols, erythritol is mostly (90%) absorbed in the small intestine. Even the 10% that remains in the intestine may not be a problem as gut bacteria are not able to metabolize it. There's more good news. Erythritol is not metabolized significantly by the body as most of it can be recovered in urine. Safety studies in animals and humans suggest that erythritol is very safe as well. Thanks to Lauren Benning (http://www.healthyindulgences.net) for writing to me about the benefits or erythritol and Kris Gunnars (http://authoritynutrition.com/erythritol/) for his excellent article on erythritol.

All of this information about food types is designed to prepare you for the next chapter in this book, where we take a quick look at some of diets that have been developed to treat digestive tract conditions. All of these diets try to limit foods that cause gastric distress, and increase your consumption of foods that do not.

Understanding the nature of the foods that your body is trying to digest will both help you understand why many diets do not fully protect your gastrointestinal tract from SIBO and IBS, and show you how the Fast Track Diet System that I've developed offers a safe, thorough and complete solution to the problem.

# CHAPTER 10:

# Comparing Diets for SIBO

My research has established that SIBO and related digestive conditions including IBS have many underlying causes, but the driving force behind SIBO is *always* poorly absorbed carbohydrates. The best way to limit SIBO — and IBS — is to deny gut bacteria the fuel they need to overrun the small intestine by limiting the consumption of hard-to-digest carbohydrates.

Several existing diets have shown promise in treating SIBO-related conditions. These include the Elemental Diet, Paleo Diet, Specific Carbohydrate Diet, Low-Starch Diet, Low-Carb Diet, the FODMAP approach and the Low Residue Diet. Each of these diets, to varying degrees, limit carbohydrate malabsorption; an approach known to be effective for treating SIBO. Unfortunately, none of them offers a completely effective treatment for SIBO or IBS.

## The Elemental Diet

The Elemental diet consists of foods that are essentially "predigested." The foods contain fatty acids rather than fats, amino acids rather than proteins, and glucose instead of carbohydrates. The diet formula also includes water and micronutrients — vitamins and minerals. Elemental diet product such as Nestlé's Vivonex can be delivered orally or enterally (by tube). Elemental diets are designed to ensure full absorption and have been used to treat a broad range of digestive conditions including: Crohn's and celiac disease, lactose intolerance, malabsorption, diarrhea, constipation, diabetes, cystic fibrosis, abdominal distention, and short bowel syndrome. Note that all of these conditions have some connection to SIBO. Drawbacks of the elemental diet approach include the high cost and unappealing (predigested!) nature of these products.

## The Paleo Diet

The proponents of the Paleo diet make a good case for eating like our ancestors. Their basic argument is that our bodies evolved to digest the foods that were available before we learned to cultivate grains. I've read two great books about the Paleo diet: *The Paleo Solution*, by Rob Wolf, and *The Primal Blueprint,* by Mark Sisson. Another excellent source of authentic Paleo information is Danny Alber's Blog, Primal North.[138]

The Paleo diet includes fish, meat (including organ meat), fowl, eggs, and traditionally raised or organically sourced vegetables, tubers, fruits, nuts, seeds, herbs, and even insects. It excludes grains (with the exception of wild rice), beans and pulses, dairy, heavily-processed oils (except olive and coconut oil), processed foods containing sugars and trans-fats, nitrates, and other additives including antibiotics, pesticides and hormones.

Clearly, this diet is a step in the right direction towards gut health! The Paleo diet removes or limits many of the difficult-to-digest carbohydrates that are tied to SIBO. But some of the foods included do contain carbohydrates that could contribute to SIBO.

Wild rice varieties contain lots of resistant starch. Many fruits such as apples, pears, plums, mangos and cherries contain relatively high amounts of fructose. Bananas can also cause significant digestive problems. Bananas, especially under-ripe bananas, contain a lot of resistant starch. Certain tubers, including sweet potatoes and yams also contain significant amounts of resistant starch.

## The Specific Carbohydrate Diet

The book *Breaking the Vicious Cycle* by Elaine Gottschall describes her experiences with Drs. Sidney and Merrill Haas, who successfully treated celiac disease (linked to SIBO) with a diet that allowed only specific sugars and starches. The Specific Carbohydrate Diet limits disaccharide or double sugars as well as grains and starch, but allows simple sugars like glucose.

In general, this dietary approach is on the right track, but it fails to limit a number of known contributors to SIBO and IBS. For example, honey is used extensively in the recipes even though honey has just as much fructose as table sugar (sucrose is made of equal parts glucose and fructose). And the diet also allows a large variety of fruits and fruit juices that contain large quantities of fructose, which is now recognized as a major contributor to the development of SIBO.

Finally, the SCD does not allow any grains or foods containing starch. It wrongly identifies amylose starch as easy to digest and amylopectin starch as difficult to digest, suggesting that amylopectin and not amylose is more likely to cause microbial fermentation. The reverse is actually true.

The GAPS Diet (Gut and Psychology Syndrome), created by Dr. Natasha Campbell-McBride, is based on the Specific Carbohydrate Diet but also includes detoxification and nutritional supplementation.

## The Low-Starch Diet

Carol Sinclair popularized the Low-Starch Diet in her book *The IBS Low-Starch Diet*. Sinclair discovered that reducing starch in her diet improved her IBS symptoms. She also collaborated with Dr. Alan Ebringer, a professor of immunology at Kings College in London, UK, who found that the diet could improve painful symptoms of ankylosing spondylitis (AS). Dr. Ebringer has made the connection between the autoimmune disease AS, intestinal overgrowth of the bacterium *Klebsiella pneumonia*, and controlling the bacteria's growth through a low-starch diet. Sinclair's book limits all starches as well as sucrose, lactose and maltose.

Unfortunately, like the Specific Carbohydrate Diet, the Low-Starch Diet does not limit fructose, and will not be completely effective in treating SIBO or IBS.

## The Low-Carb Diet

Dr. Robert Atkins made low-carbohydrate dieting famous when he published *Dr Atkins' Diet Revolution* in the 1970s. Two other ground-breaking books on low-carb dieting; *Protein Power* by Drs. Mike and Mary Dan Eades and *Good Calories Bad Calories* by Gary Taubes, show how low-carb dieting works at the biochemical level to improve human health beyond weight loss.

Studies have shown that strict (ketogenic) low-carb dieting can also improve IBS and GERD symptoms, two conditions associated with SIBO.[139] Despite impressive results, not everyone with IBS and GERD gets complete symptom relief from a low-carb diet. One possible explanation for the variations in results is that low-carb diets don't restrict fiber or sugar alcohols — both well-known contributors to digestive illness. Another reason might be a simple failure to stick with the diet. Many people are unwilling to follow a strict low-carb eating plan for extended periods of time.

## The FODMAP Approach

Susan Shepherd and Peter Gibson developed the FODMAP diet at Monash University in Victoria, Australia.[140] The acronym FODMAP represents four classes of fermentable sugars/sugar alcohols: Fermentable Oligo-, Di-, and Monosaccharides, And Polyols.[141] The FODMAP approach limits fructose, fructans, lactose, galactans and sugar alcohols.

The FODMAP approach does not limit resistant starch, and fiber, both significant contributors to malabsorption and excessive fermentation. In fact, the FODMAP diet calls for adding more resistant starch. As a recent article on the diet stated, "Part of dietary counseling is to ensure continuing adequate intake of resistant starch."[142] A trained dietitian was recommended to deliver the diet but the authors and others have since published books on the diet. [143]

## The Low Residue Diet

The Cedars-Sinai protocol, written about in *The New IBS Solution* is an example of a low residue diet. This diet is designed to support the patient while antibiotics are being administered to combat SIBO. Some of the guidelines make sense, but I don't agree with all of the recommendations.

The protocol allows 40 grams per day of sugar. This is far too much given that fructose comprised one half of sucrose. At the same time, the diet restricts sucralose (Splenda) because, it states, the sweetener will potentially feed bacterial overgrowth. There is no evidence that sucralose is metabolized by bacteria.[144] The protocol also warns patients against eating large salads and raw vegetables because "they contain too much residue," according to the guidelines. Vegetables that are not too starchy, including most green vegetables, tend to contain fiber forms that are less fermentable and are less likely to create gas, while still adding bulk to stools. Most importantly, the guidelines state that potatoes, pasta, rice, bread, and cereals are also acceptable. Most of these foods contain far too much amylose, the resistant starch. In fact, only certain low-amylose varieties of rice and potato are acceptable and behaviors that increase absorption, such as chewing slowly, need to be encouraged.

# The Fast Tract Diet

Fortunately, my research on the biochemistry of digestion points to a new way of understanding the connection between poor absorption, SIBO, and IBS. It has also led me to develop a "new kind of diet" that offers a safe, thorough, and easy to understand way to control malabsorption through avoiding certain foods.

The defining feature of the Fast Tract Diet System is the method it uses to calculate the potential for any food containing carbohydrates to cause symptoms characteristic of SIBO and IBS. Mathematically derived values for the fermentation potential (FP) of different foods helps identify and restrict difficult-to-digest carbohydrates, notably fructose, lactose, fiber, amylose starch and sugar alcohol. None of the other diets limit the full list of difficult-to-digest carbohydrates that can promote SIBO. (The Specific and Low-Starch diets don't restrict fructose, the Low-Carb diets don't restrict sugar alcohols or fiber, and the FODMAP approach doesn't limit resistant starch.)

Anyone who reads this book can reduce their symptoms by following the recipes in Appendix A, or by creating their own recipes for foods with low FP values. I've done the hard work for you — by calculating the fermentation potential of a broad range of common foods, and by combining low-FP foods in recipes and meal plans to ensure efficient and complete digestion and absorption.

The diet is based on balanced, nutritious and appetizing meals made with wholesome foods right off the grocery shelves.

Unlike purely low-carb diets, Fast Tract meals can include both low-carb foods and higher-carb foods as long as they don't contain too many difficult-to-digest carbohydrates. The Fast Tract Diet can be employed to support a number of different eating styles, while leaving fewer carbs for gut microorganisms to consume. The result is less gas, less gas pressure and more symptom control.

In a nutshell, the Fast Tract Diet System represents a safe, effective, and flexible system to control SIBO, which I believe to be the real cause of IBS.

The next three chapters will give you a more complete introduction to the Fast Tract Diet System. The first will explain how to calculate the fermentation potential (or look it up in the tables in Appendix B) of any given food, and how to use that information. The second presents a complete diet program — full of helpful tips and advice on how to get the most out of the Fast Tract Diet System including a comprehensive trouble-shooting section. Finally, the third chapter that follows provides advice on following the recipes and preparing your own recipes. Also, wheat and carbohydrate sensitivities are discussed to make sure you can tailor this diet program to your own eating style and still control SIBO and IBS. These chapters show you how you can eat well and be healthy without symptoms, even if you've been affected by IBS.

C H A P T E R   1 1 :

# Measuring Sympton Risk in Foods

"WE CAN'T SOLVE PROBLEMS BY USING THE SAME KIND OF THINKING WE USED WHEN WE CREATED THEM."

—ALBERT EINSTEIN

My interest in IBS was a natural progression of my research into acid reflux because both conditions are related and both are caused by SIBO. After writing my first book, I was fortunate enough to become friends with Drs. Mike and Mary Dan Eades, who had written about the benefits of low-carbohydrate diets for people affected by GERD in their bestselling book, Protein Power. Mike was intrigued by my idea that poor absorption of carbohydrates could lead to bacterial overgrowth and reflux symptoms. He asked me the following key question:

"Do all carbs trigger acid reflux and, if not, can you devise something like a barometer for heartburn that helps people avoid the worst carbs?"

I spent several years answering that question. The answer has relevance not only to GERD, but to IBS and many other SIBO-related disorders.

My insight for the Fast Tract Digestion book series was this: The more difficult individual carbohydrates were to digest or absorb, the more likely those particular carbohydrates would be malabsorbed and serve as a source of food or fuel for gut bacteria. The higher the amount of malabsorption, the higher the rate of fermentation and production of gas, toxins and other inflammatory substances in the digestive tract.

It turns out that avoiding five difficult to digest carbohydrates is the key to symptom relief. As I mentioned in previous chapters, they are fructose, lactose, resistant starch, fiber, and sugar alcohols (which are similar to carbohydrates). But avoiding these five carbohydrates can be quite complex without a thorough knowledge of their types and amounts in all the foods you consume.

To overcome this burden, I needed to create a simple way to measure the total amount of difficult-to-digest carbohydrates in each food that would be subject to malabsorption and fermentation by gut bacteria.

## The FP (Fermentation Potential) Breakthrough

It finally dawned on me that the glycemic index developed by Dr. David Jenkins at the University of Toronto could be used for this purpose. The GI measures the relative ease with which carbohydrates are digested and absorbed into the bloodstream, so it made sense that it could also be used to calculate the carbohydrates that are left over — not digested and absorbed into the bloodstream. I used the glycemic index[145] and nutritional information (serving size, net carbs, fiber and sugar alcohol) for individual foods to calculate what I call the Fermentation Potential or FP.

If you know the serving size, total amount of net carbs (NC), dietary fiber (DF) and sugar alcohols (SA), and the glycemic index (GI) for a food, you can easily calculate the fermentation potential (or use the tables in Appendix B). For people suffering from SIBO-related symptoms including IBS, the FP value is a systematic way to rate "symptom potential." Foods having a low FP will be much less likely to trigger symptoms than foods having a high FP.

The formula for FP looks like this:

$$FP = \frac{(100 - GI)xNC}{100} + DF + SA$$

## Can the glycemic index really help measure malabsorption?

The glycemic index of foods is based on the type of carbohydrates each food contains (sugars, starches, or fiber), how the food has been cooked or processed, the presence (or absence) of other foods, and how fast the food is eaten. The Glycemic Load (GL) measures the over-all amount of carbohydrates expected to be absorbed into the blood stream for a typical serving of the food in question.

The only way to establish the glycemic index for a particular food is to test it in people.

Typically, individuals are tested in the morning, after an overnight fast. For the first three trials, they give a baseline blood sample, and then consume 50 grams of pure glucose. The concentration of glucose in their blood is measured in additional blood samples taken at 15, 30, 45, 60, 90 and 120 minutes after the baseline sample.

Whole blood glucose levels are measured with an automatic analyzer that can accurately determine the concentration of glucose in the blood. Measuring blood glucose levels over time (producing what's known as the "blood glucose response curve") gives a much more accurate value for glucose absorption than measuring blood glucose at a single point in time.

After the three trials with glucose, known as the reference food, the individuals are tested again, this time after consuming the food being studied. These results are then compared to the trials using glucose.

Glucose doesn't need to be digested or "broken down" — it is absorbed completely and directly into the blood stream. Pure glucose is absorbed so efficiently that you can expect 100 % of a 50-gram test dose to be absorbed into the blood stream. As a result, glucose is assigned a glycemic index of 100.

The glycemic index for a specific food can then be calculated by comparing its absorption to the absorption of pure glucose.

The absorption value for 50 net carb grams of the test food is divided by the absorption for 50 grams of glucose, and then multiplied by 100 to arrive at a glycemic index.

Here's the general equation:

*GI (Glycemic Index)*

*= (absorption of 50 net carb g test food) / absorption of 50 g glucose) x (100)*

Let's look at a simple example by calculating the glycemic index of spaghetti. While spaghetti's glycemic index varies depending on the type of spaghetti and how long it's cooked, the absorption value for a 180 gram (6.35 ounce) serving containing 50-grams of net carbs is typically around 22 grams.

According to our formula:

*GI (glycemic index) = (22)/(50) x 100 = 44*

In this case, the glycemic index of spaghetti was calculated to be 44. In other words, spaghetti raised blood sugar only 44% as much as pure glucose. That means that 44% of the 50-gram net carb serving of spaghetti, or 22 grams (0.44 x 50g = 22 g), was absorbed into the blood stream. This amount is known as the Glycemic Load (GL).

This whole process is repeated for each new food tested. Since 1980, over 1000 carbohydrate-containing foods have been tested in this fashion. (The next time you see the glycemic index listed for an individual food, remember that a determined test subject was stuck with a needle 28 times to determine that number!)

The availability of good glycemic index data for many of the most common foods containing carbohydrates makes it possible to calculate the fermentation potential of these foods. If you know the total carbo-hydrates (including net carbohydrates, fiber, and sugar alcohol) of a food, and you know its glycemic index (measuring how much of it will be digested and absorbed), you can easily calculate the carbohydrates that will be "left over" to fuel fermentation.

The key question here is: "What happens to the carbohydrates that aren't absorbed?" To continue with our example, the question becomes, "if 44% of the carbohydrates in spaghetti are absorbed, what happens to the 56% (or 0.56 x 50 grams = 28 grams) that is not absorbed?" If 22 grams of carbohydrates from of a 50-gram net carb serving of spaghetti enter the blood stream, the remaining 28 grams must remain in the intestines. And what about the fiber? A serving of pasta with 50 grams of carbohydrates contains about 3 grams of fiber. Fiber is a non-digested carbohydrate that needs to be included in the calculation.

Adding the 28 grams of net carbohydrate and the 3 grams of fiber from spaghetti gives us a total of 31 grams of carbohydrate left in the digestive tract after the meal — and available to be "fermented" by intestinal bacteria. Hopefully, most of this fermentation will take place in the large intestine, where fermentation is relatively normal, but the more "fuel" is left behind, the more likely it is that some of the fermentation will take place in the small intestine, raising the chances for SIBO to develop.

(Note that the serving size used in the FP tables for spaghetti is slightly less than the serving depicted in this example, and the FP value for the smaller serving will therefore be less than 31g.)

I refer to these unabsorbed carbohydrates as having "Fermentative Potential." The unabsorbed carbohydrates represent potential food for intestinal microorganisms. And remember that as little as 30 grams of malabsorbed carbohydrates (30 FP grams) can produce 10 liters of intestinal gas. That is a huge amount of gas. Imagine ten balloons filled with one liter of gas each. Then imagine these balloons inside your intestines!

Someone eating a typical American diet (for example — oatmeal, bread, and orange juice for breakfast; a banana for a snack; cheeseburger, fries and a soda for lunch; and rice, carrots, chicken, milk and chocolate cake for dinner) easily consumes a daily FP of more than 160 grams. That is the equivalent of more than 50 balloons per day!

The FP value, measuring unabsorbed carbohydrates, is much more valuable for people with IBS or other conditions caused by SIBO than either glycemic index (GI) or glycemic load (GL). Carbs with a low FP will be much less likely to cause IBS symptoms. The most symptom friendly carb is glucose, which has a glycemic index of 100 (or 100 percent), it has a fermentation potential of zero, because it is completely absorbed into the bloodstream.

Finally, let's take a look at a few more sample calculations for common foods to see how to determine whether a given food is safe for you. These calculations are based on round numbers so that the calculation is easier to follow. For exact values, see the FP tables in Appendix B.

## Bread Comparison

**English Muffin (FP 4 g)** — *Less Symptom Potential*
Serving size = 1 oz, 30 g
NC 14 g
Fiber 1 g
GI 77
FP = $((100 - 77) \times 14)/100 + 1 = 4$ g

**Whole Grain Bread (FP 8g)** — *More Symptom Potential*
Serving size = 1 oz, 30 g
NC 13 g
Fiber 2 g
GI 51
FP = $((100 - 51) \times 13)/100 + 2 = 8$ g

Comparing two types of bread products, you can see that FP can vary quite a bit. Keep in mind that many people with diagnosed and undiagnosed celiac disease can't tolerate the gluten in wheat products. Remember to chew bread and other starchy foods well before swallowing to give the amylase in your saliva ample time to breakdown the starch.

# Yogurt Comparison

### Plain Yogurt (FP 7 g) — *Less Symptom Potential*
Serving size 8 oz, 228 g
NC 10 g
Fiber 0 g
GI 36
FP = ((100 − 36) x 10) / 100 + 0 = 7 g

### Sweetened Yogurt with Fruit (FP 23g) — *More Symptom Potential*
Serving size 8 oz, 228 g
NC 35 g
Fiber 0 g
GI 33
FP = ((100 − 33) x 35) / 100 + 0 = 23

Notice the difference between sweetened and unsweetened yogurt. The sweetened yogurt contains 16 more grams of difficult to digest carbs per serving. I recommend plain yogurt sweetened with no-calorie sweeteners. Another option is sweetening with the sugars glucose (called dextrose) or maltose as these sugars are easy to digest with FP values of 0 grams. Just keep in mind the potential negative health consequences from consuming too much sugar.

# Rice Comparison

### Asian Sticky Rice (FP 3g) — *Less Symptom Potential*
Serving size 5.3 oz, 150 g
NC 32 g

Fiber 2 g

GI 98

$FP = ((100 - 98) \times 32) / 100 + 2 = 3$ g

## Jasmine Rice (FP 0 g) — *Less Symptom Potential*

Serving size 5.3 oz, 150 g

NC 42 g

Fiber 0 g

GI 109

$FP = ((100 - 109) \times 42) / 100 + 0 = -4$ g (essentially 0 g)

## Basmati Rice (FP 17g) — *More Symptom Potential*

Serving size 5.3 oz, 150 g

NC 38 g

Fiber 1

GI 58

$FP = ((100 - 58) \times 38) / 100 + 1 = 17$ g

## Uncle Ben's White Rice (FP 20g) — *More Symptom Potential*

Serving size 5.3 oz, 150 g

NC 36 g

Fiber 0 g

GI 45

$FP = ((100 - 45) \times 36) / 100 + 0 = 20$ g

In this comparison of rice varieties, you can see that Asian sticky rice (also known as glutinous rice) and jasmine rice have low fermentation potentials indicating they are IBS friendly. Jasmine rice has an FP of 0 grams indicating that it is actually absorbed as fast as pure glucose due to its lack of amylose starch and perhaps the fluffy nature of its amylopectin starch content. One hundred percent of the carbs in jasmine rice are absorbed and zero grams remain in the intestine.

Asian sticky rice fairs almost as well with over 31 grams absorbed and only 3 grams (including 2 grams of fiber) remaining in the intestine. Just remember not to over-consume any starch-containing food, eat slowly and chew well.

Other rice varieties don't fare as well in comparison. Basmati rice and Uncle Ben's white converted rice have FP values of 17 and 20 grams respectively. Every time you consume a serving of these rice varieties between 17 and 20 grams of difficult to digest carbs become available for gut fermentation. While this might be fine for people without intestinal bacterial overgrowth, it can be a problem for people with IBS and other related conditions. For this reason, the recipes in this book use only Asian short grain sticky rice and jasmine rice.

## Pasta Comparison

**Pasta (rice-based) (FP 5g)** — *Less Symptom Potential*
Serving size 6 oz, 170 g
NC 36 g
Fiber 2 g
GI 92
FP = ((100 − 92) x 36) / 100 + 2 = 5g

**Pasta (wheat-based) (FP 28g)** — *More Symptom Potential*
Serving size 6 oz, 170 g
NC 45 g
Fiber 3 g
GI 44
FP = ((100 − 44) x 45) / 100 + 3 = 28 g

The FP for a serving of wheat-based pasta (spaghetti) is 28 grams indicating that 28 grams of carbohydrate are not leaving your intestine and can potentially cause bacterial overgrowth, gas and IBS symptoms.

This is the real reason so many people get symptoms from eating spaghetti. The rice-based pasta on the other hand, gives a much more reasonable FP of 5 grams and is clearly the better choice. Note: The FP of rice pasta will depend on the type rice used in its production, which can be difficult to determine, as well as the production method and how long it was cooked. As I have indicated, some rices have more resistant starch than others. The rice pasta used was made from brown rice, which likely was relatively low in resistant starch.

## Milk Comparison

**Soy Milk (FP 2g)** — *Less Symptom Potential*
Serving size 8 oz, 224 g
NC 2 g
Fiber 1 g
GI 44
FP = ((100 − 44) x 2) / 100 + 1 = 2 g

**Whole Milk (FP 8g)** — *More Symptom Potential*
Serving size 8 oz, 224 g
NC 11 g
Fiber 0 g
GI 27
FP = ((100 − 27) x 11) / 100 + 0 = 8 g

Comparing unsweetened soy milk to whole milk shows that soy milk will be much less apt to trigger symptoms. Skim milk fairs no better than whole milk and chocolate milk is worse with an FP of 18 g. These FP values make sense. The lactose in whole and skim milk and the additional sugar and fiber in the chocolate milk represent difficult-to-digest carbohydrates that are responsible for the higher FP values. Also note that glycemic index calculations are based on testing in healthy people who are not lactose-intolerant. This means that the FP value for milk would likely be higher if the glycemic index had been determined in lactose-intolerant people.

As you can see from these examples, fermentation potential depends less on the *amount* of carbohydrate in each food, and more on the *type* of carbohydrate, which determines how easily it can be broken down and absorbed

Now that we've taken a thorough look at fermentation potential, a key metric when trying to deal with the symptoms of IBS, it's time to look at how to incorporate this value into a diet plan that will change the way you eat and live. In the long run, a dietary approach to IBS, based on fine-tuning the inputs to the digestive process, is more likely to produce the results you're looking for.

# CHAPTER 12:

# The Fast Tract Diet

"NECESSITY IS
THE MOTHER OF
INVENTION."
—PLATO

## On The Fast Tract

Now that you understand how difficult-to-digest carbohydrates can cause IBS symptoms, I'd like to introduce you to the most important element of my system for eliminating IBS symptoms — the Fast Tract Diet.

The goal of the Fast Tract Diet is to help you change your eating habits so that your digestive system breaks down and absorbs carbohydrates more efficiently. The better this process works, the less fermentable material is "left over" for bacterial fermentation, SIBO, and eventually IBS symptoms.

The diet's basic strategy is to limit foods with high FP values and replace them with foods with lower FP values. For example, we've looked at the benefit of replacing long grain rice varieties like Basmati with short grain Asian ("sticky") rice. Long grain rices (except jasmine rice) tend to have a very high amylose content (which is difficult to digest — and can cause symptoms) while short grain rices and jasmine rice are higher in amylopectin (which is easy to digest — and less likely to cause symptoms).

There are three basic principles to keep in mind when evaluating FP values on your own.

*Both low and high carbohydrate foods can have a low Fermentative Potential.*

*Fermentative Potential (FP) is the key measure regardless of the carbohydrate count.*

*Limiting foods with high FP will help control the overgrowth of bacteria in the small intestine — and IBS symptoms.*

Though everyone is different, and able to tolerate varying amounts of difficult to digest carbohydrates, I recommend starting on the low end, consuming foods that are relatively low in FP.

**Recommended FP (grams) total for a single meal:**

*FP between 0 and 7 is considered low.*

*FP between 8 and 15 is considered moderate.*

*FP equal or greater than 15 is considered high.*

**Recommended FP (grams) for a single day:**

*FP between 20 and 30 is considered low.*

*FP between 30 and 45 is considered moderate.*

*FP equal to or greater than 45 is considered high.*

## Make the Most of Your Diet

Before you get started with the recipes from the meal plans, let's look at some basic dietary practices that will help you make the Fast Tract Diet as effective as possible.

### Minimize the Effects of Starches

There are several steps you can take to avoid consuming resistant starches. You can avoid starchy vegetables and fruits all together, but if you do include them in your diet, consume only fully ripened fruits and vegetables as they have lower amounts of resistant starch.

Make sure you eat only freshly prepared starchy vegetables (such as rice and potatoes). Cooked, then cooled, starchy vegetables can contain three times as much resistant starch. If you do consume leftover starches, heating them thoroughly helps gelatinize the retrograded starch.

Cook starchy vegetables well, because steaming, boiling or cooking starchy foods longer reduces the amount of resistant starch. This is important for potatoes, pasta, rice, and grains. You don't need to do this with non-starchy vegetables.

Avoid consuming whole grain products, as they are high in RS, and consider limiting or eliminating wheat products entirely until you determine their effect on you in a controlled manner (starting *after* your symptoms improve).

One piece of good news: Foods that don't contain carbohydrates, such as meats, fish, eggs, cheese, oils, etc., have an FP value of zero and are not limited by the diet. Also, non-starchy vegetables (refer to Table 10 in Appendix B for a list of over 50 vegetables) have very low FP values — you can eat more of these foods more often!

### Stay Hydrated

Drink plenty of water: at least six glasses per day, especially if you are physically active. Water is required for the breakdown and metabolism of every food group as well as transporting nutrients and eliminating waste from your system. In addition, water is critical for maintaining body temperature, osmotic balance (controlling salt and other electrolyte concentrations), blood pressure and normal bowel and bladder function.

Sometimes it's hard to remember to stay hydrated. I used to fill a glass with water, take a sip, and then forget about it. It's difficult to drink eight glasses a day one sip at a time! Later, I'd realize I was getting dehydrated. To improve my own water intake, I have started the habit of drinking at least one half of a glass of water as soon as I pour it.

I drink tap water, because the water in the Boston suburb where I live is of excellent quality and (lack of) taste. If it weren't, I would switch immediately to filtered or bottled water.

### Other Liquids

While water is the most important component for staying hydrated, you can also enjoy a number of other liquids while on the Fast Tract Diet. During week one of the diet, certain drinks are limited by amount. After the first week, however, drinks are only limited by the contributions of their FP values to your overall allowances.

You may be surprised to see coffee, tea and alcoholic drinks are allowed on the diet. I have found no convincing evidence that either caffeine or alcohol contributes to IBS symptoms. I believe that any IBS symptoms associated with these drinks are actually caused by additives — for example, sucrose (table sugar) in coffee and tea, or sodas and drink mixes that contain high fructose corn syrup. Nevertheless, until you have your symptoms completely under control, I recommend that you limit caffeine-containing beverages to two per day and alcohol-containing beverages to one per day in the first week of the diet.

Also avoid sweetened wines, non-light beer, sweetened soft drinks, lactose-containing milk and milk products like non lactose-free ice cream, as well as all fruit juices. Here are some general guidelines:

### Water:

*Unlimited: Six to eight glasses per day (depending on activity level) recommended to aid digestion.*

### Soft drinks:

Not Allowed: *Soft drinks containing sugar.*

Allowed: *Limit diet soft drinks to one can per day during weeks one and two. After that, unlimited. Other zero calorie drinks, unlimited.*

### Caffeinated drinks such as tea and coffee:

Not Allowed: *Regular, fat free or low fat milk, sugar, half and half.*

Allowed: *Two cups per day with light cream, non-dairy creamer, lac-tose-free milk and a low FP sweetener.*

### Alcoholic drinks:

Not allowed: *Sweet wine, sugar sweetened drinks, and non-light beer.*

Allowed: *Light beer, dry (non-sweet) red or white wine, or mixed drinks made with non-sugar sweeteners and mixes; for example rum and diet coke. Limit to one drink per day during week one and limit to two drinks per day going forward until all symptoms are gone.*

### Fruit Juices:

Not allowed: *During week one and week two.*

Allowed: *After week one and week two, fruit juices can be consumed only within overall FP limits.*

### Milk:

Not Allowed: *Lactose-containing milk.*

Allowed: *Light and heavy cream and lactose-free milk as used in recipes or within daily FP limits.*

### Soy milk:

Allowed: *Can be consumed within overall FP limits.*

## Vitamin and Mineral Supplements

Take a multivitamin daily that includes minerals. Vitamins B12, A, D, E, K and the minerals magnesium, calcium, iron, and zinc are important for digestive health. And your body's ability to use them can be affected by digestive malabsorption.

I take a generic multivitamin and mineral product that compares with Centrum every day. This supplement contains all the vitamins and minerals I just mentioned as well as lutein (a carotenoid antioxidant pigment from green leafy plants, egg yolks and animal fats) and lycopene (another carotenoid antioxidant pigment found in tomatoes and other fruits and vegetables). Your individual condition may require additional supplements. For example, you may want to take calcium if you're at risk for osteoporosis, or iron if you're affected by anemia (see note of caution below for iron).

Taking a combination multivitamin/mineral supplement is a good way to make sure your body gets the nutrients you need — and that are often lacking in contemporary diets or depleted due to malabsorption.

Be cautious in using supplements, though. Iron, for example, can be toxic at high levels, and iron supplements should be used under a doctor's supervision. Some mineral supplements are not 100% pure. Calcium supplements, for instance, may contain other minerals including trace amounts of lead. Be sure to buy your supplements from reputable sources where the product is regularly tested by an accredited laboratory.

## Probiotics

Probiotics are another alternative that can make it easier to digest carbohydrates. These products contain live microorganisms (usually freeze-dried) that are believed to improve intestinal or general health. Two common bacteria used in probiotics are *Lactobacillus acidophilus* and *Bifidobacterium bifidum*. *Bifidobacteria*, in particular, are very efficient at breaking down oligosaccharides such as lactose, sucrose, raffinose, and stachyose. The lactobacilli can help with the breakdown lactose in the small intestine. [146]

Enthusiasts claim that probiotics can reduce cholesterol, lower blood pressure, improve IBS symptoms, strengthen the immune system, and help prevent cancer.

Personally, I have found the evidence for some of these health claims is mixed or non-existent. There are, however, reasons to think that they might help with SIBO-related conditions. The bacteria in probiotics produce lactic acid that helps prevent the growth of unhealthy bacteria. Lactobacillus acidophilus and Bifidobacteria also produce little or no gas. You get the natural preservative lactic acid without the symptom-causing gas.

Only use high-quality probiotic supplements from reputable suppliers. Store them as directed. Take probiotics on a regular schedule as indicated on the label.

## Healthy Lifestyle Choices

*Avoid food and water poisoning.* Both can wreak havoc on your digestive tract by upsetting the natural balance of your gut bacteria. I trust and prefer my home water supply, but when I travel, I tend to drink bottled water simply because I don't know where the local supply comes from or how it was processed, transported or stored. The same holds true for foods, or even for foods rinsed with water that you can't trust.

*Exercise.* Exercise accomplishes two goals. Body movements help keep your intestinal contents moving, but exercise also drives your body's demand for carbohydrates. This demand induces more enzyme production, more complete digestion, and more movement of sugars from your digestive tract into your blood stream. Exercise isn't a complete solution, though. Extreme sports, weight lifting and endurance running can result in acid reflux from exertion, shaking and other movements that put pressure on your stomach and lower esophageal sphincter. This is an issue for IBS sufferers who are susceptible to acid reflux.

On a positive note: Because the Fast Tract Diet allows some high-carb (low-FP) foods, athletes who follow it can avoid the digestive symptoms sometimes associated with "carb loading" to increase glycogen storage levels.

*Rest.* Just one of the many reasons you need rest is that it helps your body have more energy for the hard work of digestion that requires strenuous, sustained and coordinated muscle contractions. Rest also reduces your stress level, the amount of acid your stomach produces between meals, and influences, if only indirectly, almost every aspect of your digestive process.

*Fast periodically.* Every few weeks or so, consume only water for several hours past your usual meal time, or even skip a meal entirely. Fasting gives your digestive system a break from the constant processing of food, giving it a chance to recover and prepare for more efficient digestion.

*Slow down!* How you eat is just as important as what you eat. Many of us race through our meals in an effort to save time for more pressing activities. But fast and furious eating is a severe disadvantage for your body's ability to digest food.

*Take smaller bites, eat slowly and chew well.* Consider counting to 20 on each mouthful. The amylase enzyme in your saliva can only act on small particles of food and only works until the starch reaches your stomach — at which point the amylase is destroyed. If your salivary amylase doesn't have the time to do its job, you'll have to rely on the pancreatic amylase in your small intestine, which is capable of finishing off the digestive process, but not the entire job of breaking down starches. I would never eat bread, rice, potatoes, corn, other wheat or grain products or pasta without chewing each bit to completion. If I didn't, these foods would absolutely give me symptoms.

## Monitor Your Progress

You may be wondering how long it takes to see results from this diet. For most people, IBS symptoms caused by over-consumption of difficult-to-digest carbohydrates should significantly improve over a period of one to three days. Some conditions that involve more extensive damage to the cells that line the intestine (advanced SIBO, celiac or Crohn's disease, cystic fibrosis, etc.) may require more time for the mucosal surface to heal.

Tracking your diet and symptoms is one of the most powerful tools you have in treating SIBO-related conditions with the Fast Tract Diet. Make a list of any digestive symptoms you have before you start the diet. Check your progress every week to see whether the symptoms have begun to subside. Also, record your meals and snacks as well as any medications or supplements you may be taking. In most cases, your symptoms should show improvement relatively quickly as you follow the diet, and you should be able to start checking symptoms off your list.

I've included a dietary journal template (Appendix C) to help you track the foods you eat and your symptoms. The journal can help you identify specific foods, potentially containing lactose, fructose, starches, fiber, or sugar alcohols that may be affecting you.

Once your symptoms have greatly improved or disappeared, you can consider adding back some favorite foods you've had to avoid. Some people are lactose tolerant and will be able to add back lactose-containing foods. Other people are tolerant of fructose and will be able to add back more fruits should they desire. Make these changes gradually, and keep careful track of how your digestive tract responds. Try not to increase different kinds of difficult to digest carbohydrates — for example, fructose and lactose — at the same time. Again, this gradual approach requires knowing which foods contain which carbohydrates. Separate any changes you make by at least a few days so that you can identify which changes affect your symptoms.

## If the Diet Isn't Working for you

After the first week on the diet, I would expect you to have experienced significant improvement in your symptoms. If not, the solution may be as simple as refocusing your efforts on following the diet — and eating fewer foods containing the five difficult-to-digest carbohydrates I have identified.

Changing your diet can be difficult. Business travel, restaurant dining, dinner with friends, or even your own preferences may make it difficult to stick to your resolutions. If you fall into this category, simple behavior-change strategies like keeping a food journal, giving yourself tangible incentives, or just clearing the foods you should avoid out of your refrigerator and pantry are more likely to succeed than simple will power.

## Tried that and it Didn't Work

If symptoms persist after a week on the diet, you should ask yourself the following questions:

*Did I follow the meal plan and recipes exactly?*

*Did I consume any additional carbohydrates (including wheat products, desserts, medicines, supplements, candy, gum, cough syrup, drinks etc.) that might have caused my symptoms to persist?*

*Was I practicing the healthy digestion techniques outlined in previous chapters such as eating slowly, chewing each bite extremely well, taking any needed supplements such as lactase if lactose intolerant, drinking enough water, exercising to improve peristalsis, etc.?*

*Do I suffer from an underlying condition that increases my IBS symptoms that requires diagnosis and treatment?* (Refer to chapter 8.)

The types of food you prepare are critical. They must truly be equivalent to the low FP foods recommended in the Week One Meal Plan. For instance, did you use short grain glutinous rice (or jasmine rice) instead of the high-FP varieties? It's important to follow the recipe for preparing this kind of rice closely to make sure the result is soft and fluffy, with a low FP. As an alternative, you can buy freshly-prepared sticky rice from a reputable sushi restaurant.

## Address Contributing Conditions

For persistent symptoms, here are a few more possibilities:

You may have a specific condition promoting SIBO, and you may want to consult with your health care provider to try to identify the problem. Any of the conditions discussed, such as motility issues, recent antibiotic use, gastric acid reduction, immune impairment, recent food poisoning or intestinal infection etc., can lead to SIBO. So can specific digestive disorders such as celiac disease and Crohn's disease, as well as systemic disorders that affect digestion, including diabetes, cystic fibrosis, etc. Diagnosing and treating such disorders may be an important part of the solution.

Food tolerance issues or enzyme deficiencies can also limit the effectiveness of the diet. A gluten-free diet may be necessary to help control the symptoms and progression of celiac disease. Or a high-quality lactase enzyme supplement may be necessary to reduce SIBO-related symptoms for people who are lactose-intolerant but continue to eat foods that contain lactose.

People who have an amylase deficiency have trouble digesting even small amounts of starch, including resistant starch (mainly amylose) and even the normally easy-to-digest starch amylopectin. An amylase enzyme supplement can greatly increase the efficiency of starch digestion for these individuals, including people with cystic fibrosis or pancreas problems that affect the digestion of starches.

If your symptoms are improving you might be able to consume leftover refrigerated starches without any trouble. But if you continue to have symptoms, avoid the leftover refrigerated or frozen rice mentioned in the recipes. Resistant starch can build up during cold storage. It's not as convenient to make small portions of rice, but your digestive system will be better off.

If you consume legumes, even in small amounts, you might consider taking Beano, a product that contains the enzyme alpha-d-galactosidase, before meals. This enzyme breaks down the complex sugars raffinose, stachyose and verbascose present in legumes down into simple sugars and sucrose that can be more efficiently digested and absorbed.

## Die Hard Symptoms

IBS symptoms that do not appear to respond to the low FP recipes in the diet plan could also be caused by duodenal or intragastric SIBO, where overgrowing bacteria are present in high numbers in the earliest part of the small intestine or even in the stomach. In this situation, even low FP foods that are normally digested and absorbed very quickly, could fuel SIBO, because the bacteria have access to food before any digestion can take place.

In this case, all carbohydrate-containing foods consumed, even glucose (dextrose), would have a reduced "effective" glycemic index and increased "effective" fermentation potential. We know this can occur based on research studies showing that glucose (FP=0 grams) can be used to detect SIBO via hydrogen breath testing, though at a reduced frequency compared to a non-digestible sugar such as lactulose. In other words, even low-FP, easy-to-digest carbs can be a problem in cases of severe SIBO. You'll have to limit these along with carbs in general to allow your system to clear bacteria from your upper small intestine.

If your symptoms are not responding to the low FP recipes, here are two additional options:

**Lower Your Daily FP Target**: Consider lowering your daily FP level to 20 grams per day. For instance, you may want to consume fewer mixed nuts, which, though low in net carbs, contain significant amounts of fiber, which adds to FP. Another tactic is to replace the rice and other starches in the meal plans with low FP vegetables, as the type of rice or the way it's being prepared or stored can generate resistant starch.

**Adopt A Very Low-Carbohydrate Diet**: For one to two weeks, consume less than 20 grams of total carbohydrates per day. Also, reduce your fiber intake during this time. Sweeten foods and desserts with **non-caloric sweeteners** only. Cease using dextrose as an option in the recipes.

When your symptoms subside, you can return to the standard low-FP approach.

**Note concerning Soy:** An ongoing debate challenges both reported health benefits of soy (lower prostate cancer in men, lower breast cancer in Asian women, etc.) and reported health detriments (lowered protein digestion from protease enzyme inhibitors, thyroid issues from estrogenic isoflavones, etc.) The debate is far from being resolved, but consuming fermented soy products in moderation and limiting unfermented soy products such as soy milk and tofu to a few servings per week may be prudent until these issues are resolved. If you have sensitivties or allergies to soy, simply replace soy in Fast Tract recipes with low FP alternatives such as ground beef, chicken, or veggies.

CHAPTER 13:

# The Fast Tract Plan

"DOING THE
RIGHT THING HAS
POWER."
—LAURA LINNEY

For your first two weeks on the diet, I recommend following the Week One and Week Two Meal Plans contained in Appendix A. They contain recipes for every meal, snack and dessert you'll need for those first weeks. They'll help you improve your symptoms immediately, while you gain experience preparing low-FP recipes.

The recipes in the meal plans represent a blend of traditional American and Japanese foods. The ingredients include fresh seafood, beef, chicken and pork, a wide variety of vegetables, soy-based foods like tofu, and low-amylose starches like Russet Burbank potatoes and jasmine or sticky rice. All of the ingredients are easy to digest and absorb because they possess low fermentative potential values. And they are easy to find in your local market or, for a few items, a grocery store that carries Asian foods.

### Preparing Recipes and Weighing Foods

The recipes are easy to prepare, and pretty much self-explanatory. Just make sure you use the specific kinds of food listed in the recipes without substitutions, particularly with regard to starches.

Ingredient amounts and serving sizes are listed in ounces and grams. I recommend buying a good kitchen, diet, or shipping scale that is accurate from a pound or two down to one tenth of an ounce. Not only do you want to make sure that you're preparing the recipes properly, but serving sizes will often need to be adjusted (downward) to make FP limits. The scale will help you check and/or modify recipes, especially as you begin to develop your own.

## Meal Plans for Week One and Week Two

I have developed complete meal plans and recipes — including meals, snacks, and desserts — for the first two weeks of the diet (see Appendix A) to make it as easy as possible for you to get started. The average daily FP level is approximately 30 grams.

Both the Week One and Week Two Meal Plans include seven breakfast, seven lunch, and seven dinner choices, as well as snacks and desserts. Some of the recipes make one or two servings, while others are written for more servings. In each case, the ingredient amounts can be adjusted accordingly to the number of desired servings — or leftovers can be refrigerated or frozen (while considering the storage limitations for starches if you have persistent symptoms).

You can also use the recipes to develop a shopping list to make sure you have all of the foods and ingredients you need on hand. During these first two weeks, make every effort to eat only the meals, snacks and desserts listed in the meal plan. The more you stick to the plan, the better your chances of getting results.

The Meal Plans provide specific instructions on allowed drinks. Note the limit of two caffeinated drinks and one alcoholic drink per day during this first week. Also note that certain drinks, sweeteners, mixes and certain types of wine are not allowed. After week one, alcoholic drinks are only limited by the FP guidelines for beer, wine and mixes as alcohol itself does not contribute to FP (though it may have a slight effect on glycemic index and therefore FP).

## Wheat

The Week One Meal Plan does not include foods that contain wheat. All wheat (and rye and barley) contains gluten while many wheat products also contain significant amounts of resistant starch. Gluten and resistant starch could be a factor in some people's IBS symptoms. Some condiments used in the meal plan recipes may contain small amounts of gluten, but in each case, gluten-free products are available if you suspect you are intolerant of even small amounts of gluten. For most people, this will not be necessary.

The Week Two Meal Plan contains a few wheat products, providing an opportunity to check whether this leads to an increase in your symptoms. After week two, you may consume small amounts of wheat-containing products — in accordance with FP limits — to determine if your own digestive system can tolerate these foods. If you suspect you have problems with wheat, you might consider reading *Wheat Belly* by William Davis.

## Carbs

Both week one and week two meal plans contain some higher carb foods such as rice, parsnips, dextrose, etc. Higher carb foods can be unhealthy for people with metabolic disorders, diabetes or other problems relating to high blood sugar levels. If you fall into one of these groups or simply prefer a lower carb lifestyle, replace the higher carb foods with lower carb options. The purpose of this book is to control SIBO and IBS symptoms for as many people as possible supporting the widest possible range of dietary preferences. But the diet is flexible for a variety of eating styles as long as FP levels are controlled.

## Moving On

Once you've gotten good results — in the form of reduced symptoms — from the Week One Plan, it's time to move on to the Week Two

Plan. (If not, return to the troubleshooting section above.) By the end of the second week, you'll have learned how to prepare a wide variety of low-FP foods.

You'll find that you're consulting the FP tables in Appendix B regularly.

First, you can use them to determine foods and serving sizes that fit your target FP values for each meal and for each day.

One good first step is to set a daily limit on total FP for each day. I recommend keeping your total FP grams per day under forty for the first few weeks.

When you're developing your own daily plans, choose serving sizes that seem reasonable, and then check the FP value. If necessary, adjust the serving sizes to meet your FP goal.

For example, let's say that you have already consumed an FP of 33 grams for the day, but want to have a piece of chocolate for dessert. The Table 14 lists 1.6 ounces (44 grams) of chocolate as having an FP value of 15 grams. If you want to keep your daily FP under 40 grams, you'll need to reduce the serving size of the chocolate. In this case, you could only eat about one half the amount or 0.8 ounces (22 grams) to limit FP to 7.5 grams. If your piece of chocolate weighed 1.6 ounces (about the size of a Hershey bar), you could just break it in half — or you could actually weigh it on a scale.

Or, if you want to have blueberries and cream but you only have 6 FP grams available for dessert, just reduce the amount from the 120 gram serving size listed in the Table 11 (FP 10 grams) to 74 grams (1/2 cup) which has an FP of 5 grams. One-quarter cup of cream would add 1 FP gram for a total of 6 grams.

The tables can also serve as a good source for creating shopping lists. For instance, before shopping for fruits, notice that the low-FP fruits include: fresh watermelon, cantaloupe, dates, strawberries, pineapple, peaches, lychee and (fresh) apricots. Other berries and fruits are acceptable, but only in limited amounts.

It might help to do a quick scan of the tables and familiarize yourself with the foods at the top of each table (low-FP, IBS-friendly) and the foods at the bottom of each table (high-FP, less IBS-friendly).

Notice that some tables, such as Table 10 (for vegetables) contain mostly low-FP, IBS-friendly foods, while other tables, such as Table 8 (for pasta) contain mostly high-FP IBS-unfriendly foods.

### Creating Your Own Recipes

At some point you'll feel the urge to create your own new recipes. One relatively easy way is to adapt the existing recipes with new ingredients or in new combinations.

Whether adapting existing recipes or creating entirely new recipes, you'll follow the same Fermentative Potential (FP) guidelines used to develop the Week One and Week Two Meal Plans. This way, your new recipes are unlikely to cause new or recurring symptoms.

Again, you'll need to consult the FP tables in Appendix B. These tables contain FP values for over 360 different types of food. The FP tables are based on food types and list serving sizes in both ounces and grams.

Use your scale to check and adjust your ingredients against the values in the tables. You can also compare to the values given for the existing recipes. (Note that the serving sizes in the tables were chosen for uniformity in comparing FP values.)

### What About Foods That Aren't Listed?

There are several reasons that specific foods may not be listed in the FP tables. These include:

1. *The glycemic index value, required to calculate the FP value, may not exist.* This could be because the food has so few carbs that the test cannot be done. (Or people can't eat enough of the food to reach the 50 grams of carbs needed for the test.)

In most cases, this means that the food doesn't contain enough carbs to be a threat and you can eat them without much concern. In many of these cases, such as low-carb vegetables, I have approximated an FP value based on an estimated GI. (The average GI for known vegetables is 62. An estimated GI of 50 for vegetables is conservative and errs on the side of caution).

*2. The food is not very common and no one has thought (or paid) to perform the GI test on the food.*

*3. The food has no carbs. In this case, that also means that the FP is zero and you can consume it without limit.* I have included some of these foods such as meats, cheeses, and seafood.

*4. The food is not common to North America and including it would be of limited value.*

In the case of 2 and 4, the GI can be estimated based on similar foods and an estimated FP can then be calculated. The best approach in these cases is to err on the side of caution with a lower GI estimate (50 or lower) giving a higher FP.

In cases where you cannot find the food in the FP tables, determine whether there are appreciable carbs in the food. If not, the food can be considered safe to consume in normal quantities. If you find a food that is not in the tables, but you are able to find the GI value, serving size, net carbs, sugar alcohol and fiber levels for the food, you can calculate the FP value yourself using the formula for FP given below (some people make their own spreadsheet with the formula for quick calculations):

$$FP = \frac{(100 - GI) \times NC}{100} + DF + SA$$

As a reminder: To calculate FP, you plug in the values for net carbs (NC), dietary fiber (DF), sugar alcohols (SA), and the glycemic index (GI) for each food. Now you can calculate the fermentation potential. If there are no sugar alcohols or fiber, the values for those variables are zero.

As you begin, keep in mind that you are embarking on a new way of eating. Don't get too stressed about the details. Over time, you will easily recognize low FP, IBS friendly foods and feel much better than you did before. I am sure of it.

**Appendix A:**

# The Meal Plan and Recipes

# Week One Fast Tract Diet Plan

### DAY 1 — Daily FP 35 grams

*Breakfast: Morning Berry Smoothie and Black Forest Ham &
Cheese roll-ups — Serves 1 — FP 9 grams*

### Berry Smoothie
$^1/_2$ cup strawberries (or blueberries)

$^1/_2$ cup plain unsweetened yogurt

$^1/_2$ cup light cream

Low FP sweetener to taste

*Combine all ingredients in a blender. Blend until smooth. Serve chilled.*

### Roll-ups

2 slices of Black Forest Ham (or other ham)

2 slices of American or Swiss cheese

*Roll the ham and cheese up together. Serve.*

### Lunch: Caesar Salad with Lime Chicken – Serves 2 — FP 4 grams

2 small heads romaine lettuce

8 strips chicken breast

$^1/_2$ lime, squeezed

1 tablespoon soy sauce

1 pinch pepper

2 tablespoons extra virgin olive oil

2 tablespoons freshly chopped parsley leaves

*Prepare marinade by combining lime juice, soy sauce and pepper. Cover
chicken with marinade and refrigerate for 2-3 hours. Sauté marinated
chicken with olive oil over medium high heat for 2 minutes on each side or
until done.*

### Caesar Dressing

$1/2$ cup extra virgin olive oil

2 tablespoons white balsamic vinegar

4 anchovy filets, minced

$1/4$ teaspoon garlic, grated

$1/2$ cup parmesan cheese, freshly grated

$1/4$ lemon, squeezed

1 pinch fresh ground pepper

1 pinch sea salt

*Mix all ingredients in a bowl until creamy. Remove ends of lettuce heads, wash and slice down the middle the long way. Lay one opened head of lettuce on each plate. Place chicken strips over lettuce. Drizzle with dressing and sprinkle with chopped parsley.*

### Snack: Sweetened Nut Mix — Makes 12 daily servings —2 ounce serving allowed per day—FP 9 grams

$1^1/2$ pounds of mixed nuts (6 ounces each of almonds, walnuts, cashews, and pecans)

1 egg white, beaten until frothy

$1^1/2$ tablespoons of butter, melted in microwave and cooled

$3/4$ cup equivalent of low FP sweetener

$3/4$ teaspoon sea salt

2 teaspoons ground cinnamon

1 teaspoons coconut oil

*Beat egg white in large bowl. Blend in salt, sweetener, cooled butter, and cinnamon. Add nuts and mix to coat. Spread the mixture on a large coconut oiled baking pan and bake at 260 degrees for 45 minutes stirring each 15 minutes. Allow mix to cool and store in an airtight container.*

*Note: 2 ounces of snack mix are allowed for each day. I recommend weighing out 2 ounce portions for each day and storing in separate baggies. As your symptoms subside, you may be able to increase this amount gradually. And you can always trade FP points by substituting other foods of equal FP with more nuts.*

*Dinner: Orange Balsamic Salmon, Sautéed Asparagus and Portobello mushrooms— Serves 2 — FP 8 grams*

### Salmon

    1 pound salmon

    1.5 tablespoons balsamic vinegar

    2.5 tablespoons soy sauce

    $^1/_8$ wedge fresh orange, squeezed

    2 pinches fresh ground pepper

*Mix balsamic vinegar, soy sauce and fresh orange squeeze and marinate salmon for 3 hours. Broil in high for 20-23 minutes.*

### Portobello Mushrooms

    2 Portobello mushrooms, sliced

    2 cloves garlic, sliced

    2 tablespoons extra virgin olive oil

    1 pinch salt

    1 pinch pepper, freshly ground

*Sauté garlic on medium high heat in olive oil for approximately 30 seconds. Add mushrooms and sauté mixture on medium to medium high heat for approximately 5 minutes.*

### Asparagus

    8 ounces asparagus

    2 tablespoons extra virgin olive oil

    1 pinch salt

    1 pinch pepper, freshly ground

*Remove ends and sauté asparagus on medium high heat in olive oil. Add salt and pepper.*

### Dessert: Cheesecake — Serves 8 — FP 5 grams

2  8-ounce containers of cream cheese, warmed to
room temperature

1 cup equivalent of low FP sweetener

3 large eggs

1 teaspoon vanilla extract

$^3/_4$ cup heavy cream

*Gently beat together all warmed ingredients, adding the eggs and cream gradually. Do not over-beat. Add the filling to pie crust (recipe below) and bake at 350 degrees for 1 hour. Cool and then refrigerate. Serve with whipped cream (recipe below) and berries if desired. Freeze leftovers.*

### Almond Crust — makes one pie

$1^1/_2$ cup ground almond flour

4 tablespoon equivalents of low FP sweetener

$^1/_4$ cup butter, melted

*Mix together almond flour, sweetener, and melted butter. Press mixture into a greased 9-inch pie pan covering both the bottom and sides of the pan.*

### Whipped Cream — Serves 8

1 cup heavy cream, chilled

Low FP sweetener to taste

1 teaspoon vanilla extract

*In a mixing bowl, combine chilled cream, sweetener and vanilla extract. Set bowl inside a larger bowl filled with crushed ice. (To keep the cream chilled) Whip the cream with an electric mixer until light and fluffy.*

### DAY 2 — Daily FP 33 grams

**Breakfast: Fried Eggs and Bacon — Serves 1 — FP 0 grams**

2 eggs

4 slices bacon (or sausage)

1 teaspoon extra virgin olive oil

*Cook bacon (or sausage) in pan until crisp (browned). Remove from pan and drain on paper towel. In the same pan, fry eggs in olive oil or butter at medium high heat over easy, sunny side up or scramble as preferred. Add a slice of cheese if desired. Serve.*

**Lunch: Greek Salad with Grilled Shrimp — Serves 2 — FP 8 grams**
**Grilled Shrimp**

1 pound large shrimp

2 tablespoons extra virgin olive oil

$^1/_4$ lemon, squeezed

2 pinches salt

2 pinches pepper, freshly ground

*Coat shrimp with olive oil, lemon juice, salt and paper. Broil on high heat for 10-12 minutes (or sauté). Place on salad.*

**Greek Salad**

$^1/_2$ head of iceberg lettuce

$^1/_2$ tomato, cut in wedges

$^1/_4$ sweet onion

2 artichoke hearts in oil

$^1/_4$ English cucumber

8  black olives

$^1/_2$ cup feta cheese

3 tablespoons extra virgin olive oil

2 tablespoons balsamic vinegar

*Mix vegetables with olive oil and vinegar. Top with feta cheese, shrimp and Greek dressing (recipe below). Serve*

### *Greek Dressing*

$^3/_4$ cup extra virgin olive oil

$^1/_4$ cup white vinegar

2 tablespoons lemon juice

1 garlic clove, minced

1 tablespoon dried oregano

1 tablespoon dried basil

1 pinch salt and pepper

*Mix the olive oil, vinegar and lemon juice in a jar. Add the garlic, oregano, basil, and salt and pepper.*

### *Snack: Yogurt w/cantaloupe – Serves 1 — FP 7 grams*

$^1/_2$ cup of yogurt

$^1/_2$ cup cantaloupe

*Cut cantaloupe into cubes and add to yogurt. Sweeten with low FP sweetener to taste and serve.*

### *Dinner: Grilled Steak, Butternut Squash and Sautéed Spinach — Serves 2 — FP 15 grams*

1 rib eye (or similar) grilling steak (about 16-18 ounces)

8 ounces butternut squash (about half of one squash), peeled and diced

8 ounces spinach

2 cloves garlic, thinly sliced

1 tablespoon extra virgin olive oil

2 teaspoons butter

2 pinches salt

2 pinch freshly ground pepper

*Pat steaks with salt and pepper. Grill or broil steaks until medium rare or desired doneness. Steam squash until fully cooked. Add butter, one pinch salt and one pinch pepper and mash. Sauté spinach and sliced garlic with one tablespoon olive oil. Add salt and pepper. Serve*

### Dessert: Creamy Custard with Strawberries — Serves 6 — FP 3 grams

4 eggs

2 cups strawberries, sliced

2 cups heavy cream

$^3/_4$ cup equivalents of low FP sweetener

2 teaspoons vanilla extract

$^1/_2$ teaspoon salt

1 teaspoon nutmeg

1 teaspoon cinnamon

*Preheat the oven to 325 degrees. Pour boiling water into a large baking tray to come up about 1/3 to the top. Whisk eggs together with other ingredients except nutmeg, cinnamon and strawberries. Pour mixture into an 8 x 8 inch baking dish and sprinkle nutmeg and cinnamon over the top. Set the baking dish inside a baking tray making sure the hot water comes up to the level of the custard in the baking dish. Bake for 45 minutes to 1 hour or until a knife inserted in the center comes out clean. Cool and chill to allow custard to set. Sprinkle with nutmeg or cinnamon and add fresh strawberries before serving.*

*Note: Be careful not to get scalded moving the dish to and from the oven.*

### DAY 3 — Daily FP 33 grams

*Breakfast: Spinach & Cheddar Cheese Omelet — Serves 1 — FP 2 grams*

  2 eggs

  1 cup fresh raw spinach

  2 ounces cheddar cheese, grated

  4 teaspoons extra virgin olive oil or butter

*Sauté spinach with two teaspoons oil or butter in a pan until tender. Remove from pan. Heat remaining olive oil or butter in a pan at medium-high heat. Whisk eggs in a small bowl and pour them into the pan. Lift eggs at their edges with a spatula and tip the pan to make sure the egg mixture is cooked. Place spinach over the eggs and sprinkle with cheese. Turn the heat down to medium. Use your spatula to fold the omelet in half. Cook for 2-3 more minutes. Slide the omelet onto a plate.*

  Note: *Serve alone or with 2-4 slices bacon or sausage.*

*Lunch: Buffalo Chicken Wings— Serves 2 — FP 6 grams*

  2 ¹/₂ pounds chicken wings

  ¹/₂ cup buffalo wing sauce (Stone Wall Kitchen or equivalent)

  ¹/₂ tablespoon butter

  ¹/₄ lemon, squeezed

  ¹/₄ cup blue cheese dressing

  2 celery stems, cut into 6 pieces each.

*Add a pinch of salt and pepper to the wings and bake for approximately 25 minutes on each side at 425 degrees on a broiling pan. Remove wings and place in a bowl. Coat with butter, lemon juice and wing sauce. Serve with blue cheese dressing and celery.*

### Snack: Kettle Corn Style Popcorn — Serves 2 — FP 6 grams

1 bag microwave popcorn

Low FP sweetener to taste

2 teaspoons butter

*Follow the microwave directions to prepare popcorn. Melt butter in microwave. Drizzle melted butter over the popcorn. Add sweetener and mix. Limit to 1 ounce per serving.*

### Dinner: Pork Roast w/pear sauce, Parmesan Cheese Broccoli and Celery Root Mash— Serves 3— FP 13 grams

1 Pork roast or tenderloin — about 1 ¹/₂ pounds

10 ounces broccoli (1 large head)

¹/₄ cup parmesan cheese, grated

7 ounces celery root (celeriac), peeled and diced

2 tablespoons extra virgin olive oil

2 tablespoons butter

2 cloves garlic, minced

2 cloves garlic, thinly sliced

1 tablespoon rosemary

1 tablespoon thyme

Salt and pepper

*Preheat oven to 350 degrees. Rub pork tenderloin with one tablespoon of olive oil and pat with rosemary, thyme, minced garlic, salt and pepper. Bake for approximately 90 minutes or until pork is fully cooked. Remove pork roast from heat and let sit for 10 minutes. Cover with pear sauce (see recipe below) before serving.*

*Steam celery root until tender. Mash and add salt, pepper and butter to taste. Sauté broccoli with garlic in olive oil on medium high heat for 2 to 3 minutes. Sprinkle with parmesan cheese.*

### Pear Sauce

1 pear, grated

Low FP sweetener to taste

2 tablespoons brandy

$^1/_8$ lemon, squeezed

*Mix all ingredients in a pan. Cook on low heat for 5 minutes.*

### Dessert: Mixed Berries with Cream — Serves 1 — FP 6 grams

$^1/_4$ cup blueberries

$^1/_2$ cup strawberries, sliced

$^1/_2$ cup of heavy or light cream

Low FP sweetener to taste

*Mix berries with cream, add sweetener and*

*Serve.*

### DAY 4 — Daily FP 29 grams

**Breakfast: Cottage Cheese, Melon and Hard Boiled Eggs — Serves 1 — FP 5 grams**

$^1/_2$ cup cottage cheese

$^1/_2$ cup cantaloupe melon, diced

2 eggs

1 pinch salt

1 teaspoon butter

*Bring approximately eight cups of water to a boil. Carefully place egg(s) in the boiling water with a large spoon. Boil egg for 12 minutes. Carefully replace hot water with cold water. Serve salted, buttered eggs with cottage cheese and melon.*

**Lunch: Bacon Cheeseburger with Sautéed Mushrooms and Parsnips chips— Serves 2 — FP 7 grams**

12 ounces pound ground beef

2 slices cheddar (or American) cheese

4 slices bacon

5 mushrooms

4 romaine lettuce leaves

2 slices of onion

2 slices tomato

2 dill pickles

1 large parsnip

*Prepare two ground beef patties and grill or pan fry in 1 tablespoon olive oil over medium high heat until cooked to desired doneness, adding cheese slice towards the end. Place cheeseburgers on bed of lettuce. Cook bacon and dry on paper towel. In a bit of the remaining bacon fat, sauté mushrooms (add onions if desired) and place on cheeseburger with bacon. Serve with pickle and parsnip chips (recipe below).*

*Parsnip chips*

*Use potato peeler to cut long thin strips of parsnips. Pat dry on paper towel and fry in 1 cup of olive oil (or remaining bacon fat) heated to temperature on medium high heat. Keep the parsnips chips moving as they cook quickly. When crisp, place on paper towel and add salt.*

*Note: Eat slowly and chew parsnip chips well to increase digestion efficiency.*

### Snack: Celery with Cream Cheese — Serves 1 — FP 1 gram

2 celery stocks, cut in thirds

6 olives, sliced

2 ounces cream cheese

*Spread cream cheese onto celery stocks. Add sliced olives. For variation, try peanut butter in place of cream cheese and olives.*

### Dinner: Scallops and Shrimp Sauté with Brussels Sprouts and Carrots— Serves 2 — FP 12 gram

$^2/_3$ pound large scallops

$^2/_3$ pound large shrimp

3 cloves garlic, sliced

4 tablespoons extra virgin olive oil

2 stems of parsley leaves, minced

2 pinches fresh ground pepper

*Sauté sliced garlic for 1 – 2 minutes in two tablespoons olive oil on medium high heat. Add shrimp and scallops and sauté 5 – 7 minutes. Sprinkle with minced parsley leaves right before they are done.*

### Boiled Carrot

1 medium carrot, three slices per inch

1 teaspoon butter

1 pinch salt

1 pinch paprika

1 pinch cinnamon

*Boil carrot in salted water for approximately 10minutes or until it soft-ens. Add butter, cinnamon and paprika and heat in the same pan on low heat to melt the butter.*

### Sautéed Brussels Sprouts

8 ounces Brussels sprouts

3 tablespoons extra virgin olive oil

1 pinch salt and freshly ground pepper

*Remove Brussels sprouts stems. Sauté in two tablespoons olive oil on medium – medium high heat for 5-7 minutes until done. Add salt and pepper.*

### Dessert: Lactose-Free Ice Cream — Serves 1 — FP 6 grams

1/2 cup lactose-free Breyers ice cream

*Serve the ice cream adding a few nuts and berries if desired.*

## DAY 5 — Daily FP 38 grams

### *Breakfast: Tofu Smoothie— Serves 1 — FP 7 grams*

$^1/_3$ cup blackberries (or $^1/_3$ cup blueberries)

$^1/_2$ container silken tofu

$^1/_2$ cup light cream

Low FP sweetener to taste

*Combine all ingredients in a blender. Blend until smooth. Serve chilled.*

*Note: Additionally, you can have up to 2 ounces cheese, 2 strips of breakfast meat (bacon, sausage, ham, etc.) or a hardboiled egg if desired.*

### *Lunch: Chef Salad — Serves 1 — FP 3 grams*

2-3 cups iceberg or leafy green lettuce

2 cherry tomatoes

3 slices English cucumber

2 slices green pepper

3 slices each of turkey and ham, sliced in strips

2 ounces mozzarella cheese

1 hard-boiled egg, quartered

4-6 black olives

2 tablespoons extra virgin olive oil

1 tablespoon balsamic vinegar

$^1/_2$ pinch of salt

$^1/_2$ pinch of freshly grounded paper

*Arrange all ingredients in a large serving bowl. Dress with mixture of olive oil and vinegar. Add salt and pepper. Alternatively, dress with Italian or Greek bottled dressing.*

### *Snack: Spiced Nut Mix — 2 Ounces Per Serving — FP 9 grams*

3 cups Rice Chex cereal

9 cup mixed nuts

3 tablespoons butter

2 tablespoons Worcestershire sauce

1 $1/2$ teaspoons seasoned salt

$3/4$ teaspoon garlic powder

$1/2$ teaspoon onion powder

*Combine Rice Chex and nuts in a large microwavable bowl. Melt butter in microwave for about 25 seconds. Add spices and Worcestershire sauce to melted butter and oil, mix and add to snack mix. Mix combination with large spoon. Heat in microwave on high for six minutes, pausing to mix every two minutes. Spread on paper towels to cool, about 20 minutes. Serve or store in an airtight container.*

*Note: I recommend weighing out 2 ounce portions for each day and storing in separate baggies. You can use either the salty snack recipe or the Sweet Nut Mix recipe. In both cases, 2 ounces per day are allowed. Once your symptoms are totally gone, you can up the serving size to 3 ounces per day.*

### *Dinner: Beef and Broccoli with Jasmine Rice – Serves 2 — FP 12 grams*

1.2 pounds rib eye or other quality steak, thinly sliced.

10 ounces (one medium head) of broccoli, cut up.

2 tablespoons extra virgin olive oil

1 tablespoon sesame oil

2 tablespoons gluten-free soy sauce

1 tablespoon sake (rice wine)

$1/2$ tablespoon equivalent of low FP sweetener

$1/4$ cup of beef broth or water

1 $1/2$ teaspoons oyster sauce

3 cloves garlic, thinly sliced

1 ounce ginger, thinly sliced

2 pinches freshly ground pepper

$^{1}/_{2}$ teaspoon white sesame seeds

1 cup jasmine rice

1 $^{1}/_{2}$ cup water

*Combine rice with water in a medium saucepan (if using rice cooker, use 1 $^{3}/_{4}$ cups water) and stir. Bring to boil uncovered on high heat. Reduce heat and simmer covered for 15 minutes. Don't remove the cover while cooking. Remove from heat and let stand covered for 5-7 minutes. Fluff with spatula before serving.*

*Mix beef, soy sauce, sake, sweetener and pepper in a bowl. Stir fry garlic and ginger in olive oil / sesame oil on high heat for 30 seconds. Add beef and continue to stir fry until the meat is half cooked. Add broccoli and $^{1}/_{4}$ cup of beef broth or water. Continue to stir fry until the broccoli is cooked al dente. Add oyster sauce and sesame seeds and stir before removing from heat.*

*Serve with jasmine rice, sprinkle beef and broccoli with white sesame seeds and red pepper if desired.*

*Note: Only consume $^{1}/_{2}$ cup of rice unless your symptoms are completely under control, in which case $^{3}/_{4}$ cup of rice is allowed.*

### Dessert: Milk Chocolate— Serves 1 — FP 7 grams

$^{1}/_{2}$ Hershey's bar or other milk chocolate bar (0.8 Ounce)

## DAY 6 — Daily FP 36 grams

*Breakfast: Asparagus and Sausage Quiche — Serves 4 — FP 7 grams*

    6 large eggs

    $^1/_2$ pound Italian sausage

    1 cup asparagus, steamed, chopped and cooled

    1 $^1/_2$ cups cheddar or Monterey Jack cheese, shredded

*Cook sausage completely at medium to medium-high heat and set aside. Whisk eggs until well blended. Add asparagus, shredded cheese and cooked, then cooled sausage. Mix well. Pour mixture into pie crust (recipe below). Bake at 350 degrees for 45 minutes. Let cool for 10 minutes.*

*Almond Crust — makes one quiche*

    1 cup ground almond flour (thinner crust OK for quiche)

    3 tablespoons butter, melted

*Mix together almond flour and melted butter. Press the mixture into a greased 8 or 9-inch pie pan covering both the bottom and sides of the pan.*

*Note: Can make this dish in advance and refrigerate or freeze for quick breakfasts.*

*Lunch: Meatballs with Roasted Peppers — Serves 2 — FP 12 grams*

    1 pound ground beef

    1 cup tomato sauce (Use a brand with the fewest overall carb count.)

    $^1/_2$ pound mixed (green, yellow and red) peppers

    $^1/_4$ sweet onion, finely chopped

    2 medium mushrooms, finely chopped

    1 egg, beaten

    $^1/_4$ cup freshly grated parmesan cheese

    1 clove of garlic, crushed and chopped

    1 teaspoon dried basil (or 1 tablespoon fresh basil)

$^1/_4$ teaspoon salt

$^1/_4$ teaspoon pepper

1 $^1/_2$ teaspoons extra virgin olive oil

$^1/_2$ teaspoon butter

*Sauté sweet onion and mushrooms in olive oil and butter. Add garlic, basil, salt and pepper and continue to sauté for another minute. In a large bowl, add this mixture to the ground beef mix briefly and add beaten eggs. Mix well and form into meatballs. Preheat the oven to 325 degrees and bake meatballs until browned and well cooked, approximately 35 minutes.*

*Place meatballs in 1 cup of tomato sauce and heat until sauce begins to boil. While the sauce simmers, coat peppers with olive oil, salt and pepper. Grill (or sauté) peppers and serve with meatballs and sauce.*

*Note: Do not consume more than $^1/_2$ cup of tomato sauce per serving.*

### Snack: Lactose-Free Ice Cream — Serves 1 — FP 5 grams

$^1/_2$ cup lactose-free Breyers ice cream

*Serve the ice cream adding a few nuts and berries if desired.*

### Dinner: Burgundy Chicken with Parsnips and Mushrooms — Serves 2 — FP 7 grams

1.2 pounds boneless chicken thigh

1 parsnip, peeled and cut into one inch slices

$^1/_4$ medium sweet onion, quartered

1 stem celery, cut in thirds (only for flavor – not to eat)

6 cloves garlic, whole with skin removed

2 tablespoons extra virgin olive oil

1 cup (dry) red wine

$^1/_4$ cup balsamic vinegar

1 $^1/_2$ tablespoons gluten-free soy sauce

1 tablespoon **equivalent of low FP sweetener**

1 pinch salt

2 pinches freshly ground pepper

*Sauté parsnip, onion, celery, and garlic in olive oil on medium high heat for one minute. Add chicken pieces (uncut), salt and pepper and sauté on medium heat for 2 minutes on each side. Add wine, vinegar, soy sauce and sweetener. Bring to boil then remove from heat. Transfer to glass baking dish and bake at 325 degrees for 45 minutes.*

### Cremini Mushrooms

5 ounces cremini mushrooms, sliced

1 tablespoon extra virgin olive oil

1 tablespoon butter

*Sauté mushrooms in butter, olive oil, salt and pepper on high heat for one to two minutes. Serve with chicken.*

### Dessert: Key Lime Pie — Serves 8 — FP 5 grams

4 egg yolks, beaten

1 ³/₄ cups light cream

¹/₂ cup lime juice (about 4 limes, key limes are not necessary)

2 teaspoons gelatin

3 teaspoons lime zest (gratings of lime skin)

4 tablespoon equivalents of low FP sweetener

2 cups whipped cream (Refer to Day 1 recipe)

Almond crust (recipe below)

*Preheat the oven to 375 degrees. Beat the egg yolks. Wisk the gelatin together with the lime juice, lime zest and sweetener. Combine and mix the light cream, egg yolks and lime juice. Pour the mixture into the prebaked pie crust (recipe below) and bake for 12 to 15 minutes. Remove and cool, then refrigerate. Add whipped cream and serve with a lime wedge.*

### Almond Crust — makes one pie

1$^{1}$/$_{2}$ cup ground almond flour

4 tablespoon equivalents of low FP sweetener

$^{1}$/$_{4}$ cup butter, melted

*Mix together almond flour, sweetener, and butter. Press the mixture into a greased 9-inch pie pan covering both the bottom and sides of the pan. Prebake the crust at 375 degrees for about 7 minutes.*

*It takes about 15 key limes to make* $^{1}$/$_{2}$ *cup of key lime juice. Substituting 3-4 regular limes seems to work fine.*

### DAY 7 — Daily FP 34 Grams

*Breakfast: Steak and Eggs— Serves 2 — FP 2 grams*

1 small rib eye (or similar) grilling steak (about 12 ounces)

4 eggs

2 tablespoons heavy cream

4 strawberries, sliced in half

2 teaspoons butter

2 pinches salt

1 pinch freshly ground pepper

*Grill or broil steaks until medium rare or desired doneness. Whisk eggs with cream and scramble in a pan with butter over medium high heat. Serve steak and eggs with strawberries.*

*Lunch: Kielbasa, Vegetable Salad— Serves 1 — FP 12 grams*

7 ounces Kielbasa

1 tablespoon extra virgin olive oil

$^1/_4$ English cumber, diamond cut

$^1/_2$ medium tomato, diced

$^1/_8$ yellow pepper, diced

$^1/_4$ small red onion, chopped

$^2/_3$ cup broccoli, chopped into medium size pieces

*Broil kielbasa with high heat on a sheet of foil for 3-4 minutes per side adding broccoli with olive oil when you turn the Kielbasa. Slice kielbasa on an angle. Slice cucumber down the middle, and then cut on an angle (diamond shape). Mix all ingredients in a bowl with 2 tablespoons dressing (recipe below).*

### Lemon Thyme Dressing

$^1/_2$ cup extra virgin olive oil

$^1/_2$ lemon, squeezed

$1^1/_2$ tablespoons white balsamic vinegar

1 teaspoon dried thyme

1 pinch salt

1 pinch freshly ground pepper

*Mix all ingredients and shake. Store remainder of dressing refrigerated.*

### Snack: Yogurt and Blueberries— Serves 1— FP 7 grams

$^1/_2$ cup yogurt

$^1/_4$ cup blue berries

Low FP sweetener to taste

*Serve yogurt with berries and sweetener.*

### Dinner: Miso Sea Bass with Bok Choy, Shiitake Mushrooms and Asian Sticky Rice— Serves 2— FP 6 grams

20 ounces Chilean Sea Bass (or other white fish)

$1^1/_2$ tablespoons white miso

$1^1/_2$ teaspoon equivalents of low FP sweetener

2 tablespoons sake (rice wine)

$^1/_8$ lemon, squeezed (1 teaspoon juice)

1 teaspoon finely sliced lemon peel

*Preheat oven to 375 degrees. Cut sea bass in half. Remove skin with sharp knife. Mix miso, sweetener, sake, lemon juice and lemon peel together for glaze.*

*Coat a broiling pan with olive oil and place fish on pan. Bake for approximately 12-15 minutes. Remove and coat with miso glaze. Broil on high for an additional 5 to 7 minutes to brown the miso glaze.*

### Asian Sticky Rice — Makes 5 servings

1 cup Asian glutinous sticky rice (no substitutions)

1 cup water

*Prepare sticky rice in advance. Rinse rice with cold water three to four times or until water runs clear. Mix rice with water and soak for 10 minutes prior to cooking in a rice cooker. Turn on the rice cooker. Don't open the lid for approximately 20 minutes. Let the rice sit for another 10 minutes. Fluff rice prior to serving. Limit to $^1/_2$ cup per serving until all symptoms are gone. At that point, $^3/_4$ cup servings are allowed.*

*Note: If you do not have a rice cooker, there are You Tube videos for directions on how to prepare sticky rice on the stove top.*

### Sautéed Bok Choy and Shiitake Mushrooms

2 stems of medium bok choy

3 ounces shitake mushrooms, quartered

2 tablespoons extra virgin olive oil

1 tablespoon sesame oil

1 ounce of ginger sliced

1 tablespoon oyster sauce

1 pinch freshly ground pepper

*Slice each bok choy stem vertically into quarters. Remove ends and wash thoroughly. Sauté ginger in olive oil and sesame oil for 30 seconds on high heat. Add bok choy and pepper and sauté on medium high heat for 2-3 minutes. Add Shiitake mushroom and continue to sauté another 2-3 minutes. Cover with oyster sauce and cook until tender.*

### Dessert: Fruit Cup — Serves 1— FP 7 grams

$^1/_3$ cup watermelon, diced

$^1/_3$ cup cantaloupe, diced

2 strawberries, sliced

$^1/_3$ cup blueberries

*Combine fruit and serve.*

# Week Two Fast Tract Diet Plan

### DAY 8 — Daily FP 27 grams

*Breakfast: Smoked Salmon with Capers — Serves 2 — FP 4 grams*

   $^1/_2$ pound smoked salmon

   $^1/_2$ ripe tomato, sliced

   $^1/_4$ sweet or red onion, thinly sliced

   1 tablespoon capers

   1 tablespoon extra virgin olive oil

   1 tablespoon balsamic or white balsamic vinegar

   2 slices French baguette (1 ounce per slice)

   1 pinch salt

   1 pinch pepper

*If not pre-cut, slice the chilled salmon into thin strips and place onto a plate. Cover with chopped tomato, onion, capers and balsamic or white wine vinegar. Add salt and pepper to taste.*

*Warm and slice the baguette. Serve the salmon with one piece of warmed baguette. Limit baguette to one piece, eat slowly and chew it well. Baguettes have a relatively low FP compared to other breads, but if you still have symptoms, skip the baguette for now. As your system heals you may be able to add it back. Try again in one week.*

*Lunch: Turkey Burger with Grilled Pineapple and Guacamole— Serves 2 — FP 11 grams*

   12 ounces ground turkey

   2 tablespoons extra virgin olive oil

   2 ounces pineapple, sliced

   1 tablespoon Italian dressing

   $^1/_2$ tablespoon Worcestershire sauce

   1 pinch freshly ground pepper

1 pinch onion powder

1 pinch garlic powder

1 pinch paprika

1 stem green onion, finely chopped

3 tablespoons feta cheese, crumbled

*Mix all ingredients except pineapple and olive oil in a bowl. Form two turkey burger patties and grill or pan fry in olive oil on medium high heat for approximately 7- 8 minutes or until done. Grill or sauté pineapple for one minute. Place pineapple on top of burger and serve with guacamole (recipe below).*

### Guacamole

1 avocado

$^1/_2$ tomato, finely chopped

$^1/_8$ onion, finely chopped

2 tablespoons cilantro, chopped

$^1/_8$ lime, squeezed

$^1/_2$ pinch garlic powder

$^1/_2$ pinch onion powder

1 pinch salt

1 pinch pepper

*Peel avocado and remove pit. Place in bowel with other ingredients and mix / mash with a fork.*

### Snack: Cheese and Pepperoni — Serves 1 — FP 1 grams

6 slices cheddar cheese

6 slices pepperoni

6 dill pickle slices

*Cut cheese and pepperoni slices and serve with pickles.*

***Dinner: Steak Kabobs and Jasmine Rice — Serves 4 — FP 7 grams***

2 pounds steak, cut into $1^1/_2$ inch cubes

1 green bell pepper, cut into $1^1/_2$ inch squares

1 red pepper, cut into $1^1/_2$ inch squares

1 large onion, cut into $1^1/_2$ inch squares

6 large mushrooms, whole with stems cut flush

$^1/_3$ cup extra virgin olive oil

$1^1/_2$ tablespoons balsamic vinegar

$^1/_4$ cup soy sauce

$^1/_2$ lemon

$^1/_2$ cup fresh or 1 tablespoon dried basil, chopped

3 cloves garlic, minced and chopped

1 cup jasmine rice

$1^1/_2$ cups water

*Prepare a marinade by combining olive oil, balsamic vinegar, soy sauce, lemon juice, basil, garlic, and salt and pepper. Marinate the meat using a large zip-lock freezer bag. Refrigerate it for at least several hours, for as long as overnight. Just before cooking, add the peppers, onions and mushrooms to the bag and shake until coated. Slide the vegetable and steak pieces onto skewers. Add more salt and pepper if needed. Place skewers on a hot grill for about 4 to 6 minutes, turning them frequently and being sure not to over-cook the meat.*

*Before grilling kabobs, combine rice with water in a medium saucepan (if using rice cooker, use $1^3/_4$ cups water) and stir. Bring to boil uncovered on high heat. Reduce heat and simmer covered for 15 minutes. Don't remove the cover while cooking. Remove from heat and let stand covered for 5-7 minutes. Fluff with spatula before serving.*

*Lay skewers over jasmine rice and serve.*

*Note: If symptoms are gone, serve up to $^3/_4$ cup rice. If symptoms persist, limit rice to $^1/_2$ cup per serving.*

### Dessert: Cheesecake — Serves 8 — FP 4 grams

2 8-ounce containers of cream cheese, warmed to
room temperature

1 cup equivalent of low FP sweetener

3 large eggs

1 teaspoon vanilla extract

³/₄ cup heavy cream

*Gently beat together all warmed ingredients, adding the eggs and cream gradually. Do not over-beat. Add the filling to pie crust (recipe below) and bake at 350 degrees for 1 hour. Cool and then refrigerate. Serve with whipped cream (recipe below) and berries if desired. Freeze leftovers.*

### Almond Crust

1¹/₂ cup ground almond flour

4 tablespoon equivalents of low FP sweetener

¹/₄ cup butter, melted

*Mix almond flour, sweetener, and melted butter. Press the mixture into a greased 9-inch pie pan covering both the bottom and sides of the pan.*

### Whipped Cream

1 cup heavy cream, chilled

3 tablespoon equivalents of low FP sweetener

1 teaspoon vanilla extract

*In a mixing bowl, combine chilled cream, sweetener and vanilla extract. Set bowl inside a larger bowl filled with crushed ice. (To keep the cream chilled) Whip the cream with an electric mixer until light and fluffy.*

### DAY 9 — Daily FP 31 grams

*Breakfast: Tofu and Sausage — Serves 2 — FP 3 grams*

8 ounces ($^1/_2$ block) tofu

8 ounces Italian sausage, sliced

2 green onions, finely chopped

2 teaspoons soy sauce

1 pinch pepper

1 teaspoon hot chili sauce (optional)

4 large strawberries

Low FP sweetener to taste

*Brown the sausage at medium-high heat until half cooked. Cut tofu into $^1/_2$ inch squares and add to sausage and sauté the mixture together until tofu becomes golden. Try to keep the tofu squares intact while cooking. Add the soy sauce (aim for the tofu as the sausage is already salty), chopped green onions and pepper and remove from heat. Serve with hot chili sauce and two strawberries sprinkled with sweetener on the side.*

*Lunch: Antipasto Salad — Serves 1 — FP 7 grams*

2 cups leafy green lettuce, mixed greens or spinach

2 cherry tomatoes

2 mushrooms

1 artichoke heart

3 black olives

3 green olives

1 pepperoncini (sweet pepper)

$^1/_4$ avocado, peeled and cut into wedges

3 slices each of salami and prosciutto, rolled up

1-2 ounces mozzarella cheese, cut in strips or sliced

2 tablespoons extra virgin olive oil

1 tablespoon white or regular balsamic vinegar

*Toss the greens with a mixture of olive oil and balsamic vinegar in a* large serving bowl. Top with vegetables and arrange meats and mozzarella cheese strips on the edge. Serve.

NOTE: Alternatively, use bottled Italian or Greek dressing.

### Snack: Spicy Nut Mix —2 Ounce Serving Size — FP 9 grams
*See day 5 for recipe.*

### Dinner: Ginger Pork with Broccoli Rabe and Sticky Rice— Serves 2 — FP 7 grams
1 pound sliced pork belly

2 tablespoons sake (rice wine)

2 tablespoons gluten free soy sauce

1 tablespoon equivalent of low FP sweetener

1 tablespoon ginger, grated

$^1/_2$ teaspoon sesame seeds

1 pinch pepper

*Prepare ginger sauce mixing sake, soy sauce, **sweetener**, ginger and pepper in a small bowl. Set aside. Sauté pork belly over medium high heat without oil or butter (the meat has enough fat) approximately 2 - 3 minutes until almost cooked. Add ginger sauce and continue cooking until done.*

### Asian Sticky Rice — Makes 5 serving
1 cup Asian glutinous sticky rice (no substitutions)

1 cup water

*Prepare sticky rice in advance. Rinse rice with cold water three to four times or until water runs clear. Mix rice with water and soak for 10 minutes prior to cooking in a rice cooker. Turn on the rice cooker. Don't open the lid for approximately 20 minutes. Let the rice sit for another 10 minutes. Fluff rice prior to serving.*

*Note: Limit to $^1/_2$ cup per serving until symptoms under control, after which $^3/_4$ cup serving is allowed.*

*Save leftover rice (for Day 12 breakfast) by packing rice loosely in a $^1/_2$ cup measuring cup, then wrapping tightly in plastic wrap. Refrigerate or* *freeze. When using the rice, thaw and warm thoroughly in the microwave to limit resistant starch formation. If reheated rice gives you symptoms, either omit rice or switch to freshly prepared rice.*

### Broccoli Rabe

    10 ounces broccoli rabe

    2 cloves garlic, sliced

    2 tablespoons extra virgin olive oil

    3 tablespoons water

*Cut off ends of stems, wash and spin dry. Sauté garlic in 2 tablespoons olive oil on medium high heat for approximately 2 minutes. Add broccoli rabe and sauté on medium high heat, stirring occasionally, for 3 minutes. Add water and reduce heat to medium. Continue sautéing until rabe is tender, approximately 2 – 3 minutes more.*

### Dessert: Key Lime Pie — Serves 8 — FP 5 grams

    4 egg yolks, beaten

    1 ³/₄ cups light cream

    ¹/₂ cup lime juice (about 4 limes, key limes are not necessary)

    2 teaspoons gelatin

    3 teaspoons lime zest (gratings of lime skin)

    4 tablespoon equivalents of low FP sweetener

    2 cups whipped cream (Refer to Day 1 recipe)

    Almond crust (recipe below)

*Preheat the oven to 375 degrees. Beat the egg yolks. Wisk the gelatin with the lime juice, lime zest and sweetener. Combine and mix the light cream, egg yolks and lime juice. Pour the mixture into the prebaked pie crust (recipe below) and bake for 12 to 15 minutes. Remove and cool, then refrigerate. Add whipped cream and serve with a lime wedge.*

### Almond Crust — makes one pie

1 1/2 cup ground almond flour

4 tablespoon equivalents of low FP sweetener

$^{1}/_{4}$ cup butter, melted

*Mix almond flour, sweetener, and melted butter. Press the mixture into a greased 9-inch pie pan covering both the bottom and sides of the pan. Prebake the crust at 375 degrees for about 7 minutes.*

*It takes about 15 key limes to make $^{1}/_{2}$ cup of key lime juice. Substituting 3-4 regular limes seems to work fine.*

## DAY 10 — Daily FP 26 grams

### *Breakfast: Tomato, Onion and Green Pepper Omelet — Serves 1 — FP 3 grams*

2 eggs

$1/4$ small tomato

$1/4$ small onion, chopped

$1/4$ small green pepper, chopped

2 ounces cheddar cheese, grated

1 tablespoon extra virgin olive oil

1 tablespoon butter

*Heat olive oil and butter in a pan on medium heat, sauté tomato, onion and green pepper for 5 minutes and set aside. Whisk eggs in a small bowl and pour them into the pan. Place sautéed vegetables toward the middle and add cheese. With a spatula, lift one side and fold the omelet in half. Cook for 2-3 more minutes. Slide the omelet onto a plate.*

*NOTE: Serve alone or with 2-4 slices bacon or sausage.*

### *Lunch: Shrimp Fried Rice and Salad — Serves 6 — FP 7 grams*

1 pound medium to large shrimp, fresh or frozen

4 cups prepared Asian sticky rice (recipe below)

2 eggs, beaten

2 scallions, chopped

3 tablespoons soy sauce

3 tablespoons extra virgin olive oil

1 tablespoon butter

Salt and pepper

Avocado and Boston Lettuce Salad (recipe below)

*Sauté whole shrimp in a hot pan with two tablespoons olive oil and two teaspoons of butter as well as salt and pepper until almost done. Add the rice (recipe below) to shrimp and continue to sauté. Move the mixture to one side and drop the eggs into the pan. Scramble the eggs quickly, and combining* with the rice just before the eggs are fully cooked. Add chopped scallions to the mixture and drizzle 2 tablespoons soy sauce around the edge of the pan. Stir egg and soy sauce into the mixture. Serve with salad.

### Asian Sticky Rice

1¹/₂ cup rice

1¹/₂ cup water

*Prepare sticky rice in advance. Rinse rice with cold water three to four times or until water runs clear. Mix rice with water and soak for 10 minutes prior to cooking in a rice cooker. Turn on the rice cooker. Don't open the lid for approximately 25 minutes. Let the rice sit for another 10 minutes. Fluff rice prior to serving.*

*Note: Wrap left over rice tightly in plastic wrap and freeze. If you use leftover rice for this recipe, microwave to warm before adding to the pan. If you have any symptoms from leftover rice, switch to using fresh rice only.*

### Avocado and Boston Lettuce Salad — Serves 4

1 avocado, peeled and sliced

1 head Boston (Bibb) lettuce

2 strips cooked bacon, finely chopped

2 stems curly parsley, finely chopped

¹/₈ small sweet onion, finely chopped

4 tablespoons extra virgin olive oil

3 tablespoons white balsamic vinegar

Salt and pepper

*Add washed lettuce to individual salad bowls and cover with bacon and avocado slices. Mix oil with vinegar, salt, pepper, chopped onions and parsley. Pour dressing over salad.*

### Peaches— Serves 1 — FP 5 grams

1 peach

*Remove pit and cut peach into wedges.*

### Dinner: White Fish Piccata — Serves 2 — FP 5 grams

1.2 pounds haddock, cod (or other white fish)

2 eggs

2 tablespoons parmesan, grated

$^1/_4$ lemon, cut in two wedges

4 red lettuce leaves

$^1/_2$ tomato, cut in two wedges

3 tablespoons extra virgin olive oil

2 pinches salt

2 pinches pepper

*Beat eggs with parmesan cheese. Cut fish into approximately 8 pieces. Add salt and pepper to both sides of fish. Dip fish in egg batter and fry on medium high heat in olive oil until well browned. Arrange pieces on plate around bed of red lettuce with a tomato and lemon wedges. Place tartar sauce in center of lettuce leaves for dipping the fish in. Squeeze the lemon wedge over fish when ready to eat.*

### Tartar Sauce

4 tablespoons mayonnaise

4 bread and butter pickle slices, finely chopped

$^1/_2$ teaspoon lemon juice

1 pinch salt

1 pinch pepper

1 pinch onion powder

*Mix all ingredients.*

### Dessert: Pineapple Macaroons — Serves 5 — FP 6 grams

2 cups unsweetened shredded coconut

2 ounce fresh pineapple, finely chopped

$^1/_2$ cup egg whites

1 stick of butter, melted

1 teaspoon vanilla or almond extract

1 cup **equivalent of low FP sweetener**

*Preheat oven to 325 degrees. Whip egg whites, vanilla extract and melted then cooled butter together. Mix in coconut, pineapple and sweetener. Spoon onto baking sheet covered with foil coated with oil. Bake for approxi-mately 15 minutes, checking regularly. The recipe makes about 15 cookies. Limit to three cookies per serving.*

## DAY 11 — Daily FP 37 grams

### Breakfast: Morning Berry Smoothie — Serves 1 — FP 9 grams
*Berry Smoothie*

$^1/_2$ cup strawberries (or blueberries)

$^1/_2$ cup plain unsweetened yogurt

$^1/_2$ cup light cream

Low FP sweetener to taste

*Combine all ingredients in a blender. Blend until smooth. Serve chilled.*

*NOTE: Additionally, you can have up to 2 ounces cheese, 2 strips of breakfast meat (bacon, sausage, ham, etc.) or a hardboiled egg if desired.*

### Lunch: Tofu and Veggie Stir Fry with Jasmine Rice- Serves 2 — FP 8 grams

1 package (12 ounces) fried tofu, cut in 1$^1/_2$ inch triangles

4 large mushrooms, sliced

3 stems green onion, sliced down the middle and cut in 3 inch lengths

$^1/_4$ small red pepper, chopped in 1 inch squares

4 ounces broccoli, chopped

1 ounce carrot, thinly sliced

1 ounce fresh ginger, peeled and thinly sliced

$^1/_4$ cup water

$^1/_4$ orange, squeezed

$^1/_2$ tablespoon orange peel, finely sliced

2 $^1/_2$ tablespoons extra virgin olive oil

1 $^1/_2$ tablespoons sesame oil

1 $^1/_2$ tablespoons gluten free soy sauce

1 tablespoon oyster sauce

2 pinches freshly ground pepper

1 pinch crushed red pepper

1 cup jasmine rice

1 $^1/_2$ cup water

*Combine rice with water in a medium saucepan (if using rice cooker, use 1 $^3/_4$ cups water) and stir. Bring to boil uncovered on high heat. Reduce heat and simmer covered for 15 minutes. Don't remove the cover while cooking. Remove from heat and let stand covered for 5-7 minutes. Fluff with spatula before serving.*

*Note: Only consume $^1/_2$ cup of rice unless your symptoms are completely under control, in which case $^3/_4$ cup of rice is allowed.*

Add olive and sesame oil to a large skillet. Sauté ginger on high heat for 30 seconds. Add vegetables and tofu and stir fry on medium high heat for approximately 1$^1/_2$ minutes. Add water, cover and steam on medium high heat for 1 minute. Add orange juice, orange peel, soy sauce, oyster sauce, black pepper and red pepper. Stir fry until vegetables are cooked al dente.

*Note: Fried tofu and oyster sauce are available at Whole Foods or Asian grocery stores.*

### Snack: Sweet Nut Mix (See recipe from Day 1) — FP 9 grams

*See day one for recipe. Limit to 2 ounces per day.*

### Dinner: Beef Stew and French Baguette — Serves 4 — FP 10 grams

2 pounds stew beef

$^1/_2$ sweet onion, chopped

1 medium parsnip, cut $^1/_2$ inch slices

1 medium carrot, cut in $^1/_2$ inch slices

10 brown mushrooms, quartered

1 $^1/_2$ cup beef broth (or two beef bouillon cubes)

1 $^1/_2$ cup dry red wine

1 tablespoon extra virgin olive oil

2 bay leaves

2 small tomatoes from can, chopped

2 pinches salt

2 pinches freshly ground pepper

4 slices French Baguette (1 ounce per slice)

4 teaspoons butter

*Cut beef to 1 ¹/₂ inch cubes. Sauté beef in olive oil with salt and pepper over medium high heat until browned. Add onion, parsnip, carrot, mushrooms and chopped tomatoes and continue to sauté for approximately 10 minutes. Add wine and beef broth. Bring to a boil.*

*Transfer to crock pot on high heat for 5 – 7 hours. Alternatively, simmer on low heat in a covered pot.*

*Warm baguette, slice and serves with butter. Only one piece per serving unless all symptoms are completely gone. If symptoms are gone, two pieces are allowed.*

*Note: Best to make this dish in the morning to allow cooking time.*

### Dessert: Rum Custard — Serves 6 — FP 1 gram

5 eggs

2 ¹/₄ cups heavy cream

2 tablespoons light rum (optional)

1 cup **equivalent of low FP sweetener**

2 teaspoons vanilla extract

¹/₂ teaspoon salt

1 teaspoon nutmeg

1 teaspoon cinnamon

*Preheat the oven to 350 degrees. Pour boiling water into a large baking tray to come up about ¹/₃ to the top. Whisk eggs together with other ingredients except nutmeg and cinnamon. Pour mixture into an 8 x 8 inch baking dish and sprinkle nutmeg and cinnamon over the top. Set the baking dish inside a baking tray making sure the hot water comes up to the level of the custard in the baking dish. Bake for 45 minutes or until a knife inserted in the center comes out clean. Cool and chill to allow custard to set before serving.*

## DAY 12 — Daily FP 30 grams

**Breakfast: Creamy Rice Cereal—** *Serves 1 — FP 7 grams*

$^1/_2$ cup Asian sticky rice, cooked

$^1/_2$ cup unsweetened coconut milk

$^1/_2$ cup light cream

$^1/_2$ peach, cut in wedges

Low FP sweetener to taste

1 pinch cinnamon (optional)

*Use leftover sticky rice or prepare fresh rice according to recipe on day 9. Add sticky rice and coconut milk to a pan on medium high heat just until it begins to boils. Lower heat and add light cream. Cook for 3 minutes on low heat. Don't allow to boil. Remove from heat and let stand for 5 minutes. Serve with peach wedges on the side.*

**Lunch: Warm Chicken, Egg and Broccoli Salad—** *Serves 2 — FP 4 grams*

$^3/_4$ pound boneless chicken thigh

2 eggs, hard boiled

4 ounces broccoli, chopped

6 leafs red leaf lettuce

2 tablespoons extra virgin olive oil

$^1/_4$ lemon, squeezed

1 clove garlic, sliced

2 pinches salt

2 pinches pepper

1 teaspoon butter

*Sprinkle chicken on both sides with salt and pepper. Sauté garlic in olive oil on medium high heat for 1 minute. Add chicken and cook for approximately 10 minutes turning occasionally. Squeeze lemon over chicken just before removing from heat. Cut chicken into one inch squares.*

Hard boil eggs in water for 12 minutes and immerse in cold water. Microwave broccoli in dish with a small amount of water and butter for 2 minutes. Peel eggs and cut into approximately eight pieces per egg.

Break up lettuce, place all ingredients in a salad bowl and serve with dressing.

### Dressing:

6 tablespoons mayonnaise

3 tablespoons light cream

2 teaspoons gluten-free soy sauce

1 pinch dried dill

1 pinch salt

1 pinch freshly ground pepper

Low FP sweetener to taste

Mix all ingredients in a small bowl and use to dress salad.

### Snack: Cantaloupe and Prosciutto— Serves 1 — FP 4 grams

4 ounces cantaloupe, cut into two wedges

2 sliced prosciutto

Wrap cantaloupe pieces in prosciutto. Serve.

### Dinner: Eggplant Lasagna and Salad — Serves 8 — FP 9 grams

1 medium eggplant (three cups)

1 pound sausage, chopped

1 pound ground beef

1 1/2 pounds mozzarella cheese, grated

2 cups whole milk ricotta cheese

28 ounces tomato sauce (bottled OK, look for lowest carb brand)

1 cup green Bell pepper, chopped

1/2 cup onion, chopped

3 garlic cloves

1 tablespoon extra virgin olive oil

1 pinch Salt and pepper

Salad (see recipe and ingredients below)

*Brown the meat on medium high heat. Sauté the vegetables and garlic in olive oil. Mix the meat, tomato sauce and vegetables together. Slice the eggplant thinly. Spread a thin coat of meat and sauce mix in a large baking dish. Add new layers of eggplant, sauce mix, mozzarella, and ricotta cheese. Repeat until all ingredients are used. Top with a layer of cheeses and salt and pepper. Bake at 350 degrees for about 45 minutes to an hour. Let cool for ten to fifteen minutes. Freeze leftovers for convenient lunch meals.*

## Tossed Salad— Serves 2

4-6 cups iceberg or leafy green lettuce

4 cherry tomatoes

6 slices English cucumber

4 slices green pepper

6 black olives

4 tablespoons extra virgin olive oil

2 tablespoons balsamic vinegar

*Toss vegetables with olive oil and balsamic vinegar in a large serving bowl. Alternatively, use Italian or Greek bottled dressing.*

## Dessert: Lactose-Free Ice Cream — Serves 1 — FP 6 grams

$^1/_2$ cup lactose-free Breyers ice cream

*Serve the ice cream adding a few nuts and berries if desired.*

## DAY 13 — Daily FP 36 grams

### Breakfast: Corned Beef Hash with Celery Root and Eggs— Serves 2 — FP 13 grams

$^1/_2$ pound corned beef

10 ounces celery root

$^1/_4$ onion, chopped

4 eggs

8 cups water

2 wedges Cantaloupe melon

4 tablespoons extra virgin olive oil

1 pinch salt

1 pinch freshly ground pepper

1 pinch onion powder

*Buy a thick cut of corned beef from the deli or, bring to a boil then simmer a whole corned beef brisket in water for 3-4 hours. Cut $^1/_2$ pound corned beef into $^1/_2$ inch squares and set aside.*

*Cut celery root into $^1/_2$ inch squares and mix with chopped onions in baking pan. Add 2 tablespoons olive oil along with the salt and pepper and mix. Bake at 400 degrees for 40 minutes covering loosely with foil.*

*Lightly brown corned beef in 2 tablespoons olive oil over medium high heat. Add vegetables with onion powder and continue to sauté for another minute or two until done.*

*Bring eight cups of water to a boil in a medium size sauce pan. Add vinegar and a teaspoon of salt. Gently drop in eggs and reduce heat to medium. Simmer for 2 to 3 minutes.*

### Lunch: Swiss Chard and Sausage Soup — Serves 4 — FP 5 grams

10 ounces Swiss chard, chopped

$^1/_2$ sweet onion, chopped

3 cloves garlic, minced

1 pound mild Italian sausage, chopped

4 slices French baguette (1ounce per slice)

8 ounces Brie cheese, sliced

24 green and black olives

2 tablespoons extra virgin olive oil

1 tablespoon Better Than Bouillon chicken base (or 4 chicken bouillon cubes)

2-4 pinches salt

2 pinches freshly ground pepper

Sauté sausage with onion in olive oil for two minutes. Add Swiss chard and continue to sauté for approximately 3 more minutes. Place mixture in a large pan and add 8 cups of water. Bring to a boil. Add bouillon base, reduce heat and simmer for approximately 20 minutes. Serve soup with Brie cheese, olives and French Baguette.

Note: Limit French Baguette serving size to 1 ounce, unless symptoms are completely gone in which case, two pieces may be consumed. Eat slowly and chew well.

### Snack: Yogurt and Berries— Serves 1 — FP 7 grams
$1/2$ cup yogurt

$1/4$ cup blackberries or blueberries

Low FP sweetener to taste

*Serve yogurt with berries and sweetener. Add a few chopped nuts if desired*

### Dinner: Barbecued Baby Back Ribs — Serves 4 — FP 8 grams
3 pounds pork baby back ribs (or pork spare ribs)

6 ounces fresh pineapple

Collard greens (recipe below)

Coleslaw (recipe below)

2 tablespoons extra virgin olive oil

3 green onions

Rub — spice mix (recipe below)

Braising liquid (recipe below)

### Rub Spice Mix

2 teaspoons dark brown sugar

1 tablespoon chili powder

1 teaspoon cumin

1 $1/2$ tablespoons smoked paprika

1 $1/2$ teaspoons salt

1 teaspoons black pepper

$1/2$ teaspoon cayenne pepper

*Mix Rub Mix ingredients together. Rub/pat the mixture onto the ribs and refrigerate for 2 hours to overnight.*

### Braising Liquid

1 cup white wine

2 tablespoons white wine vinegar

1 tablespoon Worcester sauce

1 teaspoon honey

2 garlic cloves, chopped.

*Mix the Braising Liquid ingredients and refrigerate.*

*Preheat the oven to 350 degrees. Place the ribs in foil with the edges folded up to hold liquid. Add the braising liquid around the base of the ribs and cover tightly with another piece of foil. Braise the ribs at 350 degrees for one hour. Lower the temperature to 250 degrees and continue braising for 2 more hours. Remove the braising liquid and simmer over medium high heat to reduce the volume by about two thirds. Grill (0r broil) for about 10 minutes on each side on low heat basting with the braising liquid each time the ribs are turned.*

*Place medium sized pineapple chunks on skewers and grill for a few minutes on each side. Remove ribs and pineapple from grill. Sprinkle ribs with chopped green onions, salt and pepper.*

*Note: If you have limited time here is a short cut rib recipe: Boil the ribs for 45 minutes, add a thin coat of commercial barbecue sauce and grill for 10 minutes. Try to limit the amount of barbecue sauce as it contains a lot of sucrose.*

### Collard Greens — Serves 4

6 cups collard greens, chopped

2 $\frac{1}{2}$ tablespoons extra virgin olive oil

1 $\frac{1}{2}$ cup chicken broth

$\frac{1}{2}$ teaspoon garlic powder

$\frac{1}{2}$ teaspoon onion powder

Salt and pepper

*Sauté collard greens in olive oil on high heat with salt and pepper. Add chicken broth, garlic and onion powder and continue to cook on medium heat for 15 minutes.*

### Coleslaw — Serves 4

$\frac{1}{2}$ head green cabbage, washed and finely chopped

1 small carrot, shredded

$\frac{1}{4}$ cup mayonnaise

$\frac{1}{4}$ cup sour cream

2 tablespoons white vinegar

1 teaspoon lemon juice

1 teaspoon Dijon mustard

1 pinch salt and pepper

Low FP sweetener to taste

*Mix cabbage with shredded carrots in a large bowl. Combine the remaining ingredients in a separate bowl and blend until smooth. Pour this dressing over the cabbage and carrots and toss until evenly coated.*

*Serve the ribs with pineapple, collard greens and coleslaw.*

### Dessert: Watermelon — Serves 1 — FP 3 grams

6 ounces watermelon, cut in wedges

*Serve watermelon wedges.*

## DAY 14 — Daily FP 29 Grams

*Breakfast: Eggs Benedict— Serves 2 — FP 4 grams*

2 slices Canadian bacon

2 eggs

2 egg yolks

2 Cantaloupe wedges (about 2 ounces each)

1 tablespoon lemon juice

1 tablespoon extra virgin olive oil

4 tablespoons butter, heated until it bubbles up without burning

1/2 cup white vinegar

8 cups water

1 teaspoon salt

1 English muffin, toasted

2 teaspoons butter

1 pinch pepper

*Bring ten cups of water to a low boil in a medium size sauce pan. Prepare Hollandaise Sauce by separating the yokes from two eggs and placing them in a mixing bowl. Add lemon juice and about a tablespoon of water and whisk the egg yolks until they thicken slightly while warming the bowel over the pan of boiling water.*

*Heat butter in a small pan until it bubbles up without burning for a minute or so. Cool clarified butter and slowly add it to the Hollandaise Sauce stirring as you go. Set aside covered.*

*Brown Canadian bacon in olive oil over medium high heat turning once.*

*Add vinegar and salt to water and bring to a low boil. Crack and gently drop in eggs and reduce heat to medium. Simmer for approximately 3 minutes. Remove eggs with a slotted spoon.*

*Toast and butter one English muffin. Place one piece of Canadian bacon and one egg on each half of English muffin. Cover each egg with Hollandaise sauce. Add salt and pepper to taste.*

*Note: If your symptoms are completely under control, two servings are allowed. Otherwise, consume only one half of the English muffin. You can have more eggs and meat if desired regardless of symptoms.*

### Lunch: Chicken Lettuce Wraps — Serves 2 — FP 3 grams

6 iceberg lettuce leaves

$^1/_4$ English cucumber, cut in two inch lengths, and then thinly slice to resemble "match sticks."

1 pound chicken breast, chopped

1 scallion, chopped

1 tablespoon soy sauce

2 teaspoon equivalents of low FP sweetener

$^1/_2$ teaspoon rice vinegar

$^1/_3$ can water chestnuts, chopped

3 tablespoons cilantro, finely chopped

1 tablespoon extra virgin olive oil

*Mix soy sauce, vinegar and sweetener and set aside. Sauté chicken in olive oil until half cooked. Add water chestnuts and continue to sauté. Add soy sauce mixture just before chicken is fully cooked and continue to sauté. Mix in scallions and remove from heat. Place the chicken in the middle of a lettuce leaf; add a few cucumber sticks and cilantro. Roll up and dip in the peanut sauce to eat.*

### Peanut sauce

$^1/_4$ cup creamy peanut butter

1 tablespoon extra virgin olive oil

2 teaspoons sesame oil

$1^1/_2$ teaspoons apple cider vinegar 1 teaspoon gluten free soy sauce

3 tablespoons coconut milk

1 tablespoon water

1 pinch freshly ground pepper

1 $^1/_2$ teaspoon equivalents of low FP Sweetener

1 pinch paprika

*Make sure peanut butter is at room temperature. Combine all ingredients and mix.*

*Snack: Spiced Nut Mix — 2 Ounces Per Serving — FP 9 grams*

*Refer to Day 5 Recipe. Limit to 2 ounce daily serving*

*Dinner: Seared Tuna, Sticky Rice and Seaweed and Cucumber Salad — Serves 2 — FP 7 grams*

1 pound tuna steak (must be absolutely fresh!)

2 tablespoons extra virgin olive oil

2 green onions, finely chopped

4 sheets nori (edible seaweed), fold and tear into 3 inch squares

3 tablespoons soy sauce

2 teaspoons wasabi (Japanese horseradish)

Seaweed and cucumber salad (recipe below)

Asian sticky rice (recipe below)

*Prepare a large bowl of ice water with plenty of ice and set aside. Grill or Pan-sear tuna in a very hot pan with olive oil, cooking it for about 90 seconds on each side and searing the sides of the fish briefly by holding the fish on each of its sides. Remove the tuna steaks from the heat while still red in the center, and plunge the tuna into ice water for five minutes to chill. Slice the seared tuna into thin 1/4 inch sashimi sized slices (about 3 inches long) with a very sharp knife. Place fish on a chilled serving dish. Sprinkle uncooked, chopped green onions over the top.*

*Serve the tuna with cucumber salad (recipe below) and sticky rice (recipe below) along with soy sauce mixed with wasabi for dipping the tuna. You can also wrap tuna pieces in nori (dried seaweed paper) squares and dip in soy sauce wasabi mixture.*

*Asian Sticky Rice — Serves 5*

1 cup rice

1 cup water

*Prepare sticky rice in advance. Rinse rice with cold water three to four times or until water runs clear. Mix rice with water and soak for 10 minutes prior to cooking in a rice cooker. Turn on the rice cooker. Don't open the lid*

*for approximately 25 minutes. Let the rice sit for another 10 minutes. Fluff rice prior to serving.*

*Note: See You Tube videos for preparing sticky rice without rice cooker. Also, limit serving size to $^1/_2$ cup until all symptoms are gone. At that point up to $^3/_4$ cup servings are allowed.*

### Seaweed and Cucumber Salad — Serves 2

$^1/_2$ English cucumber

2 tablespoons dried wakame (edible seaweed)

*Slice cucumber lengthwise to produce thin strips approximately $2^1/_2$ inches long. (These should look like matchsticks.) Rehydrate the wakame by adding 1 cup of cold water. Let the seaweed sit for a few minutes before draining. Mix the cucumber strips with rehydrated wakame.*

### Dressing – Serves 2

$^1/_4$ cup extra virgin olive oil

1 tablespoon rice vinegar

2 teaspoons gluten free soy sauce

$^1/_8$ lemon, squeezed

1 teaspoon ginger, minced

$^1/_2$ pinch paprika

2 pinches white sesame seeds

*Mix olive oil, rice vinegar, soy sauce, ginger, lemon and paprika together. Dress the salad just before serving.*

**Dessert: Fruit Medley — Serves 5 — FP 6 grams**

    1 cup watermelon, cubed

    1 cup cantaloupe, cubed

    1 cup strawberries, halved

    $^1/_2$ cup pineapple, cubed

    $^1/_2$ cup peaches, sliced in wedges

    $^1/_2$ cup blueberries

    1 lemon, cut in half

*Wash and cut up fruit and combine in large bowl. Squeeze the juice of two lemon halves over the fruit salad, straining out any seeds. Serve chilled with or without whipped cream.*

*Note: Limit to a half cup serving if still having symptoms, otherwise, limit to a cup.*

**Whipped Cream — Serves 2**

    1 cup heavy cream, chilled

    3 tablespoon equivalents of low FP sweetener

    1 teaspoon vanilla extract

*In a mixing bowl, combine chilled cream, sweetener and vanilla extract. Set bowl inside a larger bowl filled with crushed ice. (This keeps the cream chilled.) Whip the cream with an electric mixer until light and fluffy.*

**Appendix B:**

# Fermentation Potential Tables

**Table 1** - Fermentation potential for *"Beans and Legumes"*

| Beans and Legumes | Serving Size (oz) | Serving Size (grams) | Glycemic Index | Net Carbs per Serving (grams) | Fiber per Serving (grams) | Ferm. Potential (grams) | Relative Symptom Risk |
|---|---|---|---|---|---|---|---|
| Soy beans | 5.3 | 150 | 20 | 6 | 6 | 11 | Moderate |
| Peas, green | 5.3 | 150 | 22 | 9 | 4 | 11 | Moderate |
| Romano beans | 5.3 | 150 | 46 | 18 | 3 | 12 | Moderate |
| Mung bean | 5.3 | 150 | 31 | 17 | 1 | 13 | Moderate |
| Baked beans | 5.3 | 150 | 48 | 15 | 6 | 14 | Moderate |
| Butter beans | 5.3 | 150 | 28 | 20 | 6 | 20 | High |
| Split peas, yellow | 5.3 | 150 | 32 | 19 | 12 | 25 | High |
| Lentils | 5.3 | 150 | 22 | 18 | 12 | 26 | High |
| Chickpeas | 5.3 | 150 | 31 | 30 | 6 | 27 | High |
| Lima beans | 5.3 | 150 | 32 | 30 | 9 | 29 | High |
| Brown beans | 5.3 | 150 | 38 | 25 | 13 | 29 | High |
| Pinto beans | 5.3 | 150 | 39 | 26 | 13 | 29 | High |
| Black beans | 5.3 | 150 | 30 | 23 | 13 | 29 | High |
| Blackeyed beans | 5.3 | 150 | 33 | 30 | 10 | 30 | High |
| Kidney beans | 5.3 | 150 | 23 | 25 | 11 | 31 | High |
| Navy beans | 5.3 | 150 | 30 | 30 | 16 | 37 | High |

**Table 2** - Fermentation potential for *"Soups"*

| Soups | Serving Size (oz) | Serving Size (grams) | Glycemic Index | Net Carbs per Serving (grams) | Fiber per Serving (grams) | Ferm. Potential (grams) | Relative Symptom Risk |
|---|---|---|---|---|---|---|---|
| *Miso Soup | 8.8 | 250 | 50 | 2 | 2 | 2 | Low |
| *Chicken Soup (no noodles) | 8.8 | 250 | 50 | 2 | 1 | 2 | Low |
| Tomato soup | 8.8 | 250 | 38 | 17 | 2 | 13 | Moderate |
| Black Bean soup | 8.8 | 250 | 64 | 27 | 4 | 14 | Moderate |
| Split Pea Soup | 8.8 | 250 | 60 | 27 | 5 | 16 | High |
| Minestrone Soup | 8.8 | 250 | 39 | 18 | 6 | 17 | High |
| Lentil Soup | 8.8 | 250 | 44 | 21 | 12 | 24 | High |

* Glycemic index not available. An estimated GI of 50 was used.

Also note that you can estimate the FP of other soups by checking the FP or the ingredients. You can also make soups without noodles or beans but with lots of vegetables, and perhaps some jasmine rice, that will have a very low FP.

**Table 3** - Fermentation potential for *"Cookies and Crackers"*

| Cookies and Crackers | Serving Size (oz) | Serving Size (grams) | Glycemic Index | Net Carbs per Serving (grams) | Fiber per Serving (grams) | Ferm. Potential (grams) | Relative Symptom Risk |
|---|---|---|---|---|---|---|---|
| Rice crackers | 1 | 28 | 91 | 22 | 0 | 2 | Low |
| Puffed rice cakes | 1 | 28 | 82 | 24 | 0 | 5 | Low |
| Water crackers | 1 | 28 | 78 | 20 | 1 | 5 | Low |
| Vanilla wafers | 1 | 28 | 77 | 20 | 1 | 5 | Low |
| Soda crackers (Saltines) | 1 | 28 | 74 | 21 | 1 | 6 | Low |
| Breton wheat crackers | 1 | 28 | 67 | 16 | 1 | 6 | Low |
| Graham crackers | 1 | 28 | 71 | 20 | 1 | 7 | Low |
| Shortbread cookies | 1 | 28 | 64 | 18 | 0 | 7 | Low |
| Oatmeal cookies | 1 | 28 | 55 | 16 | 1 | 8 | Moderate |
| Stoned Wheat Thins | 1 | 28 | 67 | 19 | 2 | 8 | Moderate |
| Rice cakes, (high-amylose rice) | 1 | 28 | 61 | 24 | 1 | 11 | Moderate |
| Rye crisp bread | 1 | 28 | 63 | 18 | 6 | 13 | Moderate |

Note: Limit the quantity of flour-based snacks (especially wheat), eat slowly and chew well.

**Table 4 -** Fermentation potential for *"Breads"*

| Breads | Serving Size (oz) | Serving Size (grams) | Glycemic Index | Net Carbs per Serving (grams) | Fiber per Serving (grams) | Ferm. Potential (grams) | Relative Symptom Risk |
|---|---|---|---|---|---|---|---|
| Baguette, white, plain | 1.1 | 30 | 95 | 15 | 1 | 1 | Low |
| Middle Eastern flatbread | 1.1 | 30 | 97 | 16 | 1 | 1 | Low |
| Rice bread, low-amylose rice | 1.1 | 30 | 72 | 12 | 0 | 3 | Low |
| Wonder™, white bread | 1.1 | 30 | 80 | 15 | 1 | 4 | Low |
| Gluten-free white bread | 1.1 | 30 | 80 | 15 | 1 | 4 | Low |
| English Muffin™ | 1.1 | 30 | 77 | 14 | 1 | 4 | Low |
| White flour bread | 1.1 | 30 | 70 | 14 | 1 | 5 | Low |
| White wheat flour bread | 1.1 | 30 | 73 | 15 | 1 | 5 | Low |
| Kaiser rolls | 1.1 | 30 | 73 | 16 | 1 | 6 | Low |
| Whole meal flour bread | 1.1 | 30 | 73 | 14 | 2 | 6 | Low |
| Light rye bread | 1.1 | 30 | 68 | 14 | 2 | 6 | Low |
| Rice bread, high-amylose rice | 1.1 | 30 | 61 | 12 | 2 | 7 | Low |
| Muesli bread | 1.1 | 30 | 54 | 12 | 2 | 8 | Moderate |
| Healthy Choice™ Whole Grain Bread | 1.1 | 30 | 62 | 14 | 2 | 8 | Moderate |
| Wheat flour flatbread | 1.1 | 30 | 66 | 16 | 2 | 8 | Moderate |

| Breads | Serving Size (oz) | Serving Size (grams) | Glycemic Index | Net Carbs per Serving (grams) | Fiber per Serving (grams) | Ferm. Potential (grams) | Relative Symptom Risk |
|---|---|---|---|---|---|---|---|
| Pita bread, white | 1.1 | 30 | 57 | 17 | 1 | 8 | Moderate |
| 100% Whole Grain™ bread | 1.1 | 30 | 51 | 13 | 2 | 8 | Moderate |
| Sourdough bread | 1.1 | 30 | 53 | 17 | 1 | 9 | Moderate |
| Healthy Choice™ Hearty 7 Grain Bread | 1.1 | 30 | 55 | 14 | 2 | 9 | Moderate |
| Whole meal barley flour bread | 1.1 | 30 | 70 | 20 | 3 | 9 | Moderate |
| Pumpernickel | 1.1 | 30 | 41 | 12 | 2 | 9 | Moderate |
| Bagel, white | 2.5 | 70 | 72 | 35 | 1 | 11 | Moderate |
| Coarse wheat kernel bread | 1.1 | 30 | 52 | 20 | 4 | 13 | Moderate |
| Corn tortilla | 1.8 | 50 | 52 | 24 | 2 | 13 | Moderate |
| Coarse rye kernel bread | 1.1 | 30 | 41 | 12 | 7 | 14 | Moderate |
| Wheat tortilla | 1.8 | 50 | 30 | 26 | 0 | 18 | High |

Note: Limit the quantity of bread, eat slowly and chew well. People who are sensitive to gluten should not consume bread made from wheat, rye or barley.

**Table 5** - Fermentation potential for *"Cakes, Pastry and Muffins"*

| Cakes, Pastry & Muffins | Serving Size (oz) | Serving Size (grams) | Glycemic Index | Net Carbs per Serving (grams) | Fiber per Serving (grams) | Ferm. Potential (grams) | Relative Symptom Risk |
|---|---|---|---|---|---|---|---|
| Corn muffin, low-amylose | 2 | 57 | 102 | 29 | 2 | 1 | Low |
| Scones, plain | 2 | 57 | 92 | 18 | 0 | 2 | Low |
| Pancakes, buckwheat, gluten-free, | 2 | 57 | 102 | 16 | 5 | 5 | Low |
| Waffles | 2 | 57 | 76 | 21 | 1 | 6 | Low |
| Doughnut | 2 | 57 | 76 | 28 | 1 | 8 | Moderate |
| Crumpet | 2 | 57 | 69 | 22 | 1 | 8 | Moderate |
| Croissant | 2 | 57 | 67 | 26 | 2 | 10 | Moderate |
| Apple muffin, made without sugar | 2 | 57 | 48 | 18 | 1 | 10 | Moderate |
| Cupcake, strawberry-iced | 2 | 57 | 73 | 39 | 0 | 11 | Moderate |
| Pastry | 2 | 57 | 59 | 26 | 1 | 12 | Moderate |
| Angel food cake | 2 | 57 | 67 | 33 | 1 | 12 | Moderate |
| Bran muffin | 2 | 57 | 60 | 24 | 3 | 12 | Moderate |
| Pop Tarts™, Double Chocolate (Kellogg's) | 2 | 57 | 70 | 41 | 1 | 13 | Moderate |
| Flan cake | 2 | 57 | 65 | 39 | 0 | 14 | Moderate |
| Pound cake | 2 | 57 | 54 | 30 | 0 | 14 | Moderate |

| Cakes, Pastry & Muffins | Serving Size (oz) | Serving Size (grams) | Glycemic Index | Net Carbs per Serving (grams) | Fiber per Serving (grams) | Ferm. Potential (grams) | Relative Symptom Risk |
|---|---|---|---|---|---|---|---|
| Pancakes, prepared from mix | 2 | 57 | 67 | 41 | 1 | 14 | Moderate |
| Oatmeal muffin | 2 | 57 | 69 | 40 | 2 | 15 | Moderate |
| Banana cake | 2 | 57 | 47 | 27 | 1 | 15 | Moderate |
| Chocolate butterscotch muffins | 2 | 57 | 53 | 32 | 1 | 16 | High |
| Apple muffin | 2 | 57 | 44 | 28 | 1 | 16 | High |
| Vanilla cake | 2 | 57 | 42 | 30 | 0 | 18 | High |
| Sponge cake, plain | 2 | 57 | 46 | 33 | 0 | 18 | High |
| Chocolate cake | 2 | 57 | 38 | 27 | 2 | 18 | High |
| Blueberry muffin | 2 | 57 | 59 | 59 | 1 | 25 | High |

Note: Caution, some pancake mixes may have a lower glycemic index and hence higher Fermentative Potential.

In general, be careful with baked goods and anything made with wheat based flours. Focus on products made from low amylose rice and other low amylose gluten free products and, of course, eat slowly and chew well.

**Table 6** - Fermentation potential for *"Grains"*

| Grains | Serving Size (oz) | Serving Size (grams) | Glycemic Index | Net Carbs per Serving (grams) | Fiber per Serving (grams) | Ferm. Potential (grams) | Relative Symptom Risk |
|---|---|---|---|---|---|---|---|
| Konjac noodles in water | 1.1 | 30 | 0 | 0 | 1 | 1 | Low |
| Cracked wheat (bulgur) | 1.1 | 30 | 48 | 5 | 1 | 4 | Low |
| Tapioca, boiled | 1.1 | 30 | 81 | 25 | 0 | 5 | Low |
| Rice flour, Non-glutinous | 1.1 | 30 | 68 | 15 | 1 | 6 | Low |
| [3]Xanthan gum | 0.4 | 12 | 0 | 0 | 8 | 8 | Moderate |
| [1]Almond meal, flour | 1.1 | 30 | 22 | 6 | 3 | 8 | Moderate |
| Arrowroot | 1.1 | 30 | 65 | 22 | 1 | 8 | Moderate |
| [3]Guar gum | 0.4 | 12 | 0 | 0 | 10 | 10 | Moderate |
| [2]Amaranth flour (wheat flour mix) | 1.1 | 30 | 66 | 20 | 3 | 10 | Moderate |
| Semolina | 1.1 | 30 | 55 | 22 | 1 | 11 | Moderate |
| Durum wheat | 1.1 | 30 | 52 | 22 | 0 | 11 | Moderate |
| Buckwheat | 1.1 | 30 | 50 | 20 | 3 | 13 | Moderate |
| Wheat, whole kernels | 1.1 | 30 | 42 | 20 | 4 | 15 | High |
| [4]Coconut flour | 1.1 | 30 | 50 | 7 | 12 | 15 | High |
| Corn Meal | 1.1 | 30 | 49 | 21 | 5 | 16 | High |
| Rye, whole kernels | 1.1 | 30 | 29 | 23 | 4 | 21 | High |

[1]Almond meal has not been assigned a G.I. value. The GI value was estimated based on similar foods.
[2]Amaranth flour has a glycemic index of 66 when mixed with wheat flour at a ratio of 25% amaranth to 75% wheat flour.
[3]Xanthan and guar gum is used by the tablespoon. One tablespoon weighs approximately 12 grams or 0.44 ounces.
[4]The glycemic index for coconut flour not been measured but is estimated as 50. Shredded coconut is listed in the fruits table.

**Table 7** - Fermentation potential for *"Cereals"*

| Cereals | Serving Size (oz) | Serving Size (grams) | Glycemic Index | Net Carbs per Serving (grams) | Fiber per Serving (grams) | Ferm. Potential (grams) | Relative Symptom Risk |
|---|---|---|---|---|---|---|---|
| Cornflakes™ (Kellogg's) | 1.1 | 30 | 92 | 26 | 1 | 3 | Low |
| Rice Chex™ (Nabisco) | 1.1 | 30 | 89 | 26 | 0 | 3 | Low |
| Crispix™ (Kellogg's) | 1.1 | 30 | 87 | 25 | 0 | 4 | Low |
| Rice Krispies™ (Kellogg's) | 1.1 | 30 | 82 | 26 | 0 | 5 | Low |
| Corn Chex™ (Nabisco) | 1.1 | 30 | 83 | 25 | 1 | 5 | Low |
| Shredded Wheat™ (Nabisco) | 1.1 | 30 | 83 | 20 | 4 | 7 | Low |
| Special K™ (Kellogg's) | 1.1 | 30 | 69 | 21 | 1 | 7 | Low |
| Oat bran, raw | 1.1 | 30 | 59 | 15 | 2 | 8 | Moderate |
| Puffed Wheat (Quaker Oats) | 1.1 | 30 | 67 | 20 | 1 | 8 | Moderate |
| Cheerios™ (General Mills Inc) | 1.1 | 30 | 74 | 20 | 3 | 8 | Moderate |
| Golden Grahams™ (General Mills) | 1.1 | 30 | 71 | 25 | 1 | 8 | Moderate |
| Cream of Wheat™, Instant (Nabisco) | 8.8 | 250 | 74 | 30 | 1 | 9 | Moderate |
| Grapenuts™ (Kraft Foods) | 1.1 | 30 | 75 | 22 | 3 | 9 | Moderate |
| Quick Oats (Quaker Oats Co) | 1.1 | 30 | 65 | 14 | 4 | 9 | Moderate |
| Oatmeal | 1.1 | 30 | 54 | 20 | 0 | 10 | Moderate |
| Bran Flakes™ (Kellogg's) | 1.1 | 30 | 74 | 18 | 5 | 10 | Moderate |
| Raisin Bran™ (Kellogg's) | 1.1 | 30 | 61 | 19 | 3 | 10 | Moderate |

| Cereals | Serving Size (oz) | Serving Size (grams) | Glycemic Index | Net Carbs per Serving (grams) | Fiber per Serving (grams) | Ferm. Potential (grams) | Relative Symptom Risk |
|---|---|---|---|---|---|---|---|
| Muesli, NS8 | 1.1 | 30 | 66 | 24 | 2 | 10 | Moderate |
| Creamed porridge | 1.1 | 30 | 59 | 23 | 1 | 10 | Moderate |
| Life™ (Quaker Oats) | 1.1 | 30 | 66 | 25 | 2 | 10 | Moderate |
| Froot Loops™ (Kellogg's) | 1.1 | 30 | 69 | 26 | 3 | 11 | Moderate |
| Bran Chex™ Nabisco | 1.1 | 30 | 58 | 19 | 4 | 12 | Moderate |
| Hot cereal, apple & cinnamon (Con Agra) | 1.1 | 30 | 37 | 22 | 1 | 15 | High |
| All-Bran™ (Kellogg's) | 1.1 | 30 | 38 | 23 | 9 | 23 | High |

Note: lactose free milk is recommended for lower FP cereal preparation. Soy is an alternative for those who tolerate soy. Also, many people, even in the absence of celiac disease, are sensitive to gluten. If you think you might be in this group, omit wheat-based products. In general, eat slowly and chew well when consuming grains.

**Table 8** - Fermentation potential for *"Pasta"*

| Pasta | Serving Size (oz) | Serving Size (grams) | Glycemic Index | Net Carbs per Serving (grams) | Fiber per Serving (grams) | Ferm. Potential (grams) | Relative Symptom Risk |
|---|---|---|---|---|---|---|---|
| Rice pasta, brown | 6 | 170 | 92 | 36 | 2 | 5 | Low |
| Tortellini, cheese | 6 | 170 | 50 | 20 | 2 | 12 | Moderate |
| *Rice noodles, (Thailand) | 6 | 170 | 61 | 37 | 2 | 16 | High |
| Rice vermicelli | 6 | 170 | 58 | 37 | 1 | 17 | High |
| Udon noodles | 6 | 170 | 62 | 45 | 1 | 18 | High |
| Macaroni and Cheese | 6 | 170 | 64 | 48 | 1 | 18 | High |
| Gluten-free pasta | 6 | 170 | 54 | 40 | 1 | 20 | High |
| Ravioli, meat filled | 6 | 170 | 39 | 36 | 1 | 23 | High |
| Mung bean noodles | 6 | 170 | 39 | 43 | 1 | 27 | High |
| Spaghetti | 6 | 170 | 44 | 45 | 3 | 28 | High |
| Macaroni, plain | 6 | 170 | 45 | 46 | 3 | 28 | High |
| Fettuccini | 6 | 170 | 32 | 43 | 2 | 31 | High |

*The rice noodles were likely made from long grain rice having a high amylose content and hence a low glycemic index and high fermentative potential. Rice noodles made with low amylose rice would be great if you can find them.

In general, most types of pasta should be avoided or significantly limited due to their high FP values.

**Table 9** - Fermentation potential for *"Rice and Potatoes"*

| Rice & Potatoes | Serving Size (oz) | Serving Size (grams) | Glycemic Index | Net Carbs per Serving (grams) | Fiber per Serving (grams) | Ferm. Potential (grams) | Relative Symptom Risk |
|---|---|---|---|---|---|---|---|
| Jasmine Rice | 5.3 | 150 | 109 | 42 | 0 | 0 | Low |
| Potato, Desiree | 5.3 | 150 | 101 | 17 | 2 | 2 | Low |
| Glutinous short grain rice, white | 5.3 | 150 | 98 | 32 | 2 | 3 | Low |
| Potato, Pontiac | 5.3 | 150 | 88 | 18 | 2 | 4 | Low |
| Potato, Sebago | 5.3 | 150 | 87 | 17 | 2 | 4 | Low |
| Pelde rice, white | 5.3 | 150 | 93 | 43 | 2 | 5 | Low |
| Instant rice, white | 5.3 | 150 | 87 | 42 | 1 | 6 | Low |
| Potato, Russet | 5.3 | 150 | 85 | 30 | 2 | 7 | Low |
| Waxy rice (0-2% amylose) | 5.3 | 150 | 88 | 43 | 2 | 7 | Low |
| Calrose brown rice | 5.3 | 150 | 87 | 38 | 3 | 8 | Moderate |
| Calrose rice, white, medium grain | 5.3 | 150 | 83 | 43 | 1 | 9 | Moderate |
| Potato, Prince Edward Island | 5.3 | 150 | 63 | 18 | 2 | 9 | Moderate |
| French fries, frozen | 5.3 | 150 | 75 | 29 | 4 | 11 | Moderate |
| Pelde brown rice | 5.3 | 150 | 76 | 38 | 3 | 12 | Moderate |
| Millet | 5.3 | 150 | 71 | 36 | 2 | 12 | Moderate |
| Salted rice ball | 5.3 | 150 | 80 | 52 | 2 | 12 | Moderate |
| Potato, Ontario | 5.3 | 150 | 58 | 27 | 2 | 13 | Moderate |

| Rice & Potatoes | Serving Size (oz) | Serving Size (grams) | Glycemic Index | Net Carbs per Serving (grams) | Fiber per Serving (grams) | Ferm. Potential (grams) | Relative Symptom Risk |
|---|---|---|---|---|---|---|---|
| Roasted rice ball | 5.3 | 150 | 77 | 54 | 2 | 14 | Moderate |
| Doongara brown rice, high amylose | 5.3 | 150 | 66 | 37 | 3 | 15 | High |
| Basmati rice, high amylose, white | 5.3 | 150 | 58 | 38 | 1 | 17 | High |
| Arborio, risotto rice | 5.3 | 150 | 69 | 53 | 1 | 18 | High |
| Yam | 5.3 | 150 | 66 | 34 | 6 | 18 | High |
| Brown rice | 5.3 | 150 | 50 | 33 | 3 | 19 | High |
| Long grain (high amylose) rice | 5.3 | 150 | 55 | 40 | 1 | 19 | High |
| Converted, white rice, Uncle Ben's® | 5.3 | 150 | 45 | 36 | 0 | 20 | High |
| Sweet potato | 5.3 | 150 | 48 | 34 | 4 | 21 | High |
| Potato dumplings (with white flour) | 5.3 | 150 | 52 | 45 | 2 | 24 | High |
| Bangladeshi rice variety (28% amylose) | 5.3 | 150 | 37 | 39 | 1 | 26 | High |
| Taro | 5.3 | 150 | 55 | 45 | 8 | 28 | High |

**Table 10** - Fermentation potential for *"Vegetables"*

| Vegetables | Serving Size (oz) | Serving Size (grams) | Glycemic Index | Net Carbs per Serving (grams) | Fiber per Serving (grams) | Ferm. Potential (grams) | Relative Symptom Risk |
|---|---|---|---|---|---|---|---|
| Chili, green | 0.3 | 7 | 50 | 1 | 0 | 1 | Low |
| Bok choy | 2.8 | 80 | 50 | 0 | 1 | 1 | Low |
| Pickles, dill | 1.0 | 28 | 50 | 1 | 0 | 1 | Low |
| Olives | 1.0 | 28 | 50 | 0 | 1 | 1 | Low |
| Lettuce | 2.8 | 80 | 50 | 1 | 1 | 2 | Low |
| Mixed greens | 2.8 | 80 | 50 | 1 | 1 | 2 | Low |
| Alfalfa sprouts | 2.8 | 80 | 50 | 0 | 1 | 2 | Low |
| Celery | 2.8 | 80 | 50 | 1 | 1 | 2 | Low |
| Arugula | 2.8 | 80 | 50 | 0 | 2 | 2 | Low |
| **Pumpkin** | **2.8** | **80** | **75** | **4** | **1** | **2** | **Low** |
| Cucumber | 2.8 | 80 | 50 | 3 | 1 | 2 | Low |
| Bamboo shoots | 2.8 | 80 | 50 | 2 | 1 | 2 | Low |
| Summer squash | 2.8 | 80 | 50 | 3 | 1 | 2 | Low |
| Radishes | 2.8 | 80 | 50 | 2 | 1 | 2 | Low |
| Zucchini | 2.8 | 80 | 50 | 3 | 1 | 2 | Low |
| Garlic, 3 cloves | 0.3 | 9 | 50 | 3 | 0 | 2 | Low |
| Pepper, red, green | 2.8 | 80 | 50 | 3 | 2 | 3 | Low |

| Vegetables | Serving Size (oz) | Serving Size (grams) | Glycemic Index | Net Carbs per Serving (grams) | Fiber per Serving (grams) | Ferm. Potential (grams) | Relative Symptom Risk |
|---|---|---|---|---|---|---|---|
| Asparagus | 2.8 | 80 | 50 | 2 | 2 | 3 | Low |
| Mushrooms | 2.8 | 80 | 50 | 3 | 1 | 3 | Low |
| **Rutabaga** | **2.8** | **80** | **72** | **5** | **1** | **3** | **Low** |
| Chard | 2.8 | 80 | 50 | 2 | 2 | 3 | Low |
| Spinach | 2.8 | 80 | 50 | 2 | 2 | 3 | Low |
| Hearts of palm | 2.8 | 80 | 50 | 2 | 2 | 3 | Low |
| ¹Tomatoes | 2.8 | 80 | 50 | 4 | 1 | 3 | Low |
| Cabbage, green, red | 2.8 | 80 | 50 | 2 | 2 | 3 | Low |
| Endive | 2.8 | 80 | 50 | 1 | 3 | 3 | Low |
| Rhubarb | 2.8 | 80 | 50 | 3 | 2 | 3 | Low |
| Cauliflower | 2.8 | 80 | 50 | 3 | 2 | 3 | Low |
| Daikon | 2.8 | 80 | 50 | 3 | 2 | 3 | Low |
| **Parsnips** | **2.8** | **80** | **97** | **12** | **3** | **3** | **Low** |
| Broccoli rabe | 2.8 | 80 | 50 | 2 | 2 | 3 | Low |
| Sauerkraut | 2.8 | 80 | 50 | 2 | 2 | 3 | Low |
| Broccoli | 2.8 | 80 | 50 | 2 | 3 | 4 | Low |
| Eggplant | 2.8 | 80 | 50 | 2 | 3 | 4 | Low |
| Okra | 2.8 | 80 | 50 | 4 | 2 | 4 | Low |
| Turnips | 2.8 | 80 | 50 | 5 | 2 | 4 | Low |

| Vegetables | Serving Size (oz) | Serving Size (grams) | Glycemic Index | Net Carbs per Serving (grams) | Fiber per Serving (grams) | Ferm. Potential (grams) | Relative Symptom Risk |
|---|---|---|---|---|---|---|---|
| Artichoke | 2.8 | 80 | 50 | 6 | 1 | 4 | Low |
| Pickles, sweet | 1.0 | 28 | 50 | 7 | 1 | 5 | Low |
| ¹Onion | 2.8 | 80 | 35 | 6 | 1 | 5 | Low |
| Celery root | 2.8 | 80 | 50 | 7 | 1 | 5 | Low |
| Beans, green | 2.8 | 80 | 50 | 4 | 3 | 5 | Low |
| Brussels sprouts | 2.8 | 80 | 50 | 5 | 2 | 5 | Low |
| Beans, wax | 2.8 | 80 | 50 | 4 | 3 | 5 | Low |
| Fennel | 2.8 | 80 | 50 | 4 | 3 | 5 | Low |
| **Carrots, cooked** | **2.8** | **80** | **49** | **5** | **2** | **5** | **Low** |
| Acorn squash | 2.8 | 80 | 50 | 7 | 1 | 5 | Low |
| **Beets** | **2.8** | **80** | **64** | **7** | **2** | **5** | **Low** |
| ¹Tomato Sauce | 2.8 | 80 | 38 | 6 | 1 | 5 | Low |
| Collard greens | 2.8 | 80 | 50 | 5 | 3 | 6 | Low |
| Snow peas | 2.8 | 80 | 50 | 6 | 3 | 6 | Low |
| Kale | 2.8 | 80 | 50 | 9 | 2 | 6 | Low |
| Winter squash | 2.8 | 80 | 50 | 8 | 2 | 6 | Low |
| Avocado | 2.8 | 80 | 50 | 1 | 5 | 6 | Low |
| **Carrots, raw** | **2.8** | **80** | **16** | **5** | **2** | **7** | **Low** |
| Butternut squash | 2.8 | 80 | 50 | 11 | 1 | 7 | Low |

| Vegetables | Serving Size (oz) | Serving Size (grams) | Glycemic Index | Net Carbs per Serving (grams) | Fiber per Serving (grams) | Ferm. Potential (grams) | Relative Symptom Risk |
|---|---|---|---|---|---|---|---|
| [1]Edamame | 2.8 | 80 | 20 | 5 | 4 | 8 | Moderate |
| **Peas** | **2.8** | **80** | **54** | **7** | **4** | **8** | **Moderate** |
| **Sweet corn** | **2.8** | **80** | **60** | **18** | **1** | **9** | **Moderate** |
| **Yam** | **2.8** | **80** | **66** | **19** | **3** | **9** | **Moderate** |
| **Plantain** | **2.8** | **80** | **40** | **23** | **2** | **16** | **High** |

Fermentative Potential calculations based on measured GIs are listed in **bold** font.

Non-starchy vegetables are difficult to test for GI as subjects would need to consume very large amounts of each test food (to achieve 50 grams of net carbs). As a result, many have not been tested. In these cases, a conservative estimated GI value of 50 has been used in the calculation of fermentative potential with the exception of tomatoes, tomato sauce, edamame and onions noted below. Non-starchy vegetables are generally low in carbohydrates and moderate in fiber so the FP is low regardless of the glycemic index.

[1] The GI for tomatoes and tomato sauce was estimated as 20 based on the GI for tomato juice. The GI for edamame was estimated as 38 based on the GI for soy beans. Given the reported presence of difficult-to-digest fructooligosaccharides, I estimated a relatively lower GI of 35 for onions thus increasing the FP slightly.

**Table 11** - Fermentation potential for *"Fruits"*

| Fruits | Serving Size (oz) | Serving Size (grams) | Glycemic Index | Net Carbs per Serving (grams) | Fiber per Serving (grams) | Ferm. Potential (grams) | Relative Symptom Risk |
|---|---|---|---|---|---|---|---|
| Watermelon, fresh | 4.2 | 120 | 72 | 6 | 0 | 2 | Low |
| [1]Lemon, juice | 2.1 | 60 | 50 | 4 | 0 | 2 | Low |
| [1]Lime, juice | 2.1 | 60 | 50 | 5 | 0 | 3 | Low |
| Cantaloupe, fresh | 4.2 | 120 | 65 | 8 | 1 | 4 | Low |
| Pineapple, fresh | 4.2 | 120 | 66 | 10 | 2 | 5 | Low |
| Cranberry, fresh | 2.1 | 60 | 56 | 4 | 3 | 5 | Low |
| Peach, fresh | 4.2 | 120 | 56 | 8 | 2 | 5 | Low |
| Lychee, fresh | 4.2 | 120 | 79 | 20 | 1 | 5 | Low |
| Strawberries, fresh | 4.2 | 120 | 40 | 7 | 2 | 6 | Low |
| Apricots, fresh | 4.2 | 120 | 57 | 9 | 2 | 6 | Low |
| Pear, canned | 4.2 | 120 | 44 | 11 | 2 | 8 | Moderate |
| Papaya, fresh | 4.2 | 120 | 60 | 15 | 2 | 8 | Moderate |
| Fruit cocktail, canned | 4.2 | 120 | 55 | 16 | 1 | 8 | Moderate |
| Oranges, fresh | 4.2 | 120 | 48 | 11 | 3 | 9 | Moderate |
| Kiwi, fresh | 4.2 | 120 | 58 | 12 | 4 | 9 | Moderate |
| Apricots, canned | 4.2 | 120 | 64 | 19 | 2 | 9 | Moderate |
| [1]Blackberries, fresh | 4.2 | 120 | 40 | 5 | 6 | 10 | Moderate |

| Fruits | Serving Size (oz) | Serving Size (grams) | Glycemic Index | Net Carbs per Serving (grams) | Fiber per Serving (grams) | Ferm. Potential (grams) | Relative Symptom Risk |
|---|---|---|---|---|---|---|---|
| Strawberry jam | 1.1 | 30 | 51 | 20 | 0 | 10 | Moderate |
| Peach, canned | 4.2 | 120 | 52 | 18 | 2 | 10 | Moderate |
| Grapefruit, fresh | 4.2 | 120 | 25 | 11 | 2 | 10 | Moderate |
| [1]Blueberries, fresh | 4.2 | 120 | 40 | 12 | 3 | 11 | Moderate |
| [1]Raspberries, fresh | 4.2 | 120 | 40 | 6 | 8 | 11 | Moderate |
| Orange marmalade | 1.1 | 30 | 48 | 20 | 0 | 11 | Moderate |
| Grapes | 4.2 | 120 | 43 | 17 | 1 | 11 | Moderate |
| [1]Coconut, shredded, unsweetened | 2.1 | 60 | 50 | 7 | 8 | 11 | Moderate |
| Cherries, fresh | 4.2 | 120 | 22 | 12 | 2 | 12 | Moderate |
| Mango | 4.2 | 120 | 51 | 20 | 2 | 12 | Moderate |
| Plum, fresh | 4.2 | 120 | 24 | 14 | 2 | 12 | Moderate |
| Pear, fresh | 4.2 | 120 | 33 | 13 | 4 | 12 | Moderate |
| Apple | 4.2 | 120 | 40 | 16 | 3 | 12 | Moderate |
| Banana, ripe | 4.2 | 120 | 51 | 25 | 3 | 15 | High |
| Figs | 2.1 | 60 | 61 | 26 | 6 | 16 | High |
| Plantain | 2.8 | 80 | 40 | 23 | 2 | 16 | High |
| Banana, under ripe | 4.2 | 120 | 30 | 21 | 3 | 18 | High |
| Raisins | 2.1 | 60 | 64 | 44 | 2 | 18 | High |
| Apricots, dried | 2.1 | 60 | 30 | 27 | 4 | 23 | High |

| Fruits | Serving Size (oz) | Serving Size (grams) | Glycemic Index | Net Carbs per Serving (grams) | Fiber per Serving (grams) | Ferm. Potential (grams) | Relative Symptom Risk |
|---|---|---|---|---|---|---|---|
| [1]Dates, dried | 2.1 | 60 | 42 | 40 | 4 | 27 | High |
| Prunes, dried | 2.1 | 60 | 29 | 33 | 4 | 28 | High |

[1]The glycemic index for blueberries, raspberries and black berries has not been determined, but has been estimated based on GI value for strawberries. The glycemic index for shredded coconut, lime and lemon juice was estimated to be 50%. The glycemic index of cranberries was estimated based on the GI of cranberry juice. The glycemic index for dates was originally reported to be over 100, yielding a very low FP, but subsequent studies show it's much lower, thus the FP correction to 27 grams for a 2.1 ounce serving.

Note: Another way to lower the FP value is to reduce the serving size. For instance, ½ cup of blueberries weighs 74 grams (less than the 120 g shown in table) which has an FP of 6 grams — considered to be low.

**Table 12** - Fermentation potential for *"Dairy and Soy Products"*

| Dairy & Soy Products | Serving Size (oz) | Serving Size (grams) | Glycemic Index | Net Carbs per Serving (grams) | Sugar Alcohol per Serving (grams) | Fiber per Serving (grams) | Ferm. Potential (grams) | Relative Symptom Risk |
|---|---|---|---|---|---|---|---|---|
| [3]Heavy cream | 8.0 | 227 | 50 | 3 | 0 | 0 | 2 | Low |
| [3]Light cream | 8.0 | 227 | 50 | 4 | 0 | 0 | 2 | Low |
| [4]Soy milk, unsweetened | 8.0 | 227 | 20 | 2 | 0 | 1 | 2 | Low |
| [5]Almond drink | 8.0 | 227 | 22 | 2 | 0 | 1 | 3 | Low |
| Milk, lactose free | 8.0 | 227 | 61 | 7 | 0 | 0 | 3 | Low |
| Yogurt, plain | 8.0 | 227 | 36 | 6 | 0 | 0 | 4 | Low |
| [1]Ice cream | 2.3 | 65 | 61 | 14 | 0 | 0 | 5 | Low |
| [1]Lactose-free ice cream (Breyers) | 2.3 | 65 | 61 | 18 | 0 | 0 | 7 | Low |
| [1]Milk, whole | 8.0 | 227 | 27 | 11 | 0 | 0 | 8 | Moderate |
| [1]Milk, skim | 8.0 | 227 | 32 | 12 | 0 | 0 | 8 | Moderate |
| [1]Milk, condensed, sweetened | 8.0 | 227 | 61 | 25 | 0 | 0 | 10 | Moderate |
| [2]Carb Smart ice cream (Breyers) | 2.3 | 65 | 61 | 4 | 5 | 4 | 11 | Moderate |
| Yogurt, low-fat, fruit, aspartame sweetened | 8.0 | 227 | 14 | 15 | 0 | 0 | 13 | Moderate |

| Dairy & Soy Products | Serving Size (oz) | Serving Size (grams) | Glycemic Index | Net Carbs per Serving (grams) | Sugar Alcohol per Serving (grams) | Fiber per Serving (grams) | Ferm. Potential (grams) | Relative Symptom Risk |
|---|---|---|---|---|---|---|---|---|
| [1]Milk, chocolate, | 8.0 | 227 | 42 | 28 | 0 | 2 | 18 | High |
| Yogurt, low-fat, fruit, sugar sweetened | 8.0 | 227 | 33 | 35 | 0 | 0 | 24 | High |

[1]Lactose containing products such as milk, condensed milk and ice cream, though not likely yogurt (because its fermented removing most of the lactose), would have higher fermentative potentials if their glycemic indices were determined using people who are lactose intolerant – which they're not. If these foods give you symptoms, add dietary supplement lactase enzyme or reduce or eliminate lactose-containing foods. You can be tested for lactose intolerance. For the lactose intolerant, Breyers lactose-free ice cream is a better choice even though its FP is a little higher than regular ice cream. Cream and light cream also have lactose, but in smaller amounts.

[2]Carb smart ice cream is not the best choice, due to the presence of sugar alcohols.
[3]The GI for heavy and light cream was estimated based on the GI for lactose (46).
[4]The GI for soy milk was estimated based on tofu (20).
[5]The GI for almond drink was estimated based on the GI for similar foods (22).

**Table 13 -** Fermentation potential for *"Non-Dairy Beverages"*

| Non-Dairy Beverages | Serving Size (oz) | Serving Size (grams) | Glycemic Index | Net Carbs per Serving (grams) | Fiber per Serving (grams) | Ferm. Potential (grams) | Relative Symptom Risk |
|---|---|---|---|---|---|---|---|
| Diet soda and other zero calorie diet drinks | 8.8 | 250 | NA | 0 | 0 | 0 | Low |
| Hard alcohol - Rum, whiskey, bourbon, vodka, gin, brandy, etc. | 1.5 | 44 | NA | 0 | 0 | 0 | Low |
| *Coconut milk, unsweetened | 8.8 | 250 | 50 | 1 | 0 | 0 | Low |
| *Beer, lite | 12.0 | 336 | 50 | 3 | 0 | 2 | Low |
| *Wine, dry white | 6.6 | 187 | 50 | 3 | 0 | 2 | Low |
| *Wine, dry red | 6.6 | 187 | 50 | 4 | 0 | 2 | Low |
| Lucozade® (glucose drink) | 8.8 | 250 | 95 | 42 | 0 | 2 | Low |
| Gatorade® | 8.8 | 250 | 78 | 15 | 0 | 3 | Low |
| Quik™, chocolate mix dissolved in water | 8.8 | 250 | 53 | 7 | 1 | 4 | Low |
| *Beer, non-lite | 12.0 | 336 | 50 | 12 | 0 | 6 | Low |
| Tomato juice, no added sugar | 8.8 | 250 | 38 | 9 | 1 | 7 | Low |
| *Coconut water | 8.8 | 250 | 50 | 6 | 6 | 9 | Moderate |
| Coca Cola®, sweetened | 8.8 | 250 | 63 | 26 | 0 | 10 | Moderate |
| Grapefruit juice, unsweetened | 8.8 | 250 | 48 | 20 | 0 | 11 | Moderate |
| Cranberry juice cocktail | 8.8 | 250 | 68 | 36 | 0 | 12 | Moderate |

| Non-Dairy Beverages | Serving Size (oz) | Serving Size (grams) | Glycemic Index | Net Carbs per Serving (grams) | Fiber per Serving (grams) | Ferm. Potential (grams) | Relative Symptom Risk |
|---|---|---|---|---|---|---|---|
| Hot Chocolate | 8.8 | 250 | 51 | 23 | 1 | 12 | Moderate |
| Orange juice | 8.8 | 250 | 50 | 26 | 1 | 14 | Moderate |
| Carrot juice | 8.8 | 250 | 43 | 23 | 2 | 15 | High |
| Apple juice, unsweetened | 8.8 | 250 | 40 | 29 | 1 | 18 | High |
| Pineapple juice, unsweetened | 8.8 | 250 | 46 | 34 | 1 | 19 | High |

*Beer, wine, coconut milk and coconut water have not been tested for the glycemic index. A conservative estimated GI of 50 has been used.

Note: Unsweetened mixed drinks, light beer and dry red or white wine are the lowest FP alcoholic drink choices. Even though non-lite beer has an FP of only 6 grams, this can add up quickly if you drink more than one. Also, avoid sweetened wines as the FP will be considerably higher.

**Table 14** - Fermentation potential for *"Desserts, Snacks, Nuts and Seeds"*

| Desserts, Snacks, Nuts & Seeds | Serving Size (oz) | Serving Size (grams) | Glycemic Index | Net Carbs per Serving (grams) | Sugar Alcohol per serving (grams) | Fiber per Serving (grams) | Ferm. Potential (grams) | Relative Symptom Risk |
|---|---|---|---|---|---|---|---|---|
| Rice cracker | 1.1 | 30 | 91 | 25 | 0 | 0 | 2 | Low |
| Popcorn | 0.7 | 20 | 89 | 11 | 0 | 3 | 4 | Low |
| Pretzels | 1.1 | 30 | 83 | 20 | 0 | 1 | 4 | Low |
| ¹Pecans | 1.1 | 30 | 22 | 1 | 0 | 3 | 4 | Low |
| ¹Walnuts | 1.1 | 30 | 22 | 2 | 0 | 2 | 4 | Low |
| Peanuts | 1.1 | 30 | 14 | 2 | 0 | 2 | 5 | Low |
| Peanut butter | 1.1 | 30 | 37 | 5 | 0 | 2 | 5 | Low |
| ¹Hazel nuts | 1.1 | 30 | 14 | 2 | 0 | 3 | 5 | Low |
| Rice pudding | 2.6 | 75 | 59 | 11 | 0 | 1 | 5 | Low |
| Rice pudding | 2.6 | 75 | 59 | 11 | 0 | 1 | 5 | Low |
| ¹Ice cream | 2.3 | 65 | 61 | 14 | 0 | 0 | 5 | Low |
| ¹Almond meal | 1.1 | 30 | 22 | 2 | 0 | 3 | 5 | Low |
| ¹Almonds | 1.1 | 30 | 22 | 3 | 0 | 4 | 6 | Low |
| ²Hummus (chickpea salad dip) | 1.1 | 30 | 6 | 5 | 0 | 2 | 6 | Low |
| Cashews | 1.1 | 30 | 22 | 8 | 0 | 1 | 7 | Low |

| Desserts, Snacks, Nuts & Seeds | Serving Size (oz) | Serving Size (grams) | Glycemic Index | Net Carbs per Serving (grams) | Sugar Alcohol per serving (grams) | Fiber per Serving (grams) | Ferm. Potential (grams) | Relative Symptom Risk |
|---|---|---|---|---|---|---|---|---|
| ¹Lactose-free ice cream (Breyers) | 2.3 | 65 | 61 | 18 | 0 | 0 | 7 | Low |
| Life Savers®, candy (Nestlé) | 1.1 | 30 | 70 | 30 | 0 | 0 | 9 | Moderate |
| ¹Flax seeds | 1.1 | 30 | 0 | 0 | 0 | 9 | 9 | Moderate |
| Corn chips | 1.8 | 50 | 72 | 25 | 0 | 3 | 10 | Moderate |
| Custard | 3.5 | 100 | 43 | 17 | 0 | 0 | 10 | Moderate |
| ¹Carb Smart ice cream (Breyers) | 2.3 | 65 | 61 | 4 | 5 | 4 | 11 | Moderate |
| Pop Tarts™, (Kellogg's) | 1.8 | 50 | 70 | 35 | 0 | 1 | 11 | Moderate |
| Pizza, cheese | 3.5 | 100 | 60 | 27 | 0 | 2 | 12 | Moderate |
| Snickers Bar® (Mars) | 2.1 | 60 | 68 | 34 | 0 | 1 | 12 | Moderate |
| M & M's®, peanut (Mars) | 1.1 | 30 | 33 | 17 | 0 | 1 | 12 | Moderate |
| ¹Chia seeds | 1.1 | 30 | 0 | 1 | 0 | 12 | 13 | Moderate |
| Potato chips | 1.8 | 50 | 51 | 24 | 0 | 2 | 13 | Moderate |
| Skittles® (Mars) | 1.8 | 50 | 70 | 45 | 0 | 0 | 14 | Moderate |
| Milk chocolate | 1.6 | 44 | 43 | 25 | 0 | 1 | 15 | High |
| Mars Bar® (Mars) | 2.1 | 60 | 62 | 40 | 0 | 1 | 16 | High |
| Twix® Cookie Bar (Mars) | 2.1 | 60 | 44 | 39 | 0 | 1 | 23 | High |

[1]Almonds, almond meal, pecans, walnuts, hazel nuts, Breyers lactose free ice cream (best choice for lactose intolerance), and Carb Smart ice cream have not been assigned a GI value. The GI values were estimated based on similar foods. See additional notes on lactose-containing foods under Table 12. The glycemic index for Chia and flax seeds is assigned zero since they are essentially all fiber.

[2]Hummus appears to have a much lower FP compared to chickpeas in table one. The reason is the smaller serving size.

**Table 15 - Fermentation potential for "Sweeteners"**

| Sweeteners | Serving Size (oz) | Serving Size (grams) | Glycemic Index | Net Carbs per Serving (grams) | Fiber per Serving (grams) | Ferm. Potential (grams) | Relative Symptom Risk |
|---|---|---|---|---|---|---|---|
| Maltose | 0.5 | 14 | 105 | 14 | 0 | 0 | Low |
| NutraSweet | 0.5 | 14 | NA | 0 | 0 | 0 | Low |
| Saccharin | 0.5 | 14 | NA | 0 | 0 | 0 | Low |
| ¹Splenda | 0.5 | 14 | 100 | 14 | 0 | 0 | Low |
| Dextrose (powdered glucose) | 0.5 | 14 | 100 | 14 | 0 | 0 | Low |
| ⁴Brown rice syrup | 0.5 | 14 | 88 | 11 | 0 | 1 | Low |
| ⁵Barley malt syrup | 0.5 | 14 | 99 | 9 | 0 | 1 | Low |
| Maple syrup | 0.5 | 14 | 54 | 10 | 0 | 5 | Low |
| Sucrose | 0.5 | 14 | 59 | 14 | 0 | 6 | Low |
| ²Brown sugar | 0.5 | 14 | 59 | 14 | 0 | 6 | Low |
| Honey | 0.5 | 14 | 55 | 14 | 0 | 6 | Low |
| ³Lactose | 0.5 | 14 | 48 | 14 | 0 | 7 | Low |
| Fructose | 0.5 | 14 | 20 | 14 | 0 | 11 | Moderate |

Note: The FP of dextrose (glucose) is zero by definition because glucose is completely absorbed. Nutrasweet and saccharin have zero carbs and hence also have a fermentative potential of zero. Also, notice the extreme low GI/high FP for fructose, which is absorbed very poorly.
¹Splenda has 14 grams of carbs per 1/2 ounce but the carbs are in the form of maltodextrin, a partial breakdown product of starch. Maltodextrin is absorbed as efficiently as glucose, hence Splenda has an FP equal to zero. Also, note that 1/2 ounce of Splenda is 1/2 cup or 24 teaspoons, so a teaspoon is just over 1/2 gram.
²The glycemic index for brown sugar was estimated to be 59, the same as sucrose. 3The GI for lactose was determined in healthy volunteers, but would likely be much lower if tested in lactose intolerant people. If you are lactose intolerant, assume the FP to be equal to the net carbs.
⁴The FP of brown rice syrup is based on 52% maltotriose (GI of 60), 3% glucose (GI 100), and 45% maltose (GI 105).
⁵The FP of barley malt syrup is based on 75% maltose (GI 100), 16% glucose (GI 100), 6% sucrose (GI 59), and 2% fructose (GI 20).

**Table 16** - Fermentation potential for *"Meat, Cheese, Tofu and Seafood"*

| Meat, Cheese, Eggs, Tofu & Seafood | Serving Size (oz) | Serving Size (grams) | Glycemic Index | Net Carbs per Serving (grams) | Fiber per Serving (grams) | Ferm. Potential (grams) | Relative Symptom Risk |
|---|---|---|---|---|---|---|---|
| Steak | 6 | 170 | NA | 0 | 0 | 0 | Low |
| Eggs | 6 | 170 | NA | 0 | 0 | 0 | Low |
| Hamburg | 6 | 170 | NA | 0 | 0 | 0 | Low |
| Pork | 6 | 170 | NA | 0 | 0 | 0 | Low |
| Hotdog | 6 | 170 | NA | 0 | 0 | 0 | Low |
| Ham | 6 | 170 | NA | 0 | 0 | 0 | Low |
| Chicken | 6 | 170 | NA | 0 | 0 | 0 | Low |
| Duck | 6 | 170 | NA | 0 | 0 | 0 | Low |
| Fish | 6 | 170 | NA | 0 | 0 | 0 | Low |
| Seafood | 6 | 170 | NA | 0 | 0 | 0 | Low |
| Cold cuts | 4 | 114 | 0 | 0 | 0 | 0 | Low |
| ¹Swiss Cheese | 2 | 57 | 48 | 2 | 0 | 1 | Low |
| ¹Cheddar Cheese | 2 | 57 | 48 | 1 | 0 | 1 | Low |
| ¹Mozzarella Cheese | 2 | 57 | 48 | 1 | 0 | 1 | Low |
| ¹Cream cheese | 2 | 57 | 48 | 3 | 0 | 1 | Low |
| ¹Ricotta Cheese | 2 | 57 | 48 | 2 | 0 | 1 | Low |
| ¹American Cheese | 2 | 57 | 48 | 4 | 0 | 2 | Low |

| Meat, Cheese, Eggs, Tofu & Seafood | Serving Size (oz) | Serving Size (grams) | Glycemic Index | Net Carbs per Serving (grams) | Fiber per Serving (grams) | Ferm. Potential (grams) | Relative Symptom Risk |
|---|---|---|---|---|---|---|---|
| [1]Cottage Cheese | 5 | 114 | 48 | 3 | 0 | 2 | Low |
| [2]Tofu | 4.5 | 126 | 20 | 1 | 1 | 2 | Low |
| [3]Scallops | 8 | 170 | 50 | 4 | 0 | 2 | Low |

*The glycemic index is not applicable (NA) for foods containing no carbohydrates.

[1]Most cheeses have low overall carb counts and hence were not assessed for glycemic index. The GI for lactose (48) was used to calculate the FP for cheeses. These foods have a Fermentative Potential [FP] close to zero. The symptom potential for these foods is therefore low. The lactose content (because cheese comes from milk) may be an issue for some lactose intolerant people. Limit cheeses, such as Ricotta, with higher carbs counts if you are lactose intolerant or take lactase enzyme with cheese-containing meals. For most people, this won't be an issue because the carb counts, including lactose, are so low. Aged cheeses are the best choice.

[2]Tofu has not been tested for the glycemic index - assume a glycemic index of 20 based on soy beans.

[3]Scallops, unlike most seafood, contain carbohydrates, but have not been tested for the glycemic index - assume a glycemic index of 50%.

**Appendix C:**

# Fast Tract Dietary Journal Template

| Date | Breakfast | Lunch | Snack | Dinner | Dessert |
|------|-----------|-------|-------|--------|---------|
|  |  |  |  |  |  |
|  |  |  |  |  |  |
| FP Totals |  |  |  |  |  |
| Symptoms |  |  |  |  |  |

| Date | Breakfast | Lunch | Snack | Dinner | Dessert |
|------|-----------|-------|-------|--------|---------|
|  |  |  |  |  |  |
|  |  |  |  |  |  |
| FP Totals |  |  |  |  |  |
| Symptoms |  |  |  |  |  |

| Date | Breakfast | Lunch | Snack | Dinner | Dessert |
|------|-----------|-------|-------|--------|---------|
|      |           |       |       |        |         |
| FP Totals |      |       |       |        |         |
| Symptoms |      |       |       |        |         |

| Date | Breakfast | Lunch | Snack | Dinner | Dessert |
|------|-----------|-------|-------|--------|---------|
|      |           |       |       |        |         |
| FP Totals |      |       |       |        |         |
| Symptoms |      |       |       |        |         |

| Date | Breakfast | Lunch | Snack | Dinner | Dessert |
| --- | --- | --- | --- | --- | --- |
|  |  |  |  |  |  |
| FP Totals |  |  |  |  |  |
| Symptoms |  |  |  |  |  |

| Date | Breakfast | Lunch | Snack | Dinner | Dessert |
| --- | --- | --- | --- | --- | --- |
|  |  |  |  |  |  |
| FP Totals |  |  |  |  |  |
| Symptoms |  |  |  |  |  |

| Date | Breakfast | Lunch | Snack | Dinner | Dessert |
|------|-----------|-------|-------|--------|---------|
|      |           |       |       |        |         |
| FP Totals |      |       |       |        |         |
| Symptoms  |      |       |       |        |         |

| Date | Breakfast | Lunch | Snack | Dinner | Dessert |
|------|-----------|-------|-------|--------|---------|
|      |           |       |       |        |         |
| FP Totals |      |       |       |        |         |
| Symptoms  |      |       |       |        |         |

| Date | Breakfast | Lunch | Snack | Dinner | Dessert |
|------|-----------|-------|-------|--------|---------|
| | | | | | |
| FP Totals | | | | | |
| Symptoms | | | | | |

| Date | Breakfast | Lunch | Snack | Dinner | Dessert |
|------|-----------|-------|-------|--------|---------|
| | | | | | |
| FP Totals | | | | | |
| Symptoms | | | | | |

| Date | Breakfast | Lunch | Snack | Dinner | Dessert |
|---|---|---|---|---|---|
| | | | | | |
| FP Totals | | | | | |
| Symptoms | | | | | |

| Date | Breakfast | Lunch | Snack | Dinner | Dessert |
|---|---|---|---|---|---|
| | | | | | |
| FP Totals | | | | | |
| Symptoms | | | | | |

| Date | Breakfast | | Lunch | | Snack | | Dinner | | Dessert | |
|------|-----------|---|-------|---|-------|---|--------|---|---------|---|
| FP Totals | | | | | | | | | | |
| Symptoms | | | | | | | | | | |

| Date | Breakfast | | Lunch | | Snack | | Dinner | | Dessert | |
|------|-----------|---|-------|---|-------|---|--------|---|---------|---|
| FP Totals | | | | | | | | | | |
| Symptoms | | | | | | | | | | |

# Digestive Health Institute

Get relief without drugs or antibiotics
Take control of your health with 3 Pillar Approach

**Norman Robillard, Ph.D.**
Founder, Digestive Health
Institute

**For individual consultation or group coaching with**

**Dr. Robillard,**

call **844-495-1151 (US)**

or e-mail

info@digestivehealthinstitute.org

## 3 Pillar Approach to your holistic health

Addressing
**Underlying**
Causes

**Diet**

**Behavioral**
Modification

- Heartburn | Acid Reflux | GERD
- Laryngopharyngeal Reflux Disease (LPR)
- Irritable Bowel Syndrome (IBS)
- Small Intestinal Bacterial Overgrowth (SIBO)
- Celiac disease
- Crohn's disease
- Constipation
- Diverticulitis
- Asthma
- Rosacea
- Leaky gut | Autoimmunity

**Disclaimer:** Norm Robillard holds a Ph.D. in microbiology and has authored several books on digestive health, but is not a medical doctor. His advice is focused on balancing gut microflora through diet and behavior modification. This is not nutritional counseling. This advice should be used in conjunction with discussions with your own doctor.

Find a wealth of digestive health articles:
**www.digestivehealthinstitute.org**

Join the Digestive Health Institute Facebook page:
**www.facebook.com/DigestiveHealthInstitute**

Follow Dr. Robillard on Twitter:
**@DrNRobillard**

END NOTES

[1] Middleton SJ, Coley A, Hunter JO. The role of faecal Candida albicans in the pathogenesis of food-intolerant irritable bowel syndrome. Postgrad Med J. 1992 Jun;68(800):453-4.

[2] Manning AP, Thompson WG, Heaton KW, Morris AF. Towards positive diagnosis of the irritable bowel. Br Med J. 1978 Sep 2;2(6138):653-4.

[3] Drossman DA, Richter JE, Talley NJ, et al., eds. Functional gastrointestinal disorders: Diagnosis, pathophysiology and treatment: A multinational consensus. Boston: Little, Brown; 1994.

[4] Thompson WG, Longstreth GF, Drossman DA, Heaton KW, Irvine EJ, Müller-Lissner SA. Functional bowel disorders and functional abdominal pain. Gut. 1999 Sep;45 Suppl 2:II43-7.

[5] Saito YA; Locke GR; Talley NJ; Zinsmeister AR; Fett SL; Melton LJ 3rd A comparison of the Rome and Manning criteria for case identification in epidemiological investigations of irritable bowel syndrome. Am J Gastroenterol 2000 Oct;95(10):2816-24.

[6] Longstreth GF, et al. (2006). Irritable bowel syndrome section of Functional bowel disorders. In DA Drossman et al., eds., Rome III: The Functional Gastrointestinal Disorders, 3rd ed., pp. 490-509.

[7] Atkinson W, Sheldon TA, Shaath N, Whorwell PJ. Food elimination based on IgG antibodies in irritable bowel syndrome: a randomised controlled trial. Gut. 2004 Oct;53(10):1459-64.

[8] Badiali D, Corazziari E, Habib FI, Tomei E, Bausano G, Magrini P, Anzini F, Torsoli A. Effect of wheat bran in treatment of chronic nonorganic constipation. A double-blind controlled trial. Dig Dis Sci. 1995 Feb;40(2):349-56.

[9] Bijkerk CJ, Muris JW, Knottnerus JA, Hoes AW, de Wit NJ. Systematic review: the role of different types of fibre in the treatment of irritable bowel syndrome. Aliment Pharmacol Ther. 2004 Feb 1;19(3):245-51.

10 Bijkerk CJ, de Wit NJ, Muris JW, Whorwell PJ, Knottnerus JA, Hoes AW. Soluble or insoluble fibre in irritable bowel syndrome in primary care? Randomised placebo controlled trial. BMJ. 2009 Aug 27;339:b3154.

11 Center for Drug Evaluation and Research (CDER). Public Health Advisory: Tegaserod maleate (marketed as Zelnorm). Food and Drug Administration. March 30, 2007.

12 Drossman DA, Chey WD, Johanson JF, Fass R, Scott C, Panas R, Ueno R. Clinical trial: lubiprostone in patients with constipation-associated irritable bowel syndrome—results of two randomized, placebo-controlled studies. Aliment Pharmacol Ther. 2009 Feb 1;29(3):329-41.

13 Chey WD, Lembo AJ, Lavins BJ, Shiff SJ, Kurtz CB, Currie MG, Macdougall JE, Jia XD, Shao JZ, Fitch DA, Baird MJ, Schneier HA, Johnston JM. Linaclotide for Irritable Bowel Syndrome With Constipation: A 26-Week, Randomized, Double-blind, Placebo-Controlled Trial to Evaluate Efficacy and Safety. Am J Gastroenterol. 2012 Sep 18. doi: 10.1038/ajg.2012.254.

14 Rao S, Lembo AJ, Shiff SJ, Lavins BJ, Currie MG, Jia XD, Shi K, Macdougall JE, Shao JZ, Eng P, Fox SM, Schneier HA, Kurtz CB, Johnston JM. A 12-Week, Randomized, Controlled Trial With a 4-Week Randomized Withdrawal Period to Evaluate the Efficacy and Safety of Linaclotide in Irritable Bowel Syndrome With Constipation. Am J Gastroenterol. 2012 Sep 18. doi: 10.1038/ajg.2012.255.

15 http://www.webmd.com/ibs/guide/irritable-bowel-syndrome-ibs-medications.

16 King TS, Elia M, Hunter JO. Abnormal colonic fermentation in irritable bowel syndrome. Lancet. 1998 Oct 10;352(9135):1187-9.

17 Maxwell PR, Rink E, Kumar D, Mendall MA. Antibiotics increase functional abdominal symptoms. Am J Gastroenterol. 2002 Jan;97(1):104-8.

18 Neal KR, Hebden J, Spiller R. Prevalence of gastrointestinal symptoms six months after bacterial gastroenteritis and risk factors for development of the irritable bowel syndrome: postal survey of patients. BMJ. 1997 Mar 15;314(7083):779-82.

[19] Pimentel M A New IBS Solution. Health Point Press. 2006.

[20] Pimentel M, Chow EJ, Lin HC. Eradication of small intestinal bacterial overgrowth reduces symptoms of irritable bowel syndrome. Am J Gastroenterol. 2000;95:3503-6.

[21] Bouhnik Y, Alain S, Attar A, Flourié B, Raskine L, Sanson-Le Pors MJ, Rambaud JC. Bacterial populations contaminating the upper gut in patients with small intestinal bacterial overgrowth syndrome. Am J Gastroenterol. 1999 May;94(5):1327-31). Ghoshal U, Ghoshal UC, Ranjan P, Naik SR, Ayyagari A. Spectrum and antibiotic sensitivity of bacteria contaminating the upper gut in patients with malabsorption syndrome from the tropics. BMC Gastroenterol. 2003 May 24;3:9.

[22] Tynes LL, Gibson RL. Irritable bowel syndrome: overview of diagnosis and treatment. J La State Med Soc. 1999 Feb;151(2):76-81.

[23] DiBaise J. Nutritional Consequences of Small Intestinal Bacterial Overgrowth. Nutrition Issues in Gastroenterology, Series #69. Practical Gastroenterology Dec 2008. PP 15-28. Born P. Carbohydrate malabsorption in patients with non-specific abdominal complaints. World J Gastroenterol. 2007 Nov 21;13(43):5687-91.

[24] Ringel Y, Williams RE, Kalilani L, Cook SF. Prevalence, characteristics, and impact of bloating symptoms in patients with irritable bowel syndrome. Clin Gastroenterol Hepatol. 2009 Jan;7(1):68-72.

[25] Sullivan SN. A prospective study of unexplained visible abdominal bloating. N Z Med J. 1994 Oct 26;107(988):428-30.

[26] Rumessen JJ, Gudmand-Høyer E. Functional bowel disease: malabsorption and abdominal distress after ingestion of fructose, sorbitol, and fructose-sorbitol mixtures. Gastroenterology. 1988 Sep;95(3):694-700.

[27] Lin, HC, Zaidel, O. Uninvited Guests: The Impact of Small Intestinal Bacterial Overgrowth on Nutritional Status. Nutrition Issues in Gastroenterology, Series #7. Practical Gastroenterology. Jul 2003. PP 27-34.

[28] Pimentel M, Chow EJ, Lin HC. Eradication of small intestinal bacterial overgrowth reduces symptoms of irritable bowel syndrome. Am J Gastroenterol. 2000;95:3503-6.

[29] Lin, HC, Zaidel, O. Uninvited Guests: The Impact of Small Intestinal Bacterial Overgrowth on Nutritional Status. Nutrition Issues in Gastroenterology, Series #7. Practical Gastroenterology. Jul 2003. PP 27-34.

[30] Scarpellini E, Giorgio V, Gabrielli M, Lauritano EC, Pantanella A, Fundarò C, Gasbarrini A. Prevalence of small intestinal bacterial overgrowth in children with irritable bowel syndrome: a case-control study. J Pediatr. 2009 Sep;155(3):416-20.

[31] Collins BS, Lin HC. Chronic abdominal pain in children is associated with high prevalence of abnormal microbial fermentation. Dig Dis Sci. 2010 Jan;55(1):124-30.

[32] Chatterjee S, Park S, Low K, Kong Y, Pimentel M. The degree of breath methane production in IBS correlates with the severity of constipation. Am J Gastroenterol. 2007 Apr;102(4):837-41.

[33] Chassard C, Dapoigny M, Scott KP, Crouzet L, Del'homme C, Marquet P, Martin JC, Pickering G, Ardid D, Eschalier A, Dubray C, Flint HJ, Bernalier-Donadille A. Functional dysbiosis within the gut microbiota of patients with constipated-irritable bowel syndrome. Aliment Pharmacol Ther. 2012 Apr;35(7):828-38. doi: 10.1111/j.1365-2036.2012.05007.x. Epub 2012 Feb 8.

[34] Nucera G, Gabrielli M, Lupascu A, Lauritano EC, Santoliquido A, Cremonini F, Cammarota G, Tondi P, Pola P, Gasbarrini G, Gasbarrini A. Abnormal breath tests to lactose, fructose and sorbitol in irritable bowel syndrome may be explained by small intestinal bacterial overgrowth. Aliment Pharmacol Ther. 2005 Jun 1;21(11):1391-5.

[35] Pimentel M, Chow EJ, Lin HC. Normalization of lactulose breath testing correlates with symptom improvement in irritable bowel syndrome: A double-blind, randomized, placebo-controlled study. Am J Gastroenterol. 2003 Feb;98(2):412-9.

[36] Majewski M, Reddymasu SC, Sostarich S, Foran P, McCallum RW. Efficacy of rifaximin, a nonabsorbed oral antibiotic, in the treatment of small intestinal bacterial overgrowth. Am J Med Sci. 2007 May;333(5):266-70.

[37] Dear KL, Elia M, Hunter JO. Do interventions which reduce colonic bacterial fermentation improve symptoms of irritable bowel syndrome? Dig Dis Sci. 2005 Apr;50(4):758-66.

[38] Austin GL, Dalton CB, Hu Y, Morris CB, Hankins J, Weinland SR, Westman EC, Yancy WS Jr, Drossman DA. A very low-carbohydrate diet improves symptoms and quality of life in diarrhea-predominant irritable bowel syndrome. Clin Gastroenterol Hepatol. 2009 Jun;7(6):706-708.

[39] Shepherd SJ, Gibson PR. Fructose malabsorption and symptoms of irritable bowel syndrome: guidelines for effective dietary management. J Am Diet Assoc. 2006 Oct;106(10):1631-9.

[40] Pimentel M, Constantino T, Kong Y, Bajwa M, Rezaei A, Park S. A 14-day elemental diet is highly effective in normalizing the lactulose breath test. Dig Dis Sci. 2004 Jan;49(1):73-7.

[41] Robillard, N. Fast Tract Digestion Heartburn. Self Health Publishing. 2012. ISBN 978-0-9766425-3-4.

[42] Tursi A, Brandimarte G, Giorgetti G. High prevalence of small intestinal bacterial overgrowth in celiac patients with persistence of gastrointestinal symptoms after gluten withdrawal. Am J Gastroenterol. 2003 Apr;98(4):839-43.

[43] Rubio-Tapia A, Barton SH, Rosenblatt JE, Murray JA. Prevalence of small intestine bacterial overgrowth diagnosed by quantitative culture of intestinal aspirate in celiac disease. J Clin Gastroenterol. 2009 Feb;43(2):157-61.

[44] Ohayon MM, Roth T. Prevalence of restless legs syndrome and periodic limb movement disorder in the general population. J Psychosom Res. 2002 Jul;53(1):547-54.

[45] Basu PP, Shah NJ, Krishnaswamy N, Pacana T. Prevalence of restless legs syndrome in patients with irritable bowel syndrome. World J Gastroenterol. 2011 Oct 21;17(39):4404-7.

[46] Weinstock LB, Walters AS. Restless legs syndrome is associated with irritable bowel syndrome and small intestinal bacterial overgrowth. Sleep Med. 2011 Jun;12(6):610-3. Epub 2011 May 13.

[47] Roussos A, Koursarakos P, Patsopoulos D, Gerogianni I, Philippou N. Increased prevalence of irritable bowel syndrome in patients with bronchial asthma. Respir Med. 2003 Jan;97(1):75-9.

[48] Robillard, N. Fast Tract Digestion Heartburn. Self Health Publishing. 2012. ISBN 978-0-9766425-3-4.

[49] Sontag SJ, O'Connell S, Khandelwal S, Miller T, Nemchausky B, Schnell TG, Serlovsky R. Most asthmatics have gastroesophageal reflux with or without bronchodilator therapy. Gastroenterology. 1990 Sep;99(3):613-20.

[50] Leggett JJ, Johnston BT, Mills M, Gamble J, Heaney LG. Prevalence of gastroesophageal reflux in difficult asthma: relationship to asthma outcome. Chest. 2005 Apr;127(4):1227-31.

[51] Stobaugh DJ, Deepak P, Ehrenpreis ED. Increased risk of osteo-porosis-related fractures in patients with irritable bowel syndrome. Osteoporos Int. 2012 Sep 20.

[52] Di Stefano M, Veneto G, Malservisi S, Corazza GR. Small intestine bacterial overgrowth and metabolic bone disease. Dig Dis Sci. 2001 May;46(5):1077-82.

[53] Yang YX, Lewis JD, Epstein S, Metz DC. Long-term proton pump inhibitor therapy and risk of hip fracture. JAMA. 2006 Dec 27;296(24):2947-53.

[54] Kerckhoffs AP, Samsom M, van der Rest ME, de Vogel J, Knol J, Ben-Amor K, Akkermans LM. Lower Bifidobacteria counts in both duodenal mucosa-associated and fecal microbiota in irritable bowel syndrome patients. World J Gastroenterol. 2009 Jun 21;15(23):2887-92.

[55] Suarez F, Levitt M. Textbook of Primary and Acute Care Medicine, edited by Gideon Bosker. Part VI, Section 107.

[56] Dener IA, Demirci C. Explosion during diathermy gastrotomy in a patient with carcinoma of the antrum. Int J Clin Pract. 2003 Oct; 57(8):737-8. Bigard M-A, Gaucher P, Lassalle C. Fatal colonic explosion during colonoscopic polypectomy. Gastroenterology 1979; 77: 1307-1310.

[57] Pyleris E, Giamarellos-Bourboulis EJ, Tzivras D, Koussoulas V, Barbatzas C, Pimentel M. The prevalence of overgrowth by aerobic bacteria in the small intestine by small bowel culture: relationship with irritable bowel syndrome. Dig Dis Sci. 2012 May;57(5):1321-9. Epub 2012 Jan 20.

[58] Pimentel M. A New IBS Solution. Health Point Press. 2006.

[59] Bratten JR, Spanier J, Jones MP. Lactulose breath testing does not discriminate patients with irritable bowel syndrome from healthy controls. Am J Gastroenterol. 2008 Apr;103(4):958-63.

[60] Shah ED, Basseri RJ, Chong K, Pimentel M. Abnormal breath testing in IBS: a meta-analysis. Dig Dis Sci. 2010 Sep;55(9):2441-9.

[61] Rumessen JJ, Gudmand-Høyer E. Functional bowel disease: malabsorption and abdominal distress after ingestion of fructose, sorbitol, and fructose-sorbitol mixtures. Gastroenterology. 1988 Sep;95(3):694-700. Novillo A, Peralta D, Dima G, Besasso H, Soifer L. Frequency of bacterial overgrowth in patients with clinical lactose intolerance. Acta Gastroenterol Latinoam. 2010 Sep;40(3):221-4.

[62] NDA 21-361. Briefing Document for Gastrointestinal Drugs Advisory Committee Meeting 16 November 2011. http://www.fda.gov/downloads/advisorycommittees/committeesmeetingmaterials/drugs/gastrointestinaldrugsadvisorycommittee/ucm279646.pdf.

[63] Attar A, Flourié B, Rambaud JC, Franchisseur C, Ruszniewski P, Bouhnik Y. Antibiotic efficacy in small intestinal bacterial overgrowth-related chronic diarrhea: a crossover, randomized trial. Gastroenterology. 1999 Oct;117(4):794-7.

[64] de Boissieu D, Chaussain M, Badoual J, Raymond J, Dupont C. Small-bowel bacterial overgrowth in children with chronic diarrhea, abdominal pain, or both. J Pediatr. 1996 Feb;128(2):203-7.

[65] Pimentel M, Chow EJ, Lin HC. Eradication of small intestinal bacterial overgrowth reduces symptoms of irritable bowel syndrome. Am J Gastroenterol. 2000;95:3503-6.

[66] Scarpellini E, Giorgio V, Gabrielli M, Lauritano EC, Pantanella A, Fundarò C, Gasbarrini A. Prevalence of small intestinal bacterial overgrowth in children with irritable bowel syndrome: a case-control study. J Pediatr. 2009 Sep;155(3):416-20.

[67] Basseri R, Weitsman S, Barlow G, Pimentel M. Antibiotics for the Treatment of Irritable Bowel Syndrome. Gastroenterol Hepatol. 2011 July; 7(7): 455–493.

[68] Pimentel M, Lembo A, Chey WD, Zakko S, Ringel Y, Yu J, Mareya SM, Shaw AL, Bortey E, Forbes WP; TARGET Study Group.

Rifaximin therapy for patients with irritable bowel syndrome without constipation. N Engl J Med. 2011 Jan 6;364(1):22-32.

[69] Lauritano EC, Gabrielli M, Scarpellini E, Lupascu A, Novi M, Sottili S, Vitale G, Cesario V, Serricchio M, Cammarota G, Gasbarrini G, Gasbarrini A. Small intestinal bacterial overgrowth recurrence after antibiotic therapy. Am J Gastroenterol. 2008 Aug;103(8):2031-5.

[70] Villarreal AA, Aberger FJ, Benrud R, Gundrum JD. Use of broad-spectrum antibiotics and the development of irritable bowel syndrome. WMJ. 2012 Feb;111(1):17-20.

[71] Hviid A, Svanström H, Frisch M. Antibiotic use and inflammatory bowel diseases in childhood. Gut. 2011 Jan;60(1):49-54. Epub 2010 Oct 21.

[72] http://m.cdc.gov/en/VitalSigns/making-health-care-safer-stopping-c-difficile-infections.

[73] Khanna S, Pardi DS. The growing incidence and severity of Clostridium difficile infection in inpatient and outpatient settings. Expert Rev Gastroenterol Hepatol. 2010 Aug;4(4):409-16.

[74] Kelly CP. Can we identify patients at high risk of recurrent Clostridium difficile infection? Clin Microbiol Infect. 2012 Dec;18 Suppl 6:21-7. doi: 10.1111/1469-0691.12046.

[75] Silva Júnior M. Recent changes in Clostridium difficile infection. Einstein (Sao Paulo). 2012 Jan-Mar;10(1):105-9.

[76] http://www.cdc.gov/HAI/organisms/cre/

[77] Carman RJ, Boone JH, Grover H, Wickham KN, Chen L. In vivo selection of rifamycin resistant Clostridium difficile during rifaximin therapy. Antimicrob Agents Chemother. 2012 Aug 20. [Epub ahead of print].

[78] Liao CH, Ko WC, Lu JJ, Hsueh PR. Characterizations of clinical isolates of clostridium difficile by toxin genotypes and by susceptibility to 12 antimicrobial agents, including fidaxomicin (OPT-80) and rifaximin: a multicenter study in Taiwan. Antimicrob Agents Chemother. 2012 Jul;56(7):3943-9.

[79] http://www.salix.com/products/xifaxan550.aspx.

[80] http://www.salix.com/products/xifaxan550.aspx

[81] Booyens J, Louwrens CC, Katzeff IE. The role of unnatural dietary trans and cis unsaturated fatty acids in the epidemiology of coronary artery disease. Med Hypotheses 1988; 25:175-182. Grundy SM, Abate N, Chandalia M. Diet composition and the metabolic syndrome: what is the optimal fat intake? Am J Med. 2002 Dec 30; 113 Suppl 9B:25S-29S.

[82] United States Food and Drug Administration, September 8, 2004. FDA announces qualified health claims for omega-3 fatty acids. Press release.

[83] Rada V, Bartonová J, Vlková E. Specific growth rate of bifidobacteria cultured on different sugars. Folia Microbiol (Praha). 2002;47(5):477-80.

[84] Bouhnik Y, Alain S, Attar A, Flourié B, Raskine L, Sanson-Le Pors MJ, Rambaud JC. Bacterial populations contaminating the upper gut in patients with small intestinal bacterial overgrowth syndrome. Am J Gastroenterol. 1999 May;94(5):1327-31). Ghoshal U, Ghoshal UC, Ranjan P, Naik SR, Ayyagari A. Spectrum and antibiotic sensitivity of bacteria contaminating the upper gut in patients with malabsorption syndrome from the tropics. BMC Gastroenterol. 2003 May 24;3:9.

[85] Chatterjee S, Park S, Low K, Kong Y, Pimentel M. The degree of breath methane production in IBS correlates with the severity of constipation. Am J Gastroenterol. 2007 Apr;102(4):837-41.

[86] Chassard C, Dapoigny M, Scott KP, Crouzet L, Del'homme C, Marquet P, Martin JC, Pickering G, Ardid D, Eschalier A, Dubray C, Flint HJ, Bernalier-Donadille A. Functional dysbiosis within the gut microbiota of patients with constipated-irritable bowel syndrome. Aliment Pharmacol Ther. 2012 Apr;35(7):828-38. doi: 10.1111/j.1365-2036.2012.05007.x. Epub 2012 Feb 8.

[87] Lauritano EC, Bilotta AL, Gabrielli M, et al. Association between hypothyroidism and small intestinal bacterial overgrowth. J Clin Endocrinol Metab. 2007 Nov;92(11):4180-4.

[88] Pimentel M, Soffer EE, Chow EJ, et al. Lower frequency of MMC is found in IBS subjects with abnormal lactulose breath test, suggesting bacterial overgrowth. Dig Dis Sci, 2002;47:2639-2643.

[89] Ghoshal UC, Ghoshal U, Das K, Misra A. Utility of hydrogen breath tests in diagnosis of small intestinal bacterial overgrowth in malabsorption syndrome and its relationship with oro-cecal transit time. Indian J Gastroenterol. 2006 Jan-Feb;25(1):6-10.

[90] Lombardo L, Foti M, Ruggia O, Chiecchio A. Increased incidence of small intestinal bacterial overgrowth during proton pump inhibitor therapy. Clin Gastroenterol Hepatol. 2010 Jun;8(6):504-8.

[91] Lin, HC, Zaidel, O. Uninvited Guests: The Impact of Small Intestinal Bacterial Overgrowth on Nutritional Status. Nutrition Issues in Gastroenterology, Series #7. Practical Gastroenterology. Jul 2003. PP 27-34.

[92] Riepe SP, Goldstein J, Alpers DH. Effect of secreted Bacteroides proteases on human intestinal brush border hydrolases. J Clin Invest. 1980 Aug;66(2):314-22. Jonas A, Krishnan C, Forstner G. Pathogenesis of mucosal injury in the blind loop syndrome. Gastroenterology. 1978 Nov;75(5):791-5.

[93] Mishkin B, Yalovsky M, Mishkin S. Increased prevalence of lactose malabsorption in Crohn's disease patients at low risk for lactose malabsorption based on ethnic origin. Am J Gastroenterol. 1997 Jul;92(7):1148-53.

[94] http://www.mayoclinic.com/health/dehydration/DS00561/DSECTION=treatments-and-drugs.

[95] Marshall JK. Post-infectious irritable bowel syndrome following water contamination. Kidney Int Suppl. 2009 Feb;(112):S42-3. Marshall JK, Thabane M, Garg AX, Clark WF, Salvadori M, Collins SM. Incidence and epidemiology of irritable bowel syndrome after a large waterborne outbreak of bacterial dysentery. Gastroenterology. 2006 Aug;131(2):445-50.

[96] Bercik P, Verdu EF, Collins SM. Is irritable bowel syndrome a low-grade inflammatory bowel disease? Gastroenterol Clin North Am. 2005 Jun;34(2):235-45, vi-vii,

[97] Fisher BL, Pennathur A, Mutnick JL, Little AG. Obesity correlates with gastroesophageal reflux. Dig Dis Sci. 1999 Nov;44(11):2290-4. Teitelbaum JE, Sinha P, Micale M, Yeung S, Jaeger

J. Obesity is related to multiple functional abdominal diseases. J Pediatr. 2009 Mar;154(3):444-6.

[98] Delgado-Aros S, Locke GR 3rd, Camilleri M, Talley NJ, Fett S, Zinsmeister AR, Melton LJ 3rd. Obesity is associated with increased risk of gastrointestinal symptoms: a population-based study. Am J Gastroenterol. 2004 Sep;99(9):1801-6.

[99] Khoruts A, Dicksved J, Jansson JK, Sadowsky MJ. Changes in the composition of the human fecal microbiome after bacteriotherapy for recurrent *Clostridium difficile*-associated diarrhea. J Clin Gastroenterol. 2010 May-Jun;44(5):354-60. Bakken JS. Fecal bacteriotherapy for recurrent Clostridium difficile infection. Anaerobe. 2009 Dec;15(6):285-9. Dr. Johan S. Bakken. Personal communication on updated number of C diff cases treated with bacteriotherapy. February 2011.

[100] Borody TJ, Warren EF, Leis SM, Surace R, Ashman O, Siarakas S. Bacteriotherapy using fecal flora: toying with human motions. J Clin Gastroenterol. 2004 Jul;38(6):475-83.

[101] Grehan MJ, Borody TJ, Leis SM, Campbell J, Mitchell H, Wettstein A. Durable alteration of the colonic microbiota by the administration of donor fecal flora. J Clin Gastroenterol. 2010 Sep;44(8):551-61.

[102] Wynckel A, Jaisser F, Wong T, Drueke T, Chanard J. Intestinal Absorption of calcium from yogurt in lactase-deficient subjects. Reprod Nutr Dev. 1991; 31(4):411-8 and Kolars JC, Levitt MD, Aouji, Savaiano DA. Yogurt — an autodigesting source of lactose. N engl J Med 1984 Jan 5;310(1):1-3.

[103] Barrett JS, Irving PM, Shepherd SJ, Muir JG, Gibson PR. Comparison of the prevalence of fructose and lactose malabsorption across chronic intestinal disorders. Aliment Pharmacol Ther. 2009 Jul 1;30(2):165-74. Gibson PR, Newnham E, Barrett JS, Shepherd SJ, Muir JG. Review article: fructose malabsorption and the bigger picture. Aliment Pharmacol Ther. 2007 Feb 15;25(4):349-63.

[104] Helliwell PA, Richardson M, Affleck J, Kellett GL. Regulation of GLUT5, GLUT2 and intestinal brush-border fructose absorption by the extracellular signal-regulated kinase, p38 mitogen-activated kinase

and phosphatidylinositol 3-kinase intracellular signaling pathways: implications for adaptation to diabetes. Biochem J. 2000 Aug 15;350 Pt 1:163-9.

[105] Shepherd SJ, Gibson PR. Fructose malabsorption and symptoms of irritable bowel syndrome: guidelines for effective dietary management. J Am Diet Assoc. 2006 Oct;106 (10):1631-9.

[106] Rumessen JJ, Gudmand-Høyer E. Absorption capacity of fructose in healthy adults. Comparison with sucrose and its constituent monosaccharides. Gut. 1986 Oct;27(10):1161-8.

[107] Anderson IH, Lavine AS, Levitt MD. Incomplete absorption of carbohydrate in all-purpose wheat flour. N Engl J Med. 1981 Apr 9;304(15):891-2. Levitt MD, Hirsh P, Fetzer CA, Sheahan M, Levine AS. H2 excretion after ingestion of complex carbohydrates. Gastroenterology. 1987 Feb;92(2):383-9.

[108] Stephen AM. Starch and dietary fibre: their physiological and epidemiological interrelationships. Can J Physiol Pharmacol. 1991 Jan;69(1):116-20.

[109] Hallfrisch J, Behall KM. Breath hydrogen and methane responses of men and women to breads made with white flour or whole wheat flours of different particle sizes. J Am Coll Nutr. 1999 Aug;18(4):296-302.

[110] Englyst HN, Trowell H, Southgate DA, Cummings JH. Dietary fiber and resistant starch. Am J Clin Nutr. 1987 Dec;46(6):873-4. Bird AR, Brown IL, Topping DL. Starches, resistant starches, the gut microflora and human health. Curr Issues Intest Microbiol. 2000 Mar;1(1):25-37.

[111] Bird AR, Brown IL, Topping DL. Starches, resistant starches, the gut microflora and human health. Curr Issues Intest Microbiol. 2000 Mar;1(1):25-37.

[112] Gidley MJ, Cooke D, Darke AH, Hoffmann RA, Russell AL, Greenwell P. Molecular order and structure in enzyme-resistant retrograded starch. Carbohydrate Polymers, 28(1)1995. 23-31.

[113] Macfarlane GT, Englyst HN. Starch utilization by the human large intestinal microflora. J Appl Bacteriol. 1986 Mar;60(3):195-201. Wang X, Conway PL, Brown IL, Evans AJ. In vitro utilization of amy-

lopectin and high-amylose maize (Amylomaize) starch granules by human colonic bacteria. Appl Environ Microbiol. 1999 Nov;65(11):4848-54.

[114] Wang X, Conway PL, Brown IL, Evans AJ. In vitro utilization of amylopectin and high-amylose maize (Amylomaize) starch granules by human colonic bacteria. Appl Environ Microbiol. 1999 Nov;65(11): 4848-54.

[115] Biesiekierski JR, Newnham ED, Irving PM, Barrett JS, Haines M, Doecke JD, Shepherd SJ, Muir JG, Gibson PR. Gluten causes gastrointestinal symptoms in subjects without celiac disease: a double-blind randomized placebo-controlled trial. Am J Gastroenterol. 2011 Mar;106(3):508-14; quiz 515. Epub 2011 Jan 11.

[116] Pimentel M, Constantino T, Kong Y, Bajwa M, Rezaei A, Park S. A 14-day elemental diet is highly effective in normalizing the lactulose breath test. Dig Dis Sci. 2004 Jan;49(1):73-7. Austin GL, Dalton CB, Hu Y, Morris CB, Hankins J, Weinland SR, Westman EC, Yancy WS Jr, Drossman DA. A very low-carbohydrate diet improves symptoms and quality of life in diarrhea-predominant irritable bowel syndrome. Clin Gastroenterol Hepatol. 2009 Jun;7(6):706-708..

[117] Fridge JL, Conrad C, Gerson L, Castillo RO, Cox K. Risk factors for small bowel bacterial overgrowth in cystic fibrosis. J Pediatr Gastroenterol Nutr. 2007 Feb;44(2):212-8.

[118] Goddard MS, Young G, Marcus R. The effect of amylose content on insulin and glucose responses to ingested rice. Am J Clin Nutr. 1984 Mar;39(3):388-92.

[119] Born P. Carbohydrate malabsorption in patients with non-specific abdominal complaints. World J Gastroenterol. 2007 Nov 21;13(43):5687-91. Chang FY, Lu CL. Irritable bowel syndrome in the 21st century: perspectives from Asia or South-east Asia. J Gastroenterol Hepatol. 2007 Jan;22(1):4-12.

[120] Badiali D, Corazziari E, Habib FI, Tomei E, Bausano G, Magrini P, Anzini F, Torsoli A. Effect of wheat bran in treatment of chronic nonorganic constipation. A double-blind controlled trial. Dig Dis Sci. 1995 Feb;40(2):349-56.

121 Van Horn LV, Liu K, Parker D, Emidy L, Liao YL, Pan WH, Giumetti D, Hewitt J, Stamler J. Serum lipid response to oat product intake with a fat-modified diet. J Am Diet Assoc. 1986 Jun;86(6):759-64.

122 Leadbetter J, Ball MJ, Mann JI. Effects of increasing quantities of oat bran in hypercholesterolemic people. Am J Clin Nutr. 1991 Nov;54(5):841-5.

123 Swain JF, Rouse IL, Curley CB, Sacks FM. Comparison of the effects of oat bran and low-fiber wheat on serum lipoprotein levels and blood pressure. N Engl J Med. 1990 Jan 18;322(3):147-52.

124 Pietinen P, Rimm EB, Korhonen P, Hartman AM, Willett WC, Albanes D, Virtamo J. Intake of dietary fiber and risk of coronary heart disease in a cohort of Finnish men. The Alpha-Tocopherol, Beta-Carotene Cancer Prevention Study. Circulation. 1996 Dec 1;94(11):2720-7. Eshak ES, Iso H, Date C, Kikuchi S, Watanabe Y, Wada Y, Wakai K, Tamakoshi A; JACC Study Group. Dietary fiber intake is associated with reduced risk of mortality from cardiovascular disease among Japanese men and women. J Nutr. 2010 Aug;140(8):1445-53.

125 Walker AR. Colon cancer and diet, with special reference to intakes of fat and fiber. Am J Clin Nutr. 1976 Dec;29(12):1417-26. Burkitt DP, Trowell HC. Dietary fibre and Western diseases. Ir Med J. 1977:70-272.

126 Fuchs CS, Giovannucci EL, Colditz GA, Hunter DJ, Stampfer MJ, Rosner B, Speizer FE, Willett WC. Dietary fiber and the risk of colorectal cancer and adenoma in women. N Engl J Med. 1999 Jan 21;340(3):169-76.

127 Uchida K, Kono S, Yin G, Toyomura K, Nagano J, Mizoue T, Mibu R, Tanaka M, Kakeji Y, Maehara Y, Okamura T, Ikejiri K, Futami K, Maekawa T, Yasunami Y, Takenaka K, Ichimiya H, Terasaka R. Dietary fiber, source foods and colorectal cancer risk: the Fukuoka Colorectal Cancer Study. Scand J Gastroenterol. 2010 Oct;45(10):1223-31.

128 Giovannucci E, Rimm EB, Stampfer MJ, Colditz GA, Ascherio A, Willett WC. Intake of fat, meat, and fiber in relation to risk of colon cancer in men. Cancer Res. 1994 May 1;54(9):2390-7.

[129] Shepherd SJ, Parker FC, Muir JG, Gibson PR. Dietary triggers of abdominal symptoms in patients with irritable bowel syndrome: randomized placebo-controlled evidence. Clin Gastroenterol Hepatol. 2008 Jul;6(7):765-71.

[130] Sayar S, Jannink JL, White PJ. Digestion residues of typical and high-beta-glucan oat flours provide substrates for in vitro fermentation. J Agric Food Chem. 2007 Jun 27;55(13):5306-11.

[131] Michel C, Kravtchenko TP, David A, et. al. In vitro prebiotic effects of Acacia gums onto the human intestinal microbiota depends on both botanical origin and environmental pH. 1998 Dec;4(6):257-66.

[132] Holloway WD, Tasman-Jones C, Lee SP. Digestion of certain fractions of dietary fiber in humans. Am J Clin Nutr. 1978 Jun;31(6):927-30.

[133] Soltoft J, Krag B, Gudmand-Hoyer E, Kristensen E, Wulff HR. A double-blind trial of the effect of wheat bran on symptoms of irritable bowel syndrome. Lancet. 1976 Feb 7;1(7954):270-2.

[134] Bijkerk CJ, de Wit NJ, Muris JW, Whorwell PJ, Knottnerus JA, Hoes AW. Soluble or insoluble fibre in irritable bowel syndrome in primary care? Randomised placebo controlled trial. BMJ. 2009 Aug 27;339:b3154.

[135] Dear KL, Elia M, Hunter JO. Do interventions which reduce colonic bacterial fermentation improve symptoms of irritable bowel syndrome? Dig Dis Sci. 2005 Apr;50(4):758-66.

[136] Hyams JS. Sorbitol intolerance: an unappreciated cause of functional gastrointestinal complaints. Gastroenterology. 1983 Jan;84(1):30-3.

[137] Born P, Zech J, Stark M, Classen M, Lorenz R. Carbohydrate substitutes: comparative study of intestinal absorption of fructose, sorbitol and xylitol. Med Klin (Munich). 1994 Nov 15;89(11):575-8.

[138] http://www.primalnorth.blogspot.ca/p/primal-north-rules.html

[139] Yancy WS Jr, Provenzale D, Westman EC. Improvement of gastroesophageal reflux disease after initiation of a low-carbohydrate diet: five brief cased reports. Altern Ther health med. 2001. Nov-Dec;

7(6):120,116-119. Austin GL, Thiny MT, Westman EC, Yancy WS Jr, Shaheen NJ. A very low-carbohydrate diet improves gastroesophageal reflux and its symptoms. Dig Dis Sci. 2006 Aug;51(8):1307-12. Austin GL, Dalton CB, Hu Y, Morris CB, Hankins J, Weinland SR, Westman EC, Yancy WS Jr, Drossman DA. A very low-carbohydrate diet improves symptoms and quality of life in diarrhea-predominant irritable bowel syndrome. Clin Gastroenterol Hepatol. 2009 Jun;7(6):706-708.

[140] Shepherd S, Gibson P. Fructose malabsorption and symptoms of irritable bowel syndrome: guidelines for effective dietary management. J Am Diet Assoc. 2006 Oct ;106 (10):1631-9.

[141] Gibson, P, Shepherd, S. Evidence-based dietary management of functional gastrointestinal symptoms: The FODMAP approach. J Gastroenterol Hepatol. 2010 Feb ;25 (2):252-8 20136989.

[142] Peter R Gibson, Susan J Shepherd. Evidence-based Dietary Management of Functional Gastrointestinal Symptoms: The FODMAP Approach. J Gastroenterol Hepatol. 2010;25(2):252-258.

[143] Gibson, P, Shepherd, S. Evidence-based dietary management of functional gastrointestinal symptoms: The FODMAP approach. J Gastroenterol Hepatol. 2010 Feb ;25 (2):252-8, 20136989f.

[144] Young DA, Bowen WH. The influence of sucralose on bacterial metabolism. J Dent Res. 1990 Aug;69(8):1480-4.

[145] Foster-Powell K, Holt SH, Brand-Miller JC. International table of glycemic index and glycemic load values: 2002. Am J Clin Nutr. 2002 Jul;76(1):5-56.

[146] Rada V, Bartonová J, Vlková E. Specific growth rate of bifidobacteria cultured on different sugars. Folia Microbiol (Praha). 2002;47(5):477-80.